THE GOLDEN YEARS
OF TRUCKING

THE GOLDEN YEARS OF TRUCKING

Commemorating fifty years of service by the
Ontario Trucking Association

1926-1976

© 1977 Ontario Trucking Association

ISBN 0-9690748-0-8 Paperback
ISBN 0-9690748-1-6 Casebound

Acknowledgements

All material in this book has been prepared or commissioned by the Ontario Trucking Association. Many of the photographs and much of the history have come from "Canadian Road Transport Archive" files. The Association is grateful to those who contributed in various ways, such as the loan of rare photographs and providing historical data.

Cover

Photograph of a 1912 GRAMM, courtesy of the New Brunswick Department of Highways.

Available from:
ONTARIO TRUCKING ASSOCIATION,
555 Dixon Road,
Rexdale, Ontario
M9W 1H8

Manufactured in Canada by Webcom Limited
Price: Paperback $9.95 Casebound $14.95

CONTENTS

ONTARIO TRUCKING ASSOCIATION

An association of intercity truck owners and allied interests dedicated to the advancement of the trucking industry

1974

1926

1936

INTRODUCTION

In the spring of 1963 I conceived the idea of developing a pictorial history of trucking in Canada, with the intention of publishing it in 1967, Canada's Centennial Year. A great number of valuable photographs of trucks was acquired from many sources across the country, most of them predating 1926, the founding year of The Automotive Transport Association of Ontario.

Important industry events, however, in particular the 101-day trucking strike in 1966, diverted attention away from the proposed pictorial history and made its publication in 1967 virtually impossible.

I then decided that the association's golden anniversary in 1976 should be marked by publication of a history of the association, making use of many of the photographs previously acquired and also covering technological development of the motor truck, the truck trailer and related equipment. As the anniversary year moved closer, further distractions appeared to threaten the publishing timetable. This time the Ontario government established two select committees, one to investigate the trucking industry, the other to look into the matter of road safety, both requiring considerable Association involvement.

Despite severe limitations on my own time, considerable interest was being shown in the proposed book and, to ensure its publication, it was necessary to seek the services of qualified writers and others to help put it together. Long-time journalist Ron Kenyon, with some roots in the trucking industry, was commissioned to write the story of trucking and development of the association. His was a monumental task involving research into 50-years' accumulation of ATA minute books, newsletters, trade papers and other documents of historical interest. He was helped by his wife Sheila, well known in the public relations field, by his son Cliff, also a journalist, and by researchers Lorna Gardner of Toronto and Lorna Stephen of Vancouver. Many of the industry's old-timers were sought out and interviewed by the Kenyon team, thereby adding a personal dimension to the trucking story.

To tell the equipment story I turned to Rolland Jerry of Toronto, undoubtedly the top truck historian in Canada. His fascinating account of truck technology from the early days is drawn from his own involvement with the industry and reinforced by his valuable personal collection of trucking memorabilia.

To edit the manuscripts, select photographs, and bring it all together I retained the services of Paul Ingram, an automotive engineer with a long trucking association and, until his retirement early in 1976, editor of Bus & Truck Transport.

To publish this history book, I asked a long-time friend Doug Chesebrough, president of Mil-Mac Publications Ltd., Toronto, to solicit sponsorship among OTA members. The results of his efforts were gratifying and the list of sponsors appears on page vii.

The Golden Years of Trucking was originally scheduled for publication one month prior to our Golden Anniversary Convention in November, 1976. Again, an event of great significance to the industry intervened. The Report of the Select Committee on Highway Transportation of Goods was also scheduled for release a month before our 1976 convention. I decided then to postpone publication of this book until 1977, thereby making it possible to include a brief summary of the Select Committee Report, as well as references to the Golden Anniversary Convention.

My sincere thanks to all who have contributed in many ways to make The Golden Years of Trucking a reality. To all of those in the industry who may have despaired at the delay, I hope you will agree that it has been worth waiting for.

J. O. Goodman
Executive Vice-President
Ontario Trucking Association
Nov. 21, 1977

Sponsors

Appreciation is expressed to those listed below, who
contributed materially to the publication of this historic book:

Hon. George H. Ferguson
Premier 1923-30

Hon. George S. Henry
Premier 1930-34

Hon. Mitchell F. Hepburn
Premier 1934-42

Hon. Gordon D. Conant
Premier 1942-43

Hon. Harry C. Nixon
Premier 1943

Hon. George A. Drew
Premier 1943-48

Hon. Thomas L. Kennedy
Premier 1948-49

Hon. Leslie M. Frost
Premier 1949-61

Hon. John P. Robarts
Premier 1961-71

Hon. William G. Davis
Premier 1971-present

In the past 50 years through the governments of 10 premiers,
the O.T.A. has helped the trucking industry
to serve Ontario.
And Ontario thanks you.

Province of Ontario

Dedicated to the memory of the following former employees of The ATA who have passed on:

Donald R. MacQuarrie

Newton J. Bryson

Lt. Col. Nicol Kingsmill

James R. McLeod

C. James Higgins

Each, in his own way, made a major contribution to the development of the trucking industry.

JOG

PART I

ENTERPRISE AND ACHIEVEMENT

The dynamic development of trucking in Ontario

by Ron Kenyon

Ron Kenyon is a seasoned newspaperman, having progressed from a London England advertising agency to a writer in Canada for newspapers, magazines, industry, television and films. For 14 years he was on staff with several major Canadian daily papers and was best known as a science writer. He continued with science writing at the National Research Council in Ottawa and, later, in Toronto for the Ontario Science Centre.

Kenyon has been editor of three professional journals and a contributor to virtually all major Canadian magazines, as well as for many in Britain and the U.S. He still maintains his Toronto-based writing service and is also co-publisher, with his wife Sheila, of the *Milverton Sun*.

He became familiar with the Ontario trucking industry many years ago as the writer of the *Goodyear Report*.

1

The Vital Link

Not quite 4.30 a.m....

Harry McCreary, "Hot Dog" to his friends, climbed with long-accustomed ease up the tall side of his tractor, settled in the driving seat, switched on the big rumbling diesel and made his checks in the cab. Not quite light yet.

Harry's tractor is virtually new, only 100,000 miles on it, barely adolescence for a tractor nowadays. All the comforts too, from an adjustable air-cushion seat to a recess at the driver's hand into which a coffee cup snugly fits. Unlike the tractors of only a few years ago, this one requires few gear changes, almost like driving a car. Yet a huge rig where you ride high, like a captain on the bridge of his ship.

It was 46 years ago, in 1930, when he was 12, that Harry had started driving a truck. His dad William had started Canada Transport in 1920 and Hot Dog used to go with the driver as a "helper". The driver liked to sleep on the road, so Harry would drive until they came to a hill and the gears had to be changed. Harry didn't know how to do that, so he'd have to nudge the driver into wakefulness. Since then, Harry had driven nearly three million miles without an accident ascribed to his fault.

Even so, he was by no means one of the first in the trucking industry in Ontario. Nor was his dad.

The first motor truckers were not taken seriously by anyone, least of all by railwaymen, those aristocrats of the transportation industry, who had displaced the waterways and trails and the long torturing trips by wagon. It was the railwaymen, with their brightly burnished locomotives and elegantly Victorian coaches that had sprung up and industries developed. But the rail-proud of it, and rightly so.

All along the railway rights-of-way towns and villages had sprung up, and industries developed. But the railways had one great handicap. They were limited to going where their lines led them. A few miles from the lines, Canada was a vast unopened hinterland. It would take a horse and wagon the best part of a day to transport produce twenty miles from a farm to the railway. Similarly, it would take just as long to deliver goods from the railway station to a home, along dusty bumpy roads a score of miles from the gleaming rail lines.

Trucks were to change all that and, in doing so, they were to remake the face of Ontario and bring it prosperity. Of course they did the same for other provinces, but Ontario led by a wide margin in trucking development and so came to lead in other development as well.

There was little to suggest that this would happen when the first trucks came along. It was an age of experimentation, the 1890s. No one knew what power, other than horses, would be best for road transport. They were trying steam, electricity and the new-fangled internal-combustion engine fueled by gasoline.

Electric-battery bicycles appeared in 1898, when bicycles were all the craze. Young lovers rode off on bicycles to new-found freedom in the rural parks, just as in the twenties and thirties people of that same age were to cuddle up in rumble seats while parked in the moonlight. Diamond Jim Brady had his bicycle handlebars encrusted in diamonds. And the song "A Bicycle Built for Two" gained understandable popularity.

But electric bicycles were more utilitarian. They were intended for carrying loads and, while they were not trucks, they presaged the coming of trucks. Their range limited them to the cities and the cities weren't as big as they are now.

That same year, 1898, Bob Simpson imported a real electric-powered truck. His store, The Robert Simpson Co. Ltd. of Toronto, had been famous for years for the smart delivery wagons it used, drawn by matched gray horses. So the battery truck was a big departure, yet in line with Simpson's leadership in delivery systems. The Simpson truck was built by Fischer Equipment Company of Chicago. It was supposed to have a top speed of 14 miles an hour but if it had traveled at that speed on city streets it would certainly have been breaking the law, which then limited speed to ten miles an hour. Its range was roughly 42 miles before recharging.

Simpson's purchase was not really a practical vehicle and was probably partly a publicity stunt. An electric vehicle was not a new idea, one having been built in the late 1700s. But no feasible battery had been developed until 1880, so Simpson was early in the field of electric trucks.

Less than a year after the Simpson purchase, Parker Dye Works bought an electric delivery wagon. It is of special interest because it was built in Canada in a factory across the road from Parker's, at 710-714 Yonge Street, in Toronto.

On July 7, 1899, Parker had an accident, perhaps Ontario's first with a truck. It was reported in *The Globe*:

"Pedestrians who happened to be on Jarvis Street about eight o'clock last evening have come to the conclusion that young horses fresh from the pasture are not the only means of conveyance that will bolt suddenly or shy when least expected.

"Mr. R. Parker, of R. Parker and Co., and his driver, in their new automobile carriage, were taking a pleasant spin down the asphalt when, by some means or other, the wheels on one side became tightened, while the others revolved freely. The result was that the carriage turned triangularly and ran at full speed against the curbing.

"The fore and rear wheels of the left side were snarled and the boulevard was disfigured for several feet. The turn was too sudden to allow the brakes to be applied. Fortunately, neither Mr. Parker nor his driver were hurt."

Nothing daunted, the Parker Company bought another vehicle in August 1900 from the Canadian Cycle and Motor Company, which controlled the Canadian patent for the Winton, made in Cleveland. This vehicle spun along at about 12 miles an hour.

In the early days it seemed as though electricity or steam would power trucks of the future. The Stanley Steamer passenger car was famous in its day, and steam was used for machinery of many kinds, on farms and even for building roads. The steamroller built many of the early "macadam" roads. But steam had limitations, even for passenger cars. You had to light the fire and raise steam before you could go anywhere. You had to maintain the correct head of steam en route and, on a warm day, the heat from the fire and boiler could be ferocious.

Travel in bad weather was difficult for cars and commercial vehicles because the roads were so poor. A few roads were paved in the cities and most were passable, except during winter storms. But until the close of the First World War few commercial vehicles ventured beyond city limits. In the early days there was no real

Real horsepower in 1914. Colville Cartage (later Inter-City Truck Lines Ltd.) moved this steel vault down Bay St., Toronto, to Dominion Bank at King and Yonge Sts.

In 1914, a Commer coming up to Sunnyside from the Humber River, Toronto. At left is industry pioneer Horace Harpham.

legislation covering roads or traffic and it was easy to get lost because there were few road signs.

The first true road legislation was passed in Ontario in 1901 when the province's population was 221,583. This was rather sketchy legislation, but the following year the Ontario Legislature established a Railway Committee which, through a process of metamorphosis, emerged eventually as the Ontario Municipal Board. This board was to have great influence on the trucking industry.

In 1904 the federal government established the Board of Railway Commissioners, which was intended to regulate the railways. In 1938 it became the Board of Transport Commissioners with jurisdiction over water, air, rail and road transport. Nearly 30 years later, in 1967, the Canadian Transport Commission was formed with additional responsibilities over extraprovincial trucking. However, up to the present (1977), the commission has exercised very little authority over trucking.

Back in 1903 there were 178 horseless carriages in Ontario, mostly passenger cars, and the police chief of Toronto grumbled that they were breaking the 10-mile-an-hour speed limit of his city.

Up to this time there had been no licensing, but in 1904 Ontario introduced the precursor of the complex licensing system that was to follow. The province brought in a law requiring registration of motor vehicles, the first law of its kind in Canada. Commercial vehicles and passenger cars were not differentiated and it was not until 1915 that commercial vehicles were registered separately.

The province was not doing much to improve roads. Historically, the provincial government had had little to do with them. The municipalities looked after roads within their own borders; the rest were county roads, roughly built and maintained, cleared of snow in winter only for sleigh traffic, mired hopelessly in spring, potholed and dusty in summer.

Nevertheless, in 1909, the Bell Telephone Company bought a car in Orillia and had it driven to London. Arthur W. Robinson of London says he was selected to drive the car, which had been bought from the Tudhope Carriage Company. He says he picked up a licence and markers in Toronto and hurried to Orillia "where I was given a thorough grounding in the art and science of the automobile. This consisted of a hurried trip through the factory, followed by a demonstration of the marvel of the age, the automobile. After brief and casual instruction as to driving and traffic rules, we set out for Toronto."

More Brains
than Metal are Used
in Building this

MAXWELL
TRUCK

This truck costs little more than a first class team, wagon and harness. Costs less when you figure up-keep. Eats only when it works. Requires one-twenty-fifth the care and attention horses do. Travels the 7 or 12 or 16 miles to market, under load, in one-fourth the time.

The farm hand who formerly took all day to drive to mill with a load of grain can now go and return in two hours.

Here is a truck with all the features of $7000 trucks, and sold under the same guarantee. Worm driven. Electric lights and generator. 10-foot loading space. Gas consumption more than 19 miles to every gallon. A tire miser. Mechanical trouble practically unknown. Repair bills are too low to mention.

This Maxwell is built for the farm. Weighs 2500 pounds. Goes faster than heavier and more expensive trucks and goes where they daren't follow.

6600 Maxwell trucks are in service. 1100 on farms. Service records show a verdict of 99.6% perfect based on all the trucks now in use. You'll find no mechanical faults in the Maxwell. A safe investment and a paying one.

You save $400 the day you buy this Maxwell truck, for its price is $1415. And $1415 is $400 less than any other truck of similar capacity on the market.
$1415 Chassis only, f. o. b. Windsor, Ont.   Electric lights.   Electric generator.   Worm drive.   10-foot loading space.   2500 pounds.   More than 19 miles on a gallon of gas.

MAXWELL MOTOR COMPANY OF CANADA, LTD., WINDSOR, ONTARIO.

(Montreal Weekly Star, Circa 1918)

The car covered the 30 miles from Orillia to Barrie in two and a half hours. It started to rain on the way to Toronto and the road became a quagmire. The car became stuck on Yonge Street and had to be pulled out by a farmer and horses. It was wet for the passengers because the car had no canopy; muddy too, because the car had no mudguards. Mud flew everywhere. Near Cooksville, mud got into the cooling system, the car being air-cooled and having no protection against such eventualities. Near Hamilton the rear babbit bearing melted with heat, probably caused by caked mud, and cracked the engine block. Three weeks later, the car finally arrived, more or less triumphantly, in London, where it became the first car bought by Bell in Ontario for use in repairing telephone lines, installing new lines and for general duties.

This event pointed a way to the future, presaging an entirely new way of life for Ontario. As cars and commercial vehicles increased in number, roads gradually improved; wherever the roads went so went telephone and hydro lines, serviced by the ever-more-efficient truck. Communities that had been isolated and lighted by lamps were able to speak to the world by telephone, to light their barns and houses electrically and even start industries, though relatively remote from rail lines. The ubiquitous truck would carry goods rapidly to and from the railway or even, bypassing the railway entirely, to the customer.

All this came gradually, but it came because of the truck, which changed the face of Ontario. The truck was as vital in the twentieth century as the waterways had once been in opening up the country, as the railways had been in the nineteenth century, and as the airlines were yet to become. Historically, prosperity depends on two prime factors, cheap energy and cheap food, and the truck was the means by which Ontario gained both. Just before World War I Sir Adam Beck, through the harnessing of Niagara Falls power, had introduced the biggest and cheapest power services in the world to Ontario, but it was the trucks that pushed the lines out.

Whether the early truckers had any concept of what they would achieve is unlikely. They were rough men, horny-handed and rough-spoken, but with a love of mechanical things. Trucking gave them a chance to be independent businessmen while allowing them to indulge their yen to tinker with engines. Drivers were scarce and mechanics few, so the ability to take apart and repair a recalcitrant engine and keep a truck rolling against all odds was important.

Most truckers had only one vehicle which they drove themselves and, despite their lack of academic qualifications, they were respected and even admired. The small merchant or large manufacturer didn't care whether the trucker could parse a sentence or play a fugue on the piano so long as he could negotiate the roads and make a delivery.

The big change that put internal-combustion vehicles ahead of steamers and electrics occurred in 1908, though the latter two did not immediately disappear. In 1908, Henry Ford brought out his famous Model T passenger car which revolutionized motoring. Up to then, motoring had been a rich man's hobby. The Model T was cheap and therefore available to large numbers of people. It was tough and rugged and its high wheels negotiated the rutty roads and even farm-

ers' fields. It was soon found that the versatile Model T could be converted into a truck and conversion kits became a popular item on the automotive market.

This was a time of experiment, of do-it-yourself solutions to problems. Shortly before World War I, many truck drivers attached big beach umbrellas above their seats to give them protection from the weather. A little later, the convertible bus-truck became popular; the weekday truck was fitted with seats for weekend excursions.

The First World War revolutionized trucking in Ontario, as it did elsewhere. Motor transport was one of the great developments of that war, which started with hoofed horsepower and ended with horsepower on wheels. Thousands of men learned to drive and to love the noisy, smelly, unpredictable creatures of the automobile factories.

Ford, which had led the way with passenger cars, was aware that there was a market for trucks and as far back as 1912 had produced a light commercial vehicle which, however, had little impact in Ontario. Production of the van ended after about a year.

But in 1918, Ford of Canada tooled up for light truck production and turned out its first light truck for sale the following year. There were, of course, war-surplus trucks of many makes available to anyone who wanted to get into trucking.

One of these was the oldest cartage firm in Canada—Hendrie & Co. Ltd of Toronto. It had begun with horse-drawn vehicles in 1855, a year after William Hendrie emigrated from Scotland. The company originally carted for the Great Western Railway out of Hamilton and, a year later, expanded to Toronto, Michigan and Illinois. A group, of which William was part, made a bid for business during the building of the Canadian Pacific Railway, having to put up the enormous sum of $200,000 as a guarantee of good faith.

Hendrie & Co. got into the motor transport business in 1917 with a converted Model T Ford and soon found that trucks were more efficient; two trucks could do the job of three drays and teams.

In those days the company preferred Scotsmen. Its foreman used to meet boat trains at Union Station and when he heard a Scottish burr, he would invite its owner to drive for Hendrie.

The company was well-known in Toronto for activities other than trucking. William was president of the Ontario Jockey Club, an honor passed on in due time to his son, George C., father of the present president of the Ontario Trucking Association, George M. Hendrie.

A trucking company could get some unusual loads in the old days. One of Hendrie's most unusual was that of carting the bones of deceased members of the Chinese community to the railway station in Toronto, for shipment to China for burial. The Chinese saved up the bones and shipped them every four or five years.

In the same year that Hendrie bought its first truck, 1917, James Yuill senior came back from World War I, in which he had enlisted as a baker. His wife bought him a somewhat unusual gift with war gratuities, a converted Model T Ford truck. So Yuill started in the trucking business, a company which still functions.

James senior died in 1945 but his son, James junior, 69, remembers a good deal of the old days. He himself drove for years and, until 1971, would still take a hand at the wheel in an emergency.

Ontario operators liked the Buffalo-built Lippard-Stewart truck, also an off-shoot, the Stewart. This 1917 model with a riveted tank, had the radiator mounted back of the engine and a Renault-style hood that opened from the front for good engine access.

"When I first drove we had Internationals and 4-cylinder Chevs. Everything had to be handled—no palletizing then. And there was a lot of piano moving."

James junior is still president of the company and has two younger brothers in the business with him but, as he puts it "they are only beginners... Tom Yuill has 49 years of service and Raymond (the baby) has been with us for 45 years." Tom is still driving; Raymond is secretary-treasurer.

Another early comer to the trucking industry was Edward Lancaster, who became established in 1917 in Windsor.

In the next few years trucks proliferated, especially in 1919 and 1920, as the bulk of the men came home from war. Phil Smith, who had been a scrap-metal dealer in Oshawa, got the chance in 1919 to help move pianos from the Williams Piano Company to the Canadian National Exhibition in Toronto. It occurred to him to ask General Motors in Oshawa whether they might have anything to be carried back from Toronto to Oshawa, so that he wouldn't be returning empty. They had, and Smith soon found himself making more money in trucking than in scrap-metal dealing. He started what became, through various vicissitudes, the giant Smith Transport, now owned by Canadian Pacific.

Smith Transport became the largest trucking company in the Commonwealth.

Another company that started in 1919 was O.K. Express Ltd., founded by Peter Lobraico, now 82. He still goes to the office most days for a few hours.

"My brother bought O'Keefe Express in 1919 and we operated with a half-ton truck," says Mr. Lobraico. "Although a few customers came with the purchase, we soon realized there was not enough for both of us, so I bought out my brother. I changed the name to O.K. Express at that time.

"We operated from our home on Coxwell Avenue and my wife would answer the phone and help with the bookkeeping, in between looking after five children and doing her housekeeping..."

Mr. Lobraico says: "we never turned down a load—we needed every dollar."

The company got the delivery work for Westinghouse and operated 24 hours a day, receiving calls in the dead of night to carry repair parts to places such as a dairy where a refrigeration plant might have broken down.

"In winter, a little later on, we got the contract to sand the hills in the Beaches area. There were no heaters in the trucks so we used hot bricks, and candles to keep the windshields clear of frost." says Mr. Lobraico.

"There weren't many service stations so we did our own repairs. Weren't any maps either—just had to ask your way," he says. "There were no driver examinations."

In 1914 they called this Adam Beck's Circus—a demonstration vehicle for electrical appliances. The truck is a Gramm

This 1912 Model T Ford light duty with square brass radiator was based on the car chassis and carried a ½-ton rating. The driver is Grover Wright, founder of Wright Motor Transport, Brantford, Ont.

Popularity of the McLaughlin (Buick) car in 1910 helped the sale of Buick commercial vehicles, like this 2-cylinder model operated by J. Slichter & Sons, florists of Whitby, Ont. Buick stopped building trucks during World War I.

One of the company's more unusual cargoes was harps. It had a contract with the CBC to move equipment and, at $1 per harp, this was little enough as they were awkward to manoeuvre up and down the stairs at Massey Hall.

In 1919, T. A. Collins Transport of Hamilton started in business with a Republic truck, specializing in broken loads between Toronto and Hamilton. Tom Collins had worked for the Grand Trunk Railway and Stelco before going into trucking. His son Ray, who now operates the business with his brother Ron, says that on cold days "the helper would run alongside the truck to keep warm."

Thomas Erwin and Sons, Toronto, started in 1919. Thomas senior is dead now, but his son Tom has a good memory for the early days.

"We had a one-ton Ford truck that cost $900. When it rained, the early trucks either skidded or got stuck. The tires were smooth and had no holding power on a wet road. There was no antifreeze and, if it was cold, we had to drain the radiator when we stopped and refill it when we started. Later, about 1925 or 1926, we began using wood alcohol for antifreeze but it sometimes blew the radiator cap off and you'd lose antifreeze that cost $1.25 a gallon. Even though we mixed the wood alcohol with two-thirds water, you still didn't want to lose much because $1.25 was a lot in those days.

"We often had to rely on the goodwill of farmers. They would have to tow us out of mud or snow and often they would feed us as well. One day we took a load for a Dr. Bell to Lake Scugog and couldn't find a restaurant. A farmer's wife gave us a wonderful meal of three fresh eggs each and home-cured bacon.

"In the early days, it was tough when it rained. The first windshield wipers had to be manually operated by the driver. There was no wiper on the passenger side.

There wasn't any protection against the rain either, except a drop sheet with a celluloid window. When the rain ended you had to roll it up, but it had to be dry first.

"And on the early trucks there was a sign that read: 'Over 25 miles an hour will void your warranty'."

Some efforts were being made, even before 1920, to improve the roads and traffic flow in Ontario. The first Canadian Good Roads Congress was held in Montreal in 1914. At that time, some $60 million a year was being spent on roads across Canada and this was considered "a very large sum". It cost between $5000 and $6000 a mile to lay a good macadam road. However, under the Canada Highways Act of 1919, the federal government agreed to pump $20 million into road-building over the next five years, with nine provinces being given grants—this, in addition to what was spent by counties and municipalities.

In 1919 Toronto installed a semaphore signal system at intersections on a test basis and the following year adopted the system, which remained in use until traffic lights came into service in 1928.

The year 1919 was a memorable one for Canada. Sir Wilfrid Laurier died on February 17. On March 7 the Grand Trunk Railway went into receivership. Between May 1 and June 15 there occurred the great Winnipeg strike and, on June 28, Canada signed the Versailles Peace Treaty, officially ending her war with Germany. At the Liberal convention in Ottawa August 5-7, Hon. W. L. Mackenzie King was elected leader of the Liberal Party and on September 1 the Prince of Wales, on tour of Canada, laid the tower cornerstone for the new Parliament buildings in Ottawa. On December 20, the "Canadian National Railways" was established by Order in Council, officially getting the government into the railway business in a big way and creating a potential competitor to the trucking industry in the years ahead.

Highways and Trucking
.....a history of growth

Back in 1923, when those trucking pioneers who founded The Automotive Transport Association of Ontario (now the OTA) were developing the idea of an Ontario-wide organization, the first official Ontario road map was published. It showed 1,860 miles of provincial roads, of which 1,040 were paved and 820 gravel surfaced.

Just for the record, the speed limit in 1923 was 25 miles an hour. Also for the record is the fact that all of this mileage was in southern Ontario.

Today's provincial system of 13,000 miles includes highways and freeways in all urban and rural areas in the south; and through the pre-Cambrian shield to the north. It serves mining and other resource locations and vacation areas. Add to the provincial system 83,000

miles of municipal roads and we have a total of 96,000 miles — all of which is travellled by vehicles affiliated with the OTA.

The rise of the Ontario trucking industry went hand-in-hand with the development of the province's highway system. At the turn of the century, railways were the big leaders in transportation. But that situation began to change with the arrival on the scene in 1896 of Archibald William Campbell, better known as "Good Roads" Campbell.

Mr. Campbell's credo was "Commerce can flourish without railways, but never without good roads." As Provincial Instructor of Roadmaking, he practiced what he preached by personal on-the-job appearances to demonstrate that with proper equipment, good roads could be built for less money than bad ones.

The demands of World War I for more transportation arteries between industrial areas and shipping points and a sharp increase in the use of motor vehicles, including trucks, established a need for more and better roads. And the end of World War II was another turning point, signalling, as it did, the start of a massive highway-building program to meet the demands of a post-war economic boom.

There are now more than 582,000 licensed commercial vehicles in Ontario out of the more than 3.7 million motor vehicles using our roads and highways. The number of commercial vehicles, the many millions of miles they travel and the service they provide make the Ontario trucking industry a vital factor in the province's economic life.

Hon. James Snow
Minister

Ministry of
Transportation and
Communications

Ontario

Harold Gilbert
Deputy Minister

O.K. EXPRESS Co.

Prop P. A. Lobraico & Sons

OVER HALF A CENTURY OF PROGRESS

O K Express was started in 1919 by Peter Lobraico when he purchased a red Ford truck and goodwill for the sum of $556 and arranged for a local cleaning shop to take his business calls.

After a few years and the expansion of business, the company was operated from the Lobraico's home on Coxwell Avenue with a fleet of eight trucks.

Peter was joined by his two sons, Michael and Vincent, and in the late 40's, the business was moved to Dawes Road where space was shared in a public garage.

By 1955, O K Express bought their first property on Goodwood Park in East York. Business had boomed, with the fleet now numbering twenty, tractor-trailer equipment included.

Based on the sound foundation of a lifetime of practical experience, rather than theoretical knowledge, this family business has expanded to 225 units with a staff of over 100, now under the direction of third generation Peter Lobraico as president.

O K Express Limited
is an operating company of the
O K Transportation Group

39 Howden Road, Scarborough, Ontario

755-4101

2

The Rolling Twenties

Most people think of the 1920-30 era as the Roaring Twenties, and in Ontario they certainly roared, but it would be more accurate to call them the "rolling twenties" because it was the trucks, rolling faster and farther, that gave them much of their impetus.

Ontario had a population in 1920 of roughly 2.7 million, of whom more than 2 million were of British stock (Canada's total population was just over 8.6 million. Toronto's population was about half a million, Ottawa's 100,000, Hamilton roughly the same, London 60,000, Windsor 35,000, Kitchener, Kingston and St. Catharines about 19,000 and Belleville 12,000.

The war had brought many changes, that began making themselves felt as the twenties came in. Income tax had been imposed for the first time in 1917—two percent per year on earnings over $1500 for married people and the same percentage on earnings above $1000 for singles. Food in 1920 was fairly expensive—40¢ a pound for a sirloin steak, 71¢ a dozen for eggs, 19¢ a pound for sugar, 60¢ a pound for coffee and 15¢ a quart for milk. Yet wages were not high. A carpenter or plumber earned about 90¢ an hour and salaries in manufacturing industries and offices ranged from $8 to $12.50 a week, depending on the industry and population of the area.

Ontario was moving into the lead among the provinces. The amount of hydro power being used is a good indicator. In 1910, the recently formed OHEPC sold 750 horsepower of electricity from Niagara Falls to ten municipalities. By 1920 it was selling 208,232 horsepower to 184 municipalities and big plans were afoot to tap the Falls for more power.

In 1920, Rt. Hon. Arthur Meighen became prime minister, a post he was to hold until December 29, 1921. In Ontario, Hon. E. C. Drury was premier as head of the United Farmers of Ontario—a peculiar kind of party that combined farming and labor support in a short-lived government that fell in 1923 and never reared its head politically again.

The year 1920 was notable for one important thing. Canada was represented at the inaugural session of the League of Nations and, although world events were to prove the League of Nations of little account, this particular meeting had lasting significance for Canada. Since all nations represented had to be identifiable as

nations, it became necessary to define for the first time what a "Canadian" was. And so this was done by Parliament in 1920, a step toward national identity.

The trucking industry was girding itself for some notable advances by 1920, but they had certainly not yet occurred. More and more newcomers were getting into the trucking field.

George Parke started a small truck line between Toronto and St. Catharines, an undertaking that eventually became Consolidated Truck Lines and later Dominion-Consolidated. George was a well-known St. Catharines sportsman and a star of that city's lacrosse team that won a Canadian championship. He was a founding director of the Automotive Transport Association of Ontario and founding president of Canadian Trucking Associations in 1937, a post he held until 1944. His son, G. M. "Don" Parke, was ATA president in 1950-51 and CTA president 1952-54. Don is still a key figure in the trucking industry and recalls:

"Tires were solid and Prestolite lamps were the order of the day. If you've never ridden on solid tires I can tell you it wasn't a cushioned ride. And when darkness came, the driver went to the small cylinder of compressed gas attached to the frame, turned on the valve and then lit the headlamps with a match. There was a small spout in each lamp from which the gas flowed to provide the light, which didn't carry very far, as you can imagine."

"The gas did not provide light to the back of the truck because the metal pipe required to carry it would have broken off on the bumpy roads. The rear of the vehicle was lighted by oil lamps."

The effect of trucks on farm life began to be felt increasingly after 1920. Up to then, farmers transported produce by wagon to the railway. It could stand around for days on sidings before reaching a store in the city. In 1919 a young man named Lou Egan, demobilized by the army, bought a Ford truck and began hauling milk from Kleinburg, just outside Toronto, to the city. Within months he was joined in competition by others—by Percy Brittain, for instance.

What trucking services meant to the farmer has been summed up by just such a farmer, Thomas Bird, who had 100 acres near Georgetown.

"In the old days," said Mr. Bird, "it wasn't uncommon to take a couple of hours to get to the Grand Trunk station. You'd have to bull your way through mud to the axles or heavy snowdrifts for almost half the year, and then the train would probably be an hour or so late.

"And that wasn't the worst of it. The trains were always in a hurry. Sometimes the train would pull out before you'd finished loading your milk and unloading empty cans. Then the trainmen would start heaving empty milk cans along the track for a quarter of a mile. You had to pick them up. And you'd still have half-a-day's milk on your hands, with nothing to do with it."

George Woods, who got into trucking farm produce in 1922, has left a record of his experiences. It says trucks of the early days were "heavy metal monsters with 14-inch solid tires."

Some produce had to be kept cool and refrigeration wasn't available. The old truckers used to cover their cargo with two wet tarpaulins and put a dry one on top which, says Woods, "worked better than you might have thought."

rural background, his father having interests in lumbering and cheese factories. Cliff took a commercial course in Peterborough and was at one time an accountant for The T. Eaton Company.

In 1920 he joined his brother-in-law, Cliff Stephenson, in buying a 1½-ton Maxwell truck and started moving goods for Eaton's from Toronto and fruits and vegetables back to Toronto. The company was called Tanner Transport Ltd. and, eventually, it went bankrupt. It took Cliff Tanner 30 years to pay off his creditors, but he did it.

Another well-known trucker started in 1920 and is still in business—Bigham the Mover, of Woodstock. Fred C. Bigham started with a horse and wagon but soon bought a 1916 Model T truck, which the company still has. An ice storm that year tore down all the telephone lines around Woodstock and gave Bigham months of work putting them back up again. Fred died in 1960 and his son Gordon, who joined the firm in 1931, is president.

Some early truckers started by avoiding the "long-

Good example of an early tractor-trailer is this 1922 Selden hauling a Fruehauf trailer.

The important thing to the farmer was that the truck picked up produce from his door and delivered it to his customer, a service the railway could not provide. It meant that farms could be much farther from the railway and still earn a profit. So the farms of Ontario developed in numbers and size and more food could be produced at lower prices.

Some truckers carried farm produce one way and manufactured goods—or any other load—in the other direction. Cliff Tanner, who started out in 1920, was one of these. Cliff was president of Toronto-Peterborough Transport Co. Ltd. until shortly before he died in 1963. Born at Sunwood, Ontario in 1894, he came of a

haul" routes, preferring in-town deliveries. One was George Rodanz who learned to drive a car while still in school, an unusual thing in those days. He decided then and there to be a truck driver, another unusual decision at such an early age. Rodanz began in 1924, after leaving school at 16, by hauling packing cases around Toronto. Later, he expanded and hauled to other centres for a grocery chain and developed one of the most profitable companies on the road by the 1930s. He sold out in 1949 to concentrate on his herd of Hereford cattle. Rodanz was a president of the Royal Agricultural Winter Fair in 1961 and was elected to the Canadian Agricultural Hall of Fame in 1976.

A four-wheel drive Duplex from the early twenties. The 4x4 truck had given excellent service during WWI and Canadian operators found it could cope with bad road conditions. Built in Lansing, Mich., the Duplex survives as a fire-truck chassis. Owned by Meyers Transport, Campbellford, Ont., the driver is Harold Putherick with Archie Meyers, at age 41, up back.

A four-wheel drive Duplex from the early twenties. The 4x4 truck had given excellent service during WWI and Canadian operators found it could cope with bad road conditions. Built in Lansing, Mich., the Duplex survives as a fire-truck chassis. Owned by Meyers Transport, Campbellford, Ont., the driver is Harold Putherick with Archie Meyers, at age 41, up back.

Surprisingly, not all successful truck operators were men. One who was definitely not was Ethel Cruise who was to have four children, having married at 17 in her native Owen Sound. Her husband was a laborer who could neither read nor write. When the family moved to Toronto, Ethel bought a cartage company and started operating with horses, later changing to trucks. Ethel could drive. She drove the men who drove the trucks. She fed them lunch daily as well, working from 5 a.m. to midnight most days. She was successful and her company prospered. She died at 91 years of age in 1976.

Prior to 1920, roads weren't kept open in winter, except for sleighs. In that year the province spent $1486 on snow clearance. Three years later it invested in its own snow removal equipment and also bought snow fencing.

Also in 1923, a man who was to become well-known in the industry, started a trucking business—Harold H. Leather of Hamilton. Born in Hamilton in 1893, he was to live in the same house all his active life—941 James Street South. Now retired, he still lives there.

Leather obtained the CPR business for delivering from the railway to Beamsville, St. Catharines and the Niagara Peninsula. The reason the CPR probably made this arrangement was to avoid using the rival CNR to reach these areas. It expected less competition from trucks, which shows that the railways were still short-sighted in 1923—so Leather got the CPR business.

Leather's first truck was a National stake-body vehicle, built by National Steel Car in Hamilton—"a good truck", he says. Later, he bought Reos and, when parts

became difficult to obtain during World War II, he changed to Internationals and stayed with them until he sold his company to Laidlaw Transport in 1973.

Aside from his pioneering work in the trucking industry, Leather is proud of two things. First is that he was awarded an MBE during World War II for his work as chairman of the Canadian prisoner-of-war packaging plants operated for the Red Cross. The six plants dispatched food parcels to prisoners all over the world and Canadian parcels became famous for their excellence. His second pride is his son, Capt. Ted Leather, who stayed in England after the war, entered politics and became Sir Edward Leather, Governor of Bermuda.

By 1924-25 the number of trucks operating in Ontario had increased amazingly. J. P. Bickell, registrar of motor vehicles, reported that in 1925 there were 34,690 trucks owned in the province, of which 5740 were operated by cartage, express and hauling contractors, the rest being privately owned.

This proliferation also gave rise to public animosity against trucks, based partly on a failure of the public to understand their importance, partly because truckers were not organized and not always considerate of others, as they were later to become.

In Canada, Ontario easily led the way in numbers of trucks and, significantly, it was also leading the way to expansion and prosperity. Trucks could not create prosperity where no potential existed but, just as the railways in the 19th century had opened up the fabulous wealth of the West, so trucks in the 20th century released the hidden wealth of Ontario that the railways could not economically reach.

A 1921 Chev 490 of fond memory for many. Cost: a little
under $1100.

This 1922 GMC with van body is notable for, among other
things, its ornate paint job. Robert Elder built the body.

Another popular four-wheel drive make, the FWD. This 1920 model with chains all around, to improve the limited traction with solid tires, has a 4-cylinder Wisconsin engine under the floor. The gas tank is up behind the driver, Noah Mark.

Because of growing public misunderstanding and antagonism, the government served notice in 1924 that it would introduce legislation that no truck of more than eight tons would be licensed after January 1, 1926. This announcement created not only a problem for truckers but a rallying point as well.

There was also another rallying point. Truckers were involved in a rough, tough, cutthroat business. There was no control of routes, bills of lading, hours of work, or much else. You got what business you could from your competitor by whatever method you could. Owners who wanted to provide efficient service and better labor conditions found these things impossible. Competitors would steal the business, using dangerously overloaded vehicles, mechanically defective equipment and drivers and helpers who were grossly underpaid and overworked.

The stage was being set for some sort of association of truckers that would protect them from damaging forces inside and outside their industry.

Outside, the railways were becoming formidable opponents, but still not realizing that trucking could become the big threat it would, in fact, become in the future.

The railways cunningly suggested that roads should not be built to serve communities already being looked after by railways.

In a statement issued in March 1923, the Railway Association of Canada said: "Railwaymen believe in the movement to improve highways. But they know that only some and not all roads can be improved in any given year, and that it is vitally important to establish some sort of principle by which to decide which roads should have preference. They know that the new roads create a new common carrier for whom no means of regulation have been devised. They believe that the public is closely concerned in having those points discussed and decided.

"Some roads must be improved before others. Should preference be given to roads parallel to existing lines of steam and electric service? Or to roads running at right angles into poorly served territory?

"Should the money be used to create merely additions or luxurious refinements to transportation lines already ample?

"Or should it open new territory to the benefit of rapid transit?

"More facilities for fat and prosperous regions?

The Reo Speed Wagon was a popular truck in the postwar years and on into the thirties. Typical of the breed, this 1920 model was durable and reliable. Shown is Howard Bescoby, founder of Bescoby's Transport, Toronto.

"Or a beginning of better facilities for backward and scantily served regions.

"Railwaymen believe the limited funds available should, as a general rule, be devoted to build 'right-angle' extensions into new territory. Facilities for more farms and townsmen—not more facilities for old well-served communities."

Reading between the lines it isn't hard to see that the railways wanted to protect their service to "fat and prosperous" regions and to leave to the truckers the hinterland where they would have great difficulty even making ends meet. On the other hand, building right-angle roads to the railways would bring profit to the railways because trucks would then be funneling business to them.

In fact, trucks could, and did open up the hinterland. But they were equally wanted in the cities where they soon found powerful allies in the merchants and manufacturers, the very fat and prosperous regions that the railways had hoped to keep to themselves.

The fact was that trucks were more convenient for merchants, delivering promptly door-to-door and in small lots, if necessary, instead of merchants having to wait while the railway made up a boxcar. Stan Corney of Motorways (Ont.) Ltd., who started as a helper in 1925 and began driving a truck in 1926, points out that the trucker did a good deal of handling in those days.

He carried mostly groceries for Carroll's, which became Grand Union and later Steinberg's. In those days vinegar came in big barrels, sugar in 100-lb bags, lard in big containers, figs in wooden boxes. The trucker did his own loading and unloading at his pick-up and delivery points. No wonder merchants in the cities liked trucks and wanted them.

The year 1926 was a pivotal one in a number of ways, not only for the country but for the trucking industry. Sir Adam Beck, that great architect of hydro-electric power in Ontario, died. The Canadian grain harvest was the second largest in history (the next year it was even bigger). Prosperity had arrived. Prices in stores actually declined by eight percent and, in a move that must be unprecedented in the field of taxation, the federal government lowered income taxes.

This was also the year of Canada's Diamond Jubilee, with wild celebrations; it saw the opening of the Peace Bridge across the Niagara River between Canada and the United States.

Canada was still poised fortunately between a powerful Britain and a friendly neighbor, the United States, which yet presented no economic threat.

In 1926 a telephone cost $2.40 a month and there were more than a million telephones in Canada. Steak had dropped to 28¢ a pound, sugar to 11¢ a pound and the average city rent was $27 a month. The national population had reached 9 million, Ontario somewhat over 2 million and Toronto close to 600,000. The country had 608,000 cars and trucks—only the U.S., Britain and France had more. Of the Canadian vehicles, most were concentrated in Ontario, which had 388,728.

Trucking fleets, as distinct from one-truck owners, began to appear in larger numbers; "long-distance" hauling sent trucks scurrying from city to city, though long-distance in those days would scarcely compare to long-distance in a later day. Six-cylinder engines for trucks were in vogue and semitrailers, even trailer-trains, were coming in. Tank trucks appeared in the late twenties and gasoline, which had been transported by truck in vertical drums, now was transported horizontally.

The trouble was that roads were still not good and traffic control was poor. The explosion of traffic in Ontario was more evident by its nuisance value than in the good it was doing. Its noise was apparent, while the fact that it was putting Ontario into an unprecedented era of prosperity was less obvious.

In 1926 Ontario had only 63,928 miles of roads, some little better than cart tracks, as 59,000 miles of the total were of dirt or gravel. A trucker still had to cross a bridge with extreme caution, especially if his truck was overloaded as many were. The bridge could so easily collapse.

Phil Smith used to tell a story of being behind a truck owned by Cliff Tanner. The Tanner truck suddenly broke through a bridge. Smith managed to stop with his own front wheels over the edge of the break.

Cold continued to present problems. Ray Tanner, grandson of Cliff, remembers staying overnight with a farmer because his engine froze up and, next morning, having to start the engine by warming it with a Quebec heater, manhandled under the truck.

The Canada Year Book of 1926 noted that "Only the lack of an adequate road system is postponing a great increase in traffic for both passengers and freight service" and added: "The automotive industry is just becoming a factor in the transportation of passengers and freight in this country. Railways have found that the handling of less-than-carload lots of freight is often an unprofitable business. It follows that commercial trucks are being used in greater numbers to carry lighter shipments between some of the larger centres served by adequately surfaced highways... There can be no doubt that motor vehicles are now carrying much of the short-haul traffic formerly carried by steam and electric railways. In addition, a certain amount of traffic formerly carried over water routes has been diverted to the more modern carriers."

Speaking at a Canadian Good Roads Association convention in Edmonton in 1926, S. L. Squire Ontario's deputy minister of public works and highways, remarked that "the traffic on highways has increased over one thousand percent in ten years."

Alf Reeves, president of the National Automobile Chamber of Commerce, told a meeting of truck operators that "trucking is a form of transportation that the public demands and is going to get."

There were tremendous pressures for more and better trucks, more and better roads, better and more efficient trucking services. There was opposition from the railways on grounds of competition, opposition from the public on grounds of noise and congestion. The pressures were conflicting but pressures nonetheless that faced an unorganized trucking industry.

By 1926 the truckers badly needed an effective association, with good men to lead it. Most of the truckers were not organizers. They were not men able to talk with governments or cajole civil servants. But such men were urgently needed.

3

An Association Is Formed

There is a difference of opinion as to who really proposed an association of truckers in Ontario. Most probably Don MacQuarrie, one of the key proponents, was right when he credited the idea to Frederik C. Foy.

In an article MacQuarrie wrote ten years later, he said: "Probably most of the credit for the original idea of organization belongs to Fred C. Foy, at that time manager of Ontario Transport Company Limited. He sounded out various other operators and it is interesting to note the reactions of one operator:

"On one occasion Mr. Foy and the writer were invited in no uncertain terms to leave an office before the manager found it necessary to assist them out with the toe of his boot. This operator is now one of the prominent members of the association."

Fred Foy was one of Canada's more colorful and remarkable characters. According to his son, Fred C. junior (usually known as "Peter") who now lives in Victoria, B.C., Fred was born August 28, 1885, of a family that came originally from Tipperary, Ireland. The Foys had considerable influence in Toronto. Fred's father, also Fred C., was a medalist in law at Osgoode Hall and became Toronto city clerk, first president of the Royal Canadian Yacht Club and first president of the Toronto Club.

Fred's uncle, J. J. Foy, was Ontario's attorney-general and another uncle, Barlow Cumberland, owned the house in Port Hope later bought by the Hon. Vincent Massey, one-time Governor-General of Canada. Fred's grandfather, F. W. Cumberland, had been ADC to Lord Dufferin when he was governor-general and organized the 10th Royal Grenadiers, which merged with the Toronto Regiment in 1921. Grandfather Cumberland produced a plan for Toronto harbor which was rejected, but later bought by the City of Chicago. He owned extensive lands which became part of the University of Toronto. His widow lived in a house called "Earnscliffe", later donated to the university. Convocation Hall now stands on the site.

Frederik, who was to become important to the trucking industry, attended St. Michael's College, learning among other things Greek and Latin, which was the custom of the day. His father wanted him to be a musician, but young Frederik had a mind of his own. He would slip off to play second base for the Toronto

Maple Leafs, which was the farm team for the New York Giants.

In the First World War, Frederik enlisted in the Royal Flying Corps but was never posted out of Toronto. After the war he was involved in dredging operations off Toronto Islands, though how he became involved in that is unclear. Young Frederik got into a lot of unlikely things.

With his brother-in-law, Charles Wilson, he formed the Ontario Transport Company Limited and it was at this point that he entered the trucking scene. He and his family were well connected and, about 1926, he helped George Parke obtain a licence from the government to transport liquor to the Niagara Peninsula. Moreover, he helped Parke obtain a licence for a bonded warehouse so that he could store the liquor too.

Foy was entirely different from most other truck operators—scholarly, easy-spoken, of excellent family and with a sophisticated interest in the arts. It's easy to understand why he was one to whom the truckers looked for help in forming an association.

Don MacQuarrie, a second key person in organizing the association, was not a trucker at all. He was a chartered accountant, in partnership with a Mr. Petman, with offices at 105 Victoria Street, Toronto.

MacQuarrie was born at Valetta in Essex County, his father a Presbyterian minister. There were seven children, six boys and a girl. MacQuarrie's widow, Iva, says he was a "skinny kid". His mother had died when he was twelve and the family had little money. MacQuarrie thought of going into medicine but the war intervened and he later found an interest in accounting instead.

Like some others who have been key figures in the trucking industry, MacQuarrie never drove a truck in his life and was not particularly inclined toward mechanical things. He was not even interested in cars. But some of his accounting clients were in the trucking business and so he developed an interest in the industry and its people.

MacQuarrie made a good foil to Foy. MacQuarrie was also cultured, but whereas there was a quicksilver quality about Foy's personality and an upper-crust look about him, MacQuarrie was of poor family, a hard worker and utterly sincere. Truckers of that day were

*Although this White "speed truck" has a
1929 licence, it's probably a 1926 model.
Pneumatic tires brought great changes in
truck design, although this one still has
acetylene headlights and oil lamps on
the cowl.*

rough diamonds and they appreciated MacQuarrie,
whereas they might not always have felt the same about
Foy. Their four-letter words didn't bother MacQuarrie,
though he was not a man to use them. Unlike the
average trucker, MacQuarrie was only five feet, four
inches tall and slimly built.

Taking up again the story MacQuarrie has left of the
formation of the Automotive Transport Association of
Ontario (later the Ontario Trucking Association): "Late
in July 1926, an informal meeting of interested operators was held in the office of the Toronto Storage Company."

Toronto Storage was owned by George Parke. Present
at the meeting were Parke, Fred Foy and Reg Dean
from Ontario Transport, Alex Mellway of Mellway
Brothers, Jim Stacey of Stacey Transport, Phil Smith of
Smith Transport, Wilf Goodman of *Bus and Truck* magazine, and MacQuarrie himself.

"This meeting was important because it was really
the founding of the association," says MacQuarrie. "It
was decided to hold a further meeting in Hamilton
before any definite organizational steps were taken.
This Hamilton meeting was held late in August 1926,
and The Automotive Transport Association of Ontario
became an actuality. Fred C. Foy was elected president,
Phil Smith was first vice-president and Herb Cleland of
Cataract Express, Niagara Falls, was second vice-president. On the board of directors were the above three
and F. G. Baldrey of Preston; Edward Goodale of Hamilton; Alex Mellway, George Parke and Jim Stacey, all
of Toronto."

MacQuarrie was elected secretary-treasurer and it
was decided to use his offices at 105 Victoria Street,
Toronto, as association offices, where they remained for
the next eight years.

Other reports have been left of the meeting, one of
the most authoritative probably by Wilf Goodman, who
wrote in *Bus and Truck* that the meeting took place in
the offices of the Hamilton Chamber of Commerce, that
there was a good deal of suspicion about the true mo-
tives of the organizers and that some warned strongly
against the association trying to introduce standard rate
schedules.

Truckers were independent men, some little more
than pirates of the road, and they liked competition,
fair or foul, that assured their business.

Fred Foy, persuasive, confident, positive in approach,
perhaps a little awe-inspiring, acted as chairman. He
pointed out, says Goodman, that "while various members were in direct competition with one another—and
hard competition at that—they could join together prof-
itably for their common good."

And so the association was formed. It was not really
an impressive beginning. Reports vary as to how many
people attended. Some say 20, some 15. They controlled
fewer than 200 trucks of the 34,000 or so in the province.

But Foy passed off the poor attendance as the result
of the weather, which was appalling for August, with
heavy rain and thick mud on the roads. It was heartening, he said, that so many had come. This was undoubtedly the diplomat in Foy speaking out and one wonders

how many believed him. For a buck, any of the truckers would brave far worse weather than that. Bad roads were part of the business and bad weather nothing but a challenge.

Inauspicious as the first meeting may have been, it was a beginning and its duly appointed executive at once showed itself a power. It was ready to take on anyone.

On September 9, in a speech at the Canadian National Exhibition, T. E. McDonnell, vice-president and general manager of the Canadian Pacific Express Company, asked for a better deal for railways. He claimed that for-hire trucks could operate as they wished, vary their rates anyhow they chose and "take the cream of the traffic—and your railways dare not refuse the skim milk."

He said: "The present condition is manifestly unfair and my chief hope is that the reputation of the Canadian businessman is such that he will not for long tolerate unfair treatment of his railways, with which his interests are so closely related."

Foy bared his teeth and that of the new association in what must have come as a shock to the giant railways.

"We accept the same responsibility towards, and give the same amount of protection to, the goods we carry as do the railways and in some cases we give more protection," he replied tartly.

"I think that Mr. McDonnell when he gave his speech, was not fully informed . . . The advantages of shipping by truck are so numerous as to admit of no argument. We can pick up a load in Toronto and deliver it to Hamilton the same day, for the same rate that the railways want for two days and four extra handlings. On short hauls there can be no question of the superiority of the truck."

The association thus drew blood for the first time in what was to be a battle for decades between the railways and the trucks.

In a way, the railways had advantages. They were well organized; they had federal government support. In fact, the federal government had placed itself in an invidious position by becoming the owner of Canadian National. It had entered the transportation field, not only in competition with Canadian Pacific, but more particularly with the trucking industry, both of which its duty was to control from a governmental point of view. Its decisions were inevitably suspect, and this increased the problems.

Up to 1926, the federal government had granted more than 47 million acres of land to the railways, had given financial aid to the tune of over $225 million and had guaranteed railway bonds worth over $484 million, which meant that the railways could sell the bonds more easily. The government really had an interest, therefore, in seeing Canadian Pacific prosper, as well as Canadian National.

And despite this massive aid, Canadian National Railways in 1926 had a deficit of nearly $30 million. The government did not want to go to the taxpayers for more money for the railways and so it was, understandably, supporting their stand against the trucks and buses.

Ranged beside the truckers, however, were even more powerful interests—the people themselves—the farmers, storekeepers, manufacturers, everyone in need of furniture moving from home to home.

There was no doubt that regulation of trucking was needed in Ontario. The ATA itself believed in regulation, despite the objection of some of its own members. The Government of Ontario also saw a need for regulation but, rather like a man who wants to pick up a porcupine, was discreetly aware of a prickly problem.

Hon. George S. Henry, the minister of public works and highways, admitted he had had complaints from locomotive drivers that trucks didn't stop at railway crossings, thereby creating a hazard to the trains. There were complaints, too, from the motoring public who, decked out in their Sunday best, were bent on "touring", only to find the road blocked by a truck which covered them in dust and sometimes mud. Horses were still prominent on streets and roads and some were still not accustomed to motor vehicles, especially big and noisy trucks. Some horses shied and bolted. At night horse-drawn traffic was not required to carry lights, so accidents involving trucks were not uncommon. This latter problem was rectified sensibly in 1927 when legislation was passed requiring the lighting of horse-drawn vehicles. This did not please the owners of these vehicles; since they had been on the roads long before the trucks, they assumed some form of divine right-of-way.

On the other hand, Mr. Henry himself was a farseeing man of excellent judgment. He realized what trucks were doing for the province. They had, he said, "largely revolutionized social life." Himself a farmer, he noted that the rural districts had gained the most.

Mr. Henry had considered introducing a bill to control trucking at a session of the Legislature in 1926, but delayed it after departmental studies showed how complicated it would have to be. Some trucks operated as for-hire common carriers in one direction and as contract carriers in the other. There were privately owned trucks, operating solely for one business or one farmer; there were trucks entirely for-hire by anyone. There were trucks that were buses on Sundays. Then there were trucks that ran only in cities, some that operated only between cities and some "tramp" trucks that ran all over the place as the owners' fancy and the availability of goods took them.

Numerous meetings were held among interested groups, including the railways, but the problems remained. Truckers loved their freedom, the railways disliked the truckers' freedom. At what point should it be curtailed for the good of the industry and the public at large?

On October 14, 1926, the ATA held its own meeting to talk over the matter and this was followed by a larger general meeting on October 17. These preceded one of the most significant conferences in the trucking industry of Ontario, called by the Department of Public Works and Highways and presided over by the deputy minister, S. L. Squire. Truckers, shippers, manufacturers, the railways and others were there, the object being, as the editor of *Canadian Railways and Marine World* was later told "to discover, if possible, a recognized place for each of the transportation interests."

Don MacQuarrie left a brief note about this meeting. He said it was attended by representatives of the Canadian Manufacturers' Association, the electric railways, the Ontario Motor League, the Board of Trade and the "new body", the ATA. "It is rather interesting to note that most of the principles laid down at that meeting have since become part of the regulations governing

This 1929 Hug tractor was an unfamiliar make but an example of a good American assembled truck. Hug was better known for its dump trucks and off-highway vehicles. But some commercial units were built and they sold well in Ontario in the late twenties. The trailers are Brantford.

public commercial vehicle operations in Ontario," he said.

This was the true significance of the meeting. The shippers and manufacturers lined up solidly behind the truckers. An attempt to have trucks banned by law from operating over a range of more than 75 miles was defeated roundly. The ground rules were laid down for the Public Commercial Vehicles Act, which was introduced the following year. The act, after many changes, began to bring order to the chaotic and cutthroat competition that so handicapped the industry and made it difficult for reputable operators to compete fairly.

Foy was by no means fooled by this apparently easy victory. At a monthly board meeting of the ATA he warned: "The battle has just begun and the support of every truckman in the province is required to defeat such proposals as might work hardships on the industry generally."

Within the ATA, the differences of opinion over the need for regulation erupted violently. Phil Smith, an ATA founder and big-fleet operator, resigned from the association in July 1927 over this issue. He refused to stop cutting rates, was exposed to severe criticism from some colleagues in the association and went his own way.

Smith, however, was to encounter more problems. On Oct. 15 of the same year, having merged his own Smith Transportation Co. with the transport division of Toronto Storage and Transport and with Stacey Transport, he found himself in trouble. The new company, Smith

Transportation Ltd. with 110 trucks, was unwieldy and unmanageable and, in Feb. 1928, went out of business. Undaunted, Smith started up a new Smith Transport, which survived to become the largest carrier in the British Empire, eventually selling it to the Canadian Pacific Railway.

The year 1927 was the most euphoric of the 20th century in Canada. Nearly everyone was convinced prosperity was to be permanent, a result of good business practices coupled with an ideal form of government. Things could only go on improving.

In the trucking industry, trucks were bought with little foresight—15 percent down and two years to pay. Roy A. Hauer of Mack Trucks warned against this risky procedure in such a cutthroat business and announced that the larger manufacturers had decided against giving so much credit in the future. Terms would become 25 percent down and complete payment would be required in 18 months. with trade-in allowances included as part of the cash down-payment.

But J. E. Smith, the Montreal manager of the Ford Motor Company of Canada, saw things more the way most people did—prosperity unlimited: "Canada is on the eve of a period of great prosperity," he told the Eastern Canadian Motor Show delegates. "Businessmen see this condition coming and are providing themselves with necessary transportation."

The speech could scarcely have been more ill-timed. Faced with higher down-payments and having already bought so many trucks, the industry could do without buying for a while and truck sales plummeted. It was not until 1930 that there was any improvement in sales and even then only in the export market. Truck sales did not really improve noticeably until 1932.

But, as we said, nobody (or hardly anybody) believed such a thing could happen in 1927. Everything seemed to be going up, from flappers' dresses to the Ontario speed limits, which were raised to a frightening 35 miles an hour. There were protests, of course, but it seemed as though the human body did not, as some thought, disintegrate at such rates of speed. So the speed limit stayed.

One thing the government felt should stop increasing was the size of trucks. The Hon. Mr. Henry grumbled that big trucks should be controlled and so a bill was introduced to limit vehicle length to 33 feet and combinations of vehicles to 65 feet. The bill also provided that no vehicle, other than one publicly owned, could weigh more than eight tons. However, the bill was delayed and eventually defeated.

What was happening in Ontario was having a distinct impact on the rest of Canada. Ontario still had by far the most vehicles. Commercial vehicles numbered 43,442 in Ontario in 1927, compared to only 18,200 in Quebec.

But unquestionably the most important event of 1927 in Ontario was the passage of the new PCV Act which, imperfect though it was and full of loopholes, laid the groundwork for regulation of trucks and a more orderly operation of the industry.

It provided for licensing and insurance regulations, as well as fines for breaking the law. The fines were low, $100 being the maximum for a third offence; but it was a beginning.

The association was not entirely happy with the PCV Act. At its annual meeting, ATA members pointed out that PCV operators were defined as "running between two or more municipalities" whereas many carriers had no definite runs. Like tramp steamers, they picked up loads anywhere and then looked for another load. The act did not seem to cover them and they were a great nuisance to the regular trucking lines. One of the latter might, and often did, ensure its prosperity by arranging a return load in advance of a journey, only to find that some "tramp" trucker had got in first and picked up the return load ahead of the contract truck, which would have to return empty at a loss.

The term "contract carrier" was not clear in the new act, which had loopholes by which carriers could circumvent the intent of the law.

A 1928 Durant light-duty truck equipped with relatively new four-wheel brakes.

"But How Do I Know He's Reliable?"

A Message Addressed to the Shippers of Ontario — Time, Money and Anxiety Can be Saved by Dealing With Responsible Truck Operators — Avoid Sending Shipments by Irresponsible Concerns

As one of the leading shippers of the province you perhaps employ, from time to time, the services of road transport companies. You will have found that on some hauls a truck is the ideal unit of transportation and that the majority of truck operators are equipped to give you speedy and economical service.

Unfortunately, however, truck transportation has developed in haphazard fashion and the industry has attracted a few irresponsible operators in addition to the many who maintain a high standard of business ethics. In consequence, when considering a new truck operator, shippers must frequently ask themselves the question:

"But how do I know he's reliable?"

Naturally you hesitate to do business with a concern without some kind of guarantee that it is financially responsible and managed in an efficient and businesslike way. You want to avoid, in your own interests, placing business with fly-by-nights and suffering, in consequence, unsatisfactory service and possibly heavy loss.

In choosing your transportation company you rightly demand:

Efficient and responsible service at reasonable rates.

Of course, there are many truck operators in Ontario whose integrity you may check by investigation, but for your benefit and protection an organization exists which is composed exclusively of responsible road transport men. It is known as the Automotive Transport Association of Ontario and its members are drawn from all parts of the province. In doing business with any of them you have the assurance that they will give you efficient and responsible service at reasonable rates.

Below are listed the members and the routes they cover. As new members are admitted into the organization their names, and particulars regarding them, will be forwarded to you.

Members of the Automotive Transport Association of Ontario

Name	Routes Covered
Alderman Transport, 207 Cannon Street, Hamilton	Various.
Baldry Transport, 1357 King Street, Preston	Hamilton, Galt, Preston, Kitchener and Hespeler.
Bigham, The Mover, 243 Riddell Street, Woodstock	Vicinity of Woodstock.
Bird and Dance, Norfolk Street, Hamilton	Toronto, Niagara Falls.
E. F. Blackwell Carting Co., 125 Arthur Street, Brantford	Brantford, Hamilton.
Briggs Transport, 36 Vermont Ave., Toronto	Toronto to Barrie.
Cataract Express, 383 River Road, Niagara Falls	Toronto to Niagara Falls.
Comet Transport, Marshall St., London	London to Windsor
Finch and Sons, Brantford	Toronto to Brantford.
Giles Express, 22 Brucedale Ave., Hamilton	Hamilton to Toronto.
Goodale Transport, 18 Wright Ave., Hamilton	Hamilton, Guelph, Galt and Kitchener.
Hamilton Brantford Electric Delivery, 12 Walnut St., Hamilton	Hamilton to Brantford.
Hoars Motor Transport, 18 Gladstone Ave., Toronto	Toronto to Cobourg.
Invicta Transport, 85 Lombard St., Toronto	Toronto, Galt, Preston and Kitchener.
Larke Transport, 286 Adelaide St. W., Toronto	Toronto to Oshawa.
Mellway Brothers, Ltd., 512 Lansdowne Ave., Toronto	Toronto to London.
McIvor's Transport, Welland	Toronto, Welland and Port Colborne.
Ontario Transport, Ltd., 54 King William St., Hamilton	Toronto, Hamilton, Niagara Falls and Welland.
Sayle Transport, 206 Sheridan St., Brantford	Brantford, Woodstock and London.
Smithson Transport Line, Port Dover.	
Smith's Transportation, Ltd., Oshawa.	
Stacey Transport, 8 Duke St., Toronto	Toronto, Hamilton, Guelph and London.
Stratford Motor Transport, Stratford	Toronto, Stratford and London.
Toronto Storage and Transport, Ltd., 17 River St., Toronto	Toronto, St. Catharines and Niagara Falls.

The PCV Act, though passed in 1927, was not proclaimed until the following year; even then licences were granted indiscriminately and violations were so common that its usefulness was limited. Nevertheless, it was a start, a milestone in the long effort to create a viable, responsible trucking industry.

One important postscript to the PCV licensing startup was that, initially, the railways were offered PCV licences because they were considered the senior members of the transportation industry and the government was anxious not to injure their prospects. But though the railways saw some future for the truck in short-haul delivery of commodities to railway stations and sidings, they declined to admit that long-haul trucks could offer them real competition. They believed the railway would remain the long-haul transport medium of the future. They even asserted that long-haul trucking was a passing fad and "not here to stay".

They therefore refused the opportunity to obtain PCV licences and launch themselves into the trucking industry, which they could have done at the time at cut-rate prices. Thus they missed an opportunity to get into trucking and remained in competition with the trucks, which was to create more than a measure of ill will in the years ahead.

The beginning of the year 1929, indeed most of the year, remained a golden one for North America. Times were exceptionally good. After the enactment of the PCV Act and its proclamation in 1928, the government issued a great many licences. By the fall of 1928, some 700 PCV licences had been granted.

As the ATA had gloomily predicted, the PCV Act had giant loopholes in it and the pirate truckers drove through them promptly. If things were good in the trucking industry it was because the economy in general had never been better. Despite the cutthroat competi-

tion that continued, not many companies failed and a dealer was able to report that he had not been forced to repossess a single truck.

Yet there were signs of change. Truck sales remained sharply down.

There was a squabble between the municipalities, short of money, and the provincial government over the gasoline tax. The Ontario government had raised the tax from three cents a gallon to five cents. The municipalities wanted a share on the grounds that vehicles from outside their municipalities were using their roads. The government firmly declined to part with a cent.

One of the oddball laws proposed in 1929—and there were to be many such proposals in the years to come—was that truckers should be required to report the moving of household goods to the clerk of the municipality within 24 hours. The idea was to make it easier for creditors to find people who owed them money. The bill did not pass.

The railways seem to have had an ambivalent attitude toward trucks. They did not want to get into the long-haul field. Yet Sir Henry Thornton, president of the CNR, suggested to a Canadian Good Roads Association convention that trucks should become an adjunct to the railways and saw a useful possibility in co-operation between road and rail. This very possibility could have been ensured if the railways had taken the proffered PCV licences. The railways, highly organized, could have taken over much of the industry and had trucks operating more or less where they wished. It is a curious footnote to history that they did not see this, or at least did not act upon it until the mid-50s.

And then, at the end of 1929, came the huge Wall Street stock market crash and everyone was in trouble, the truckers, the railways and their clients.

YORK CARTAGE
and subsiduary company

Yesterday

1922 William C. Norris Ltd. started in Montreal, with one truck, and hauled farm products into Kra[...] Foods.

1936 York Cartage Toronto, was started by R. Harris with one truck hauling gravel, and general cartage f[...] Canada Packers.

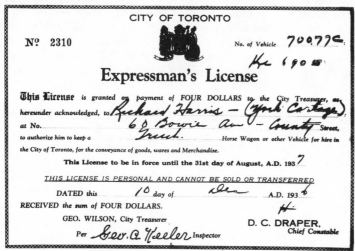

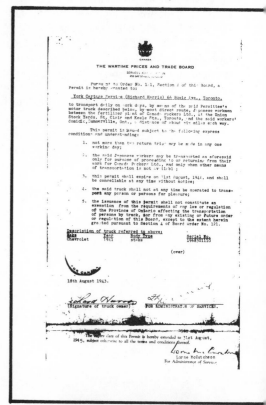

SERVICE LTD. (823 2240)

William C. Norris Ltd (Montreal).

Today

70 President of York Cartage Charles D. Bates had 10 pieces of equipment.

76 with its subsidiary company, Yellow Bird Trailer Rentals and W.C. Norris, they now have 150 trailers, tractors, and 30 strait trucks with sales of over 5 million dollars.

York Cartage was started as a local cartage company, and now serves Ontario and Quebec.

HARKEMA

Then & Now

1926

1976

Fifty years ago, a handful of trucking pioneers began forming the Ontario Trucking Association. In those days the Harkema companies didn't exist. But Sid Harkema did. And as you can see from the picture, he was in love with trucks even at that tender age.

Then, in 1954, with a few more years under his belt, Sid laid the foundations of the Harkema Group. With only one truck, but many innovative ideas and a great deal of determination, he began to build a number one trucking company.

Now, twenty-two years later, Sid has a whole fleet of trucks to "play around" with. But when Sid Harkema tells you that he loves every last one of them, believe it. Sid Harkema is not just "playing around"!

KEEP ON TRUCKING

HUSBAND TRANSPORT LIMITED

SERVING THE SHIPPING PUBLIC FOR ALMOST HALF A CENTURY

Started in the early 30's, Husband Transport Limited has grown into one of the major trucking companies in Canada, serving Ontario, Quebec, and the U.S.A.

Head Office;   10 Centre Street, London, Ontario N6A 4S1
telephone (519) 433-4581

For Decades

IMPERIAL IRL ROADWAYS

has proudly served Canada

In the 1940's the Kravetsky family opened their first terminal in Winnipeg, Manitoba. Some years later they purchased Imperial Roadways Ltd. Servicing Ontario, Quebec, Manitoba and Western Canada.

"As Canada grows, so do we. We salute and participate in the 50th Anniversary year of trucking in Ontario."

4

Trucks in The Depression

The country was far too busy in the general catastrophe of the Great Depression to notice what was happening to the infant trucking industry, either its contributions or its troubles. Yet the depression had a deep and lasting effect on the industry.

In 1930 wheat prices plummeted, which may seem to have nothing to do with trucking, but it affected the country as a whole and that inevitably affected trucking and the railways. Whereas in 1929 wheat had commanded a price of $1.05 a bushel, the farmers got only 44 cents a bushel in 1930. Farm prices of all kinds slumped and Canada was still largely a farming economy, with many people living and working on farms.

Rural communities and the merchants in them were hard hit, with people not able to buy. The trucks helped many a merchant stay in business. Where once he had to buy and stock large orders of goods, because the railways could not provide rapid service if he ran out, trucks could give him fast service on small shipments. Working capital was preserved as he did not have to keep large stocks of every item on hand.

It was difficult nonetheless for many truckers to stay in business, because few of their customers could afford to pay much. Truck owners found themselves squeezed by falling profits or downright losses and, like everyone else, they cut wages, made more demands on their men in terms of work, operated with overloaded vehicles and put off maintenance and the purchase of new equipment. In this desperate effort to remain financially afloat they were by no means alone—the whole country was doing the same thing. There was no unemployment insurance in those days, only welfare, and families received 25 cents welfare money a week for a child.

Everyone was hurting and business came to a standstill, or very nearly, just as it did in other countries of the Western World.

One effect of changes in the trucking industry was a drop in prestige of the trucker. A driver could be earning $15 for a 60-hour week, his helper $8 a week. Trucking companies could get away with lower wages and poorly trained drivers and helpers because trucks had become more dependable. They did not need the road repairs that drivers of an earlier day often had to make. Truck drivers no longer had to be mechanics as well.

By the early 1930s the efforts of manufacturers and the tightening of government regulations were bringing about striking changes in trucks. As early as 1930 the Department of National Defence was testing 6-wheel trucks made in England and equipped with 4-cylinder L-head engines, with transmissions providing four speeds forward and one in reverse. In the early thirties there were many trucks being made or assembled in Canada and competition was keen. Streamlining was being talked about. High pressure "non-skid tires" were coming in, though balloon tires were still in vogue.

Changes in the Ontario Highway Traffic Act of 1930 required motor vehicles to have "a device for cleaning rain, snow and other moisture from the windshield" and to have a rear-view mirror (the latter had previously been required only for trucks). The PCV Act was also amended to spell out loading regulations more clearly and to introduce a rule that owners of commercial vehicles must have their names and addresses on both sides of their vehicles. The definition of a public commercial vehicle was clarified to cover any motor vehicle or trailer operated on a public highway for hire, pay, or gain, or on behalf of any person for transportation of goods, wares or merchandise. The change made contract carriers, as well as common carriers, subject to PCV regulation.

The laws, however, were still loosely enforced. Piracy of cargoes was common, in fact more common than ever, spurred by the effects of the depression.

Livestock transportation was becoming important to the industry. *Truck Transportation* observed, with uncanny insight, that this was well worth looking into. In later years, most livestock was to be carried by truck. Howard G. Knill was one of those who, in 1933, began hauling livestock. He operated out of Paris, Ont. As an example, H. S. Knill Co. Ltd., as the firm is known today, shows what trucking brought to the cattle industry alone. Knills delivered registered cattle all over Canada and the United States, to the Mexican border. Knill trucks take cattle, that may be worth $200,000 apiece for a registered Holstein bull, to California for shipment to Japan, which has been building up its herds. It can make delivery from Ontario to California far more rapidly than the railway.

The transporting of livestock, which started so hum-

A 1930 Mack. A trend toward passenger car styling features is
apparent in the fenders and bumper.

A 1936 Reo Speed Wagon of 1½ to 2-ton rating, coupled to a
Kitchener-built Dominion trailer. A similar vehicle to this Reo
model was the Mack Junior.

bly in the early 1930s, is such big business today that a group of livestock truckers recently built a $500,000 rest station at Thunder Bay, capable of holding 1500 head. This is to service the huge trade in feeder cattle brought annually from the West to Ontario.

Refrigerated trucks were coming into use. Where once cargoes had been kept cool by wet tarpaulins, later by ordinary ice packing, dry ice became available and was first used in 1931 for refrigeration.

Tank trucks were becoming ever more sophisticated and capable of carrying larger loads. And semitrailers were beginning to look very businesslike with rounded, streamlined forward sections.

The greater efficiency of trucking and the disastrous effects of the depression inevitably heightened ill-feeling between the railways and the trucking industry. Their relative roles had not been, and probably could not have been clarified, since the trucking industry was developing and changing so rapidly.

In a highly competitive society, it was inevitable that a breach would widen between the railways and their labor unions on the one hand, and those sympathetic to the truckers on the other. The federal government, caught in between, was suspect by the truckers because it was the owner of a railway line.

The railway unions were powerful, whereas trucking employees were not unionized. In a way, railway labor unions increased the rail problems as their members were quite highly paid and did not favor pay cuts or longer working hours to help offset the economic chaos of the depression. Conversely, truckers were forced to do both things.

In 1930 Canadian National disbursed over $268 million in salaries and wages, an average of about $28.50 per week per employee, a good sum at a time when a married man with three children could own his own house and drive a car on $25 a week. This is not to say, of course, that the average member of a labor union was

The road haulage of new cars was big business from the late twenties on. This early trailer carries an impressive load of 1929 Oldsmobiles. The tractor appears to be a Buick-engined GMC T-80 4-tonner. Car trailers became shorter in later years with two-level loading.

The railways, with heavy costs and obviously vital to the transportation needs of the country, became increasingly hostile to the trucks as their business slipped away, eroded largely by the depression and to a smaller extent by truck competition.

Tonnage carried by the publicly owned Canadian National Railways dropped from 115 million tons in 1929 to 96 million tons. The CN deficit, which had been $46 million in 1929, pushed the railway into the red by $68 million in 1930. This was distressing to the railway, which found it increasingly difficult to maintain a service it had rightly been proud of. It was also embarrassing to the federal government, already beset by financial problems.

Figures for the operations of privately owned railway lines are not as readily available as for Canadian National, but there is no doubt they were all feeling a severe pinch.

getting $28.50 a week, since higher-paid executives and supervisory staff were included in the averaging. Nevertheless, there was little comparison between the pay and working conditions of a railwayman and employees of the average trucking company.

Determined to maintain their position in the transport industry, the railways and their labor unions used every possible argument to take business away from the trucks. But the railways were not convincing; they could not even claim greater safety or fewer losses. Figures for freight damage and loss on railways are hard to come by. However, an indication of their safety record can be found in the official Canada Year Book. In 1930, 463 people were killed and 11,063 injured on the country's steam railways and such figures were not uncommon in the years preceding and following 1930.

The government, concerned over the railway deficit, in 1931 appointed a Royal Commission on Transportation under the chairmanship of Sir Lyman P. Duff, a distinguished lawyer born in Meaford, Ont., who was to become in 1933 the Chief Justice of Canada.

The Duff Report, delivered the following year, made a number of points, some of which were to assist truckers in the long run. It did give some immediate comfort to the railway point of view but the comfort was more in spirit than practicality.

For instance, Duff said that trucks could operate as collectors and distributors for railways and he assumed they would operate over a distance of about 50 miles. This assumption was outdated—trucks were operating over distances of far more than 50 miles. And the idea that trucks would serve as collectors and distributors for railways was quite impracticable and not acceptable to merchants or industry, let alone the trucking industry.

Far more to the point, he recommended that trucking needed regulation and this regulation should be the responsibility of the provinces from a constitutional point of view. Thus, he effectively spiked any intention the federal government might have had at that time of regulating trucking in a big way. Since the federal government was suspect by the truckers, this was an important gain for them. It was especially so in Ontario, where the provincial government had shown an enlightened attitude toward the development of the industry and the province had benefited as a consequence.

A Duff Commission recommendation less welcomed by the truckers was that common carriers should pay more tax. He noted that in Ontario common carrier trucks were paying in fees and gas tax only about $215 a year if they traveled 30,000 miles, an amount which he thought to be not enough. The Ontario government, short of money, was certain to act on that recommendation.

One of the most important Duff Commission recommendations was that PCV licences should be granted only on proof of public necessity. This recommendation was instrumental in causing the Ontario government to amend the PCV Act the following year to require proof of "public necessity and convenience" before a licence could be issued. It did not at the time put effective teeth into the legislation, but an all-important step had been taken in the right direction.

By 1931 the railways were viewing trucks as the reason for many of their troubles although, in truth, trucks were not a major factor. The depression was the biggest single factor at the time. Though the trucking business was growing, some of it was "new" business which would not have been accessible to the railways anyway. Even the total business of the trucking industry was still small compared to the huge volumes of the railways.

But by 1931 the railway unions had mounted a campaign against trucks and were complaining all over the country that their jobs were being imperilled by them. In St. Thomas, Ont., a city kept alive by railways, the unions threatened to boycott merchants who received their goods by trucks.

This kind of threat was repeated elsewhere and led to some strange situations. The Railway Association of Canada had set up a committee, with representatives from all the railways. Its purpose was to oppose trucking and the committee was spearheaded by economists from Canadian National. One official of the association

lived in Stratford and it was an open secret that he used his free railway pass to go to Kitchener to buy groceries. They were cheaper in Kitchener, where they were brought in by truck.

In Timmins, a newspaper published a story about ketchup displays in two different counters. In one it was offered at 16 cents a bottle. It had been delivered by truck. The other display offered ketchup at 19 cents a bottle, it having been delivered by rail. The paper asked, a little unkindly perhaps, where the wives of railway employees were buying their ketchup? But in the depression every cent counted and even people who sincerely believed in the railways' case found themselves inexorably drawn to goods delivered by truck.

The ATA and the trucking industry fought back against the railway campaigns. One of its champions was Wilfrid H. Male, who had become a director of the ATA in 1932.

Born in Toronto October 2, 1898, "Wilf" Male had served in the Royal Canadian Army Service Corps in World War I and, in 1917, had been employed in the traffic department of Gutta Percha Rubber Ltd. He entered the trucking business in 1928 as traffic manager of Red Star Transport, which shortly after went out of business. In August of 1930 he joined Colville Cartage. He was a big man with a high broad forehead and a strong jaw, a man of dynamic character, a good administrator, a logical thinker and a forceful speaker.

In 1932, Male showed the depth of his understanding of the road transport industry in a masterly speech, one of many he later made. Figuring up to the end of 1930, he said, and computing land grants at a modest three dollars an acre, the Canadian government had subsidized the railways to the tune of one and three quarter billion dollars. There were 43,000 miles of railway lines in operation and "this represents aid to the extent of $43,458 a mile".

Noting that Ontario had 45 percent of all the motor vehicles registered in Canada, he computed that the Ontario government had spent $156 million on roads from 1920 to 1930.

"If this amount had been expended solely for the benefit of the common carrier trucks, there would be every reason to be up in arms. Only ten percent of Ontario registrations are trucks and of these 95 percent are privately owned, leaving only five percent as common carriers. Five percent of ten percent is only half of one percent. One half of one percent of $156 million is $780,000 which, spread over the 79,754 miles of provincial highways, represents less than $10 a mile.

Male was not the only champion rising vocally for the truckers. Harold T. Hoar, president of the ATA in 1932 and who had succeeded Charlie Middleton, the second president, turned the railway arguments around. The railways had argued that trucks should be limited to short hauls because the railways, they claimed, could handle long-distance freight better than trucks. Hoar suggested tartly that someone should find out the length-of-haul a truck could economically make, and the railways should be allowed to handle only the remainder.

The railways, he said, "forget that the public will always demand the transportation agency that can provide the most economical and efficient service.

"The railways have made drastic cuts in their charges

to get back business that was unprofitable to them at their old rates. But, as they are subsidized for their losses by public funds, to say the least it is unfair competition."

Hoar, the president of Hoar Transport, Toronto, and an expert on truck transport, gave it as his opinion that trucks could operate more cheaply than railways on LCL shipments up to 150 miles, and tractor-trailers could be as efficient as railways for distances up to 250 miles.

"The railroad performs only one portion of the service in most cases. The truck does the rest and it is right there that the superiority of the service has established itself. It provides complete service without assistance from any other agency."

Hoar's assault on the railway propaganda was the more effective because he carried it out in a series of radio talks. Radio was still a growing medium. Indeed, it had almost paced the development of trucking. Both had been of limited efficiency in the middle twenties. Both had made great strides and by 1932 radio, like trucking, was well established.

In December 1933 there was a conference in Ottawa of provincial and federal governments on the whole subject of truck transport. The matter was becoming a political football and the federal government was embarrassed.

Just before this conference, the ATA in Ontario had taken a step forward. It had hired its first full-time employee, Gordon L. Fabian, and his role had been largely to check up on "pirate" truckers, who were still taking business from regulated carriers. Fabian, hired in the autumn of 1933, spent most of his early months as executive director of the ATA, scouring Ontario highways for pirates and reporting them to the Department of Highways.

He was an unusual sort of person. Joe Goodman, who succeeded him, has said: "Fabian was a character. He was a heavy-set fellow, always preaching. He'd stay up day and night watching for people breaking the trucking laws."

Fabian traveled thousands of miles in this work and some measure of his endeavors can be seen in a brief presented to the federal-provincial conference by the Transportation Department of the Canadian Manufacturers' Association. This body noted that: "An organization representing the motor truck operators (the Automotive Transport Association) has recently attempted to ensure and place before the Department of Highways information indicating the extent to which the existing regulations are being violated, and it is understood that some three hundred cases have recently been presented to the department which, it is believed, is actively dealing with them."

The Department of Highways did co-operate, although it was a strange situation with the ATA doing part of the department's own work in identifying the lawbreakers.

In its brief, the Canadian Manufacturers' Association, which had a direct interest in ensuring good trucking services, spelled out the needs of the truckers as well as they could have done it themselves: the need to prove public necessity and convenience in granting PCV licences; the need for establishing and publishing tariffs and tolls charged by each company; the need for non-discrimination in transporting goods; the need for ad-equate insurance and bonding; the need for a proper system of accounting and returning information to government; and the need for a uniform bill of lading.

These needs were not all met at once, but progress was made. Concurrently with the development of regulations and better organization of the industry, trucks were still advancing in technology.

Loblaw Groceterias in Toronto ordered a Leyland highway truck with a diesel engine. The Beaver tractor chassis was designed to haul a 10-ton semitrailer and Loblaw's put it into service between Toronto and Brockville.

Silverwood-Burke Dairies of Hamilton introduced 12 specially designed vehicles for house-to-house delivery, to take over the work of 18 horse-drawn rigs on milk routes. The dairy found it made deliveries in less time and with extra load capacity.

Despite this early use of the truck for milk delivery, the horse remained, in most places, the preferred means of locomotion for house-to-house delivery. A reason for this was that many horses knew the milk and bread routes nearly as well as the drivers and would walk slowly along a street, stopping at the proper houses

1936 Dodge Model TT with Dominion semitrailer.

while the driver jumped off to make his deliveries.

The struggle between the trucking industry and the railways never lay dormant for very long. At the end of 1933, trucks were making steady progress while the railways were showing huge losses. In 1932 Canadian National alone had a deficit of more than $101 million and this dropped only slightly in 1933, to some $97 million. The railways and their supporters launched an even more vociferous campaign, appearing at clubs to make speeches, courting the press and radio stations and calling for public support against the inroads of trucking.

The truckers were not organized well enough to combat these tactics. But the industry probably benefited to the extent that it was forced to organize more thoroughly and to co-operate internally to a greater extent. This was not easy to achieve because its founders had been strong-minded people who wanted to run their own affairs. It was partly the opposition of the railways that convinced more and more of them that they had to speak with one voice, that they had to root out the faults the railways so skilfully exposed and that they must give better service than ever.

The efforts of various groups, including the ATA, to

*A 1936 Ford V-8 two-ton tractor (produced only in Canada)
with a Dominion semitrailer.*

*An early highway tractor was International's D-45 model, in-
troduced in 1937 and widely used until 1940.*

bring about government regulation of the trucking industry came a big step closer at the end of 1933, when
the Ontario government transferred authority for PCV
licences to the Ontario Municipal Board. The board said
in a later report that: "In or about 1933, it became
quite apparent that truck licences were being granted
by the Department of Highways in excess of the public
demand and, as a result, a policy was adopted to grant
only such licences in future as the services of the public
required.

"The result of this policy was that every application
for a truck licence or a bus licence must be inquired
into, especially to ascertain whether or not there was a
public service to be rendered. . . .

"That the granting of licences might be taken entirely out of politics, and inasmuch as the Ontario Municipal Board was probably better equipped than any
other board connected with the government to make
the necessary inquiry, the Legislature passed an act

directing that every application for a bus or truck licence should be referred to the Ontario Municipal
Board, and upon inquiry by the board . . . the said board
may grant or refuse a certificate. If the certificate be
granted, the Department of Highways can then, in its
discretion, issue the licence applied for."

The railways soon realized that an opportunity for
them lay in this legislation. They began showing up at
every hearing to object to the licensing of trucks. The
ATA was forced to give what support it could to legiti-
mate licence applications and so the OMB hearings
became a battleground between railways and truckers.

Although the ATA was nominally an Ontario organization it was also the spearhead of the trucking industry
in Canada. By 1933 there was no doubt that the association needed to grow; it did not have the facilities or
manpower for the huge job it faced. One full-time employee could not cope with the task.

5

The ATA Affected All Canada

By 1934 few doubted that Fabian needed help. He was crusading against pirate truckers, which took up an inordinate amount of time; there was no time left to deal with the total job of executive director, that called for increasing organizational work.

Morley Pape of Coville Transport, a volunteer who worked closely with Fabian, says it was decided that Fabian needed a full-time secretary. Pape himself had been one of the architects of the ATA. Born in Toronto in 1900, he had started in the grocery trade. In 1930 he had answered an ad for a bookkeeper at Coville Transport. Like others who influenced the trucking industry, he was not a truck driver and had no particular background in the mechnical side of the industry.

In those days Coville had trucking runs from Toronto to Barrie, Gravenhurst and Penetangueshene and, as a Coville company representative, Pape soon began to attend ATA meetings.

"They said to me at one meeting: 'You're the only one here who can speak good English, so they made me ATA secretary.' "

The job had just been relinquished by Don Mac-Quarrie.

It was through this work as unpaid secretary that Pape became a close associate of Fabian's.

The choice of Fabian's secretary came about in a strange way and the man hired was, in some respects, an unlikely choice and yet a particularly intelligent one. No man, even since the advent of personnel experts and psychological testing, has ever been more perfectly fitted for a job.

This was still a time of depression and any advertisement printed in the paper could be counted upon to attract hordes of applicants, like wasps descending on an open jam jar in August.

A three-man ATA committee was set up to make the choice. It consisted of Fabian, George Parke and Pape.

On the day the committee met, there was a lineup of men waiting to be interviewed—just as these same hopeful, yet hopeless men had waited in similar lineups day after day for other jobs. Some were probably highly qualified; in those days it wasn't just the unskilled who were out of work.

The interviewing went slowly.

At 2:45 p.m. precisely, the door of the interview room opened unexpectedly. A short dark-haired man of 20, with glasses and a bouncy manner said: "My appointment was for a quarter to three, so I thought I should let you know I was here."

He had walked past all the other waiting men and entered unannounced.

This was Joe Goodman. Born in Toronto, he had attended secondary school and taken a couple of years' training at Central High School of Commerce where he had learned shorthand, his only real claim to being a secretary. He knew nothing whatever about trucks. He was better known in the sports world as an amateur wrestler and a part-time sports writer.

After he left school, Joe's first job had been with an importer of fancy foods and chocolates. In the dirty thirties the public couldn't afford such things so the job, along with the importer, had folded. Joe was looking for something else.

Joe says of his intrusion into the committee room: "I'd passed forty waiting men to get there and the committee seemed mad at me. One of the members yelled: 'Get to the end of the line'. So I went. But a couple of minutes later someone tapped me on the shoulder and said: 'Come with me'."

He was taken directly back to the committee room. Something had impressed them about Joe—his nerve.

"There were these three big guys sitting there," he says. "They started giving me the third degree about why I had barged in like that. I said I didn't consider I had been barging in. I didn't think it was any of my business what those other guys in the lineup were waiting for. I told them I had an appointment for a quarter to three and I thought I should announce myself.

"One of the committee members said: 'You know, this is the only guy we've seen today that's got any initiative'. Then they talked to me. They found out I could do reporting and could write minutes because I had been involved with the Toronto Boy Municipal Council and various sports organizations. They offered me the job at $15 a week, which was big money for a young man in those days. But money was a secondary consideration with me; I had been earning $35 a week out of writing."

That night Joe spoke about the job to a friend, Don Parke, who was a team official in the Toronto Rugby

Union of which Joe was league secretary. "Don said to me: 'The big fat man on the committee was my dad'."

On the whole, Goodman and Fabian got along well. Goodman says: "He had a good sense of humor and he was a kindly sort of guy. But he had lots of financial problems, although he was making $45 a week. The association began getting complaints about him and he left."

At least there was one benefit in this. There was more space in the office, which was just one small room at 105 Church Street in Toronto, where the Engineers' Club is now.

It was necessary to go to the Ontario Municipal Board hearings on PCV licensing and both Fabian and Goodman attended these hearings while Fabian was still at the ATA. The board dealt with applications for two days in each month. Today, the Ontario Highway Transport Board deals with applications on a full-time basis with hearings being conducted in as many as five courts at one time.

When Fabian left the ATA, Goodman attended the board hearings alone. He was given the title of acting executive secretary and $22 a week. Meanwhile, the ATA began looking for a new executive director. But a year went by and a suitable applicant could not be found, though with so many men out of work one suspects that the ATA didn't try very hard. After all, with Goodman doing the job it was saving money.

After a year, it became clear the association affairs were being competently handled by Goodman and he was appointed executive secretary—another man in a key position who had never driven a truck and knew nothing about the mechanical side of the industry. Yet, in the years to come, Goodman was to prove himself as nearly indispensable to the association as any man could ever be.

He had a seemingly iron constitution, unlimited vitality and a high degree of organizing ability. Goodman made himself the kingpin (though he won't admit it even today) of the industry in Ontario and, indeed, in Canada. A bachelor, he made the industry his life.

What other association could you telephone in Toronto on a Saturday, when most association offices are closed, and be told by a pleasant-voiced receptionist: "Mr. Goodman is at a meeting today but he'll be in the office at 10.30 tomorrow."

Assuming she has made a mistake, you say: "Tomorrow's Sunday."

"I know," she replies. "He plans to be here."

You think this doesn't happen? It happened to me in 1976.

But back in the thirties, when Joe became executive secretary, he was twenty-two years old and untried. He faced enormous challenges . . . to organize the industry . . . to fight the quickening battle with the railways . . . to negotiate with governments for regulation of the trucking industry . . . to prevent, on the other hand, useless government red tape. . . .

On one occasion he appeared before a Senate committee. Highway No. 2, then the principal route for trucks going from Toronto to Montreal, passed through the centre of Brockville, an important railway city. There were complaints about the noise of the trucks. One of the committee members said to Goodman: "Son, is there anything we can do about these trucks that go through our city at night? They're disturbing our people, stopping them from sleeping."

Joe thought he had an answer to that.

"I've been staying at the Manitou Hotel in Brockville and I couldn't sleep because they shunt railway cars right behind the hotel in the middle of the night."

The committee member smiled gently. "I know son, but we're all used to that," he said.

This double standard on the part of politicians was to prevail for many years, especially in centres that were railway divisional points. St. Thomas was a railway town and, years after the Brockville incident, Goodman complained to an Ontario cabinet minister about the unfair treatment of trucking in St. Thomas, especially about the untrue criticisms of trucks that the minister himself had made.

"Oh, Joe," said the minister, "you mustn't mind that. I've got to say those things. Twenty-eight thousand of the 32,000 constituents who elect me either work for, or depend on the railways."

By 1934 the chief classes of truck freight being carried in Ontario were, in order of importance: general merchandise, groceries, milk, gasoline and oil, baked goods, fruit and vegetables, livestock, lumber, furniture, grain, flour, feed, automobile supplies, building supplies, coal, wood and meats. The truck had become efficient on runs up to 300 miles although—because the railways had reduced their rates to compete—the cost of trucking was slightly higher than that of the railways on trips of more than 150 miles.

The year 1934 was a busy one for the ATA. Up to July of that year it had held 42 executive meetings in a 12-month period, some lasting all day. It had reported to the Department of Highways 700 violations for punitive action. These violations included: excessive hours of labor, operation of trucks without licences, illegal transfers of licences and use of defective equipment. The ATA felt the trucking industry had a right to government help through regulation and protection. In the preceding few years trucks, though numbering only about 11 percent of the vehicles on Ontario roads, provided about 30 percent of the government's revenue from motor vehicles.

The years 1933 to 1936 were unpleasant on the whole, not only for Canada but for the world at large. The Canadian unemployment rate, which had been only 2.5 percent in 1928, reached 25 percent in the depths of the depression, the spring of 1933. Few would have dared to say at the time that the depression gradually lifted after 1933, although it was true. By 1936 the unemployment rate was 16.7 percent, still far too high but not as high as in 1933. Many families with savings at the beginning of the depression lost everything long before 1936. Thus, easing of the depression was not felt to any extent by the average family.

The year 1936 deserves to be especially remembered for it seems to have marked the end of many things familiar in the world, even of philosophies, and the beginning of others. It was a year in which the pendulum of our times passed through centre and began swinging the other way.

The year began with the death of King George V in January, the last of the truly majestic monarchs; a man who did not travel, did not make broadcasts, appeared in portraits in the full regalia of monarchy and somehow embodied the end of the image of royalty passed down by Queen Victoria. He was succeeded by Edward VIII, whose abdication in December of the same year had much of human tragedy in it, but whose short reign had little of the old imperial majesty.

In July 1934, the bloody Spanish Civil War broke out, the opponents aided on one side by the Russians, on the other by the Nazi Germans and Fascist Italians. Italy invaded Ethiopia and Germany marched into the demilitarized Rhineland, actions that revealed the impotence of the League of Nations and set the stage for World War II.

There were two other memorable events that year. On June 1 the world's biggest liner, the Queen Mary, arrived at New York on her maiden voyage and, on July 30, President Franklin D. Roosevelt became the first American president ever to visit a Canadian governor-general in Ottawa, in this case Lord Tweedsmuir.

In the twenties the world had been a confident, rollicking place; in the thirties sad sack, lacklustre. In 1936 it suddenly changed direction, speeded up and rumbled like a juggernaut of doom that people could only helplessly watch.

By 1936 there were some 70,000 commercial vehicles in Ontario, if you include fire trucks and road machines. Sales of new commercial vehicles were up sharply.

Improvement in the trucking industry in Ontario was evident by 1936 when the number of licensed operators rose to 2707 and vehicles registered under the PCV Act increased to 5665. Most of the new vehicles were serving farmers or hauling road-building materials. The cement mixer, which could mix cement while in transit, was coming into vogue about this time.

The ATA, despite its small staff but with the help of many volunteers, set about determinedly to enhance the status of drivers and develop more effective safety programs.

Joe Goodman reported: "In a safe-driving campaign being conducted by the association among a representative group of drivers, figures for the 12-month period ending October 31 disclosed 225 drivers registered. Of this number, 171 drove 5,029,265 miles without a single accident; the remaining 54 drivers covered 1,450,159 miles, being involved in 71 accidents, not all of them being of their responsibility and the average damage amounting to less than $50. There were no fatalities."

This marked the beginning of a strong and continuing campaign by the association to promote safe driving for which it has since become recognized around the world.

There was yet another significant event in 1936 in which the ATA was chiefly instrumental—the move to form the Canadian Automotive Transportation Association, now known as the Canadian Trucking Association.

On September 2 George E. Parke, president of the ATA, sent a letter to officials of provincial associations:

"The outstanding reason why a motor transport organization, Dominion-wide in its scope, should be formed without delay is the increasing influence of the Dominion government in the regulation of our industry. This has been especially evident since the Hon. C. D. Howe, an aggressive administrator, took over the direction of the Department of Transport. While the Dominion has not direct jurisdiction over motor transport, it has great influence over provincial policy and will have still greater influence as time goes on.

"The fact that it made motor transport one of the main subjects on the agenda of the last two Dominion-Provincial Conferences bears witness to this tendency, as well as some recent public utterances of Hon. C. D. Howe, intimating that the Dominion would have to take a hand in co-ordinating motor transport with the other means of transportation operating in Canada.

"It may not be generally known, but it is a fact that Mr. Howe's department is now drafting a model public commercial vehicles act and when it is completed the weighty influence of the Dominion government will be brought to bear on each of the provinces to see that they adopt it. The Dominion makes so many large money grants to the provinces that none of them can afford to go counter to its wishes on any large problem such as this one, on which it takes a stand.

"This spring, the federal government in the United States, through its Interstate Commerce Commission, took over the regulation of interstate motor carrier business in that country. The same trend toward the increase of federal influences is in evidence in Canada.

"The Dominion government is the owner of a large money-losing railway system that competes with the motor transport business and, unless the motor transport industry soon takes steps to organize a Dominion body that can speak with one strong voice in its interests, it will find that it will come out very much second best in its competition with the railways."

A furore had been caused by the apparent determination of the federal government to get into the regulation of the trucking industry. The method it chose to do this was to assert that trucks that crossed provincial boundaries, or operated between Canada and the U.S., should come under federal jurisdiction. In the truckers' opinion, it would be a short step from there to further controls. To have the government, with its big stake in a money-losing railway system, exercising wide powers over trucking put the truckers into a panic such as occurs when a wolf turns up in a herd of grazing deer.

The result of the federal government's action was to unite the trucking industry. On a cold day in January 1937 the truckers, in response to Parke's letter, met in Winnipeg and formed the Canadian Automotive Transportation Association. Initially, they financed the venture with $250 in annual dues from the ATA, while the other provincial associations agreed to put up $100 each. The new association hired M. J. Patton as an Ottawa spokesman-watchdog, with the title of executive secretary. Patton had previously worked for the ATA in Ottawa as an economist-consultant.

He carried on for the CATA for about a year and was replaced by Joe Goodman, who then had a dual executive role for both the ATA and the CATA until January 1, 1948, when John Magee was appointed executive secretary. Magee had been hired two years previously as director of public relations for the CATA. He served the national association until his appointment to the Canadian Transport Commission in 1968.

Thus the ATA influence was truly decisive in the trucking industry across Canada during the national association's vital formative years.

The CATA lost no time in making its feelings known about federal intervention. In a statement before the Senate Standing Committee on Railways, Telegraphs and Harbors, February 19, 1937, it said: "The transport industry is in favor of regulation but it does not want a multiplicity of regulating bodies. It objects to the Dominion entering as still another regulating authority with another set of license fees, another set of fines, another set of operating regulations, another inspecting staff and another rate and licensing tribunal before which time must be spent in making submissions. . . ."

Meanwhile, in Ontario the pressure on the government from the railways and particularly the railway unions was intense. Premier Mitchell Hepburn finally threw up his hands, says Goodman, and cried: "I'm not going to listen any more. We're going to appoint a royal commission."

He established the Chevrier Royal Commission on Transportation, under the chairmanship of Mr. Justice E. R. E. Chevrier. Its terms of reference included: to investigate the transportation of freight by motor vehicles for gain as well as the tolls and rates charged; and to report on methods of licensing such vehicles and what further regulations should be made to prevent unfair competition with one another and with other forms of passenger and freight transportation.

The aggressive railways and unions had not succeeded in their apparent objective of stemming the growth of the trucking industry. Instead, they had brought about an inquiry by Mr. Chevrier and his colleagues which would give everybody a chance to speak up. The trucking industry was not opposed to that.

Annual Banquet of the ATA of Ontario at the King Edward Hotel, Toronto, Nov. 26, 1932.

CONGRATULATIONS TO THE TRUCKING ASSOCIATION ON THEIR 50TH ANNIVERSARY,

FROM SOMEONE WHO JUST TURNED 50 THEMSELVES.

Fifty years ago, way back in 1926 to be precise, we formed Inter-City Forwarders Limited to operate throughout South Western Ontario.

That same year saw a handful of pioneers form what is now the Ontario Trucking Association. Looking back over those fifty years of trucking, we have to admit that it's kind of a nice feeling knowing that we've both come a long way since then.

May the next fifty be just as successful.

INTER-CITY TRUCK LINES.

From a specialized mine service operation in 1956, Commercial has branched into Specialty Trucking, Bulk Carriage and General Freight under Class C, D, K and T authorities between Northern Ontario and Southern Ontario.

COMMERCIAL CONSTRUCTION (WOODSTOCK) LIMITED

AN EMPLOYEE PROFIT SHARING COMPANY

Our first ore carrier

our latest ore carrier

We're only 15 years old but sure are looking forward to our 50th Anniversary.

MARITIME-ONTARIO FREIGHT LINES LIMITED

AN EMPLOYEE PROFIT SHARING COMPANY

KINGSWAY TRANSPORTS LIMITED AND SUBSIDIARIES

123 REXDALE BOULEVARD
REXDALE, ONTARIO M9W 1P3

LEADING THE TRUCKING INDUSTRY ~ THEN & NOW

200 years of combined service
to the industry that moves Canada

Don Reid
President

Tim Robinson
Vice President

Bruce Murray
Secretary Treasurer

Ms. Erika Tatar
Chief Underwriter

Jim Tilley
Loss Prevention

Marcel Plamondon
Loss Prevention Manager

Ed Cox
Loss Prevention

Louis Dumas
Claims Manager — Quebec

Clem St. Hilaire
Loss Prevention

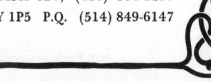

UNITED CANADA *INSURANCE COMPANY*

155 UNIVERSITY AVENUE, TORONTO, ONTARIO M5H 3B7, (416) 864-1287
360 ST. JAMES ST., SUITE 1260, MONTREAL H2Y 1P5 P.Q. (514) 849-6147

6

The Wheels of War

By 1938 and into 1939 there was still high unemployment and wages were low. Very little housing had been built since 1929 and many families were doubled up in houses. Toronto was not a particularly exciting place, its populace moving about by streetcar, many of them heated by stoves in winter. Its downtown buildings on the railway side were blackened from the smoke of steam locomotives. The old avenues, once gracious with their huge Victorian houses—like Jarvis Street—were deteriorating. Hamilton was a steel town, perhaps warmer in spirit than Toronto, but not much to look at. London, "the forest city", had charm because of its many trees and yellow brick houses. It had little industry but considerable wealth and so it was an oasis of a sort, although culturally, at the time, it had relatively little to offer.

At the lacklustre end of the thirties, Mr. Justice Chevrier set about finding a solution to the problems of road transport in the province.

It had been intended to hold sittings in several centres but the commission became bogged down in Toronto, where it stayed for 69 days.

"It nearly bankrupted us," says Joe Goodman. "What with preparing briefs, paying legal fees and having to attend hearings constantly, we were left nearly penniless at the ATA."

The Government of Ontario became impatient too. The attorney general, after the hearings had gone into their 60th day, told the commission it was spending too much time and money and ordered it to speed up. By that time the sittings had cost the Ontario taxpayer more than $50,000.

Yet Chevrier was doing his best with a difficult task. He had to sift through mountains of evidence produced by the various powerful interests which mounted massive campaigns. Much of the evidence was biased, yet skillfully presented. Experts had to be engaged by both sides.

Eventually, in 1939, Chevrier produced his 293-page report. One significant recommendation was that the province should establish a separate highway transport board. Another was that the Ontario trucking industry should be properly regulated.

"The Commission is convinced that the supervision of standards of equipment, service, hours, conditions of labor and details of operating methods of those making use of the highways for commercial purposes has become a duty devolving upon the public authority," said the report.

But the Chevrier Commission seemed to have been set up under an unlucky star. Despite the efforts of Mr. Chevrier to do a good job, his recommendations were to be swept away for a long time by the intrusion of the Second World War. It was to be 16 years before his recommendation for a separate transport board for Ontario was carried out. Some of his other recommendations came about piecemeal over the years; some were never introduced.

At first the effects of the outbreak of war were not obvious, because there was a lengthy "phoney-war" period with a deceptive quiet between Germany and the Western Allies. The Germans were clearing up the debris of Poland and gearing for an onslaught on the West. The Allies, not prepared for war, were apparently hoping the Germans would decide to back down. The Royal Air Force was limited to dropping leaflets on Germany, rather than bombs. The period lasted about six months.

During this time the ATA introduced, toward the end of 1939, the first edition of its *Ship-By-Truck Directory* that listed truck lines, where they operated and other information pertinent to shippers. In subsequent years the directory became of great importance to shippers and carriers.

As 1940 came in the war at sea was under way, but otherwise the deceptive quiet continued. The ATA was still struggling to improve government regulation of the industry and it introduced tougher standards of its own. In changed requirements for association membership, announced in the ATA Bulletin in January 1940, it was noted that "The board of directors may refuse membership to any applicant or, on refunding the fees paid, may cancel the membership of any member if the conduct of such member or proposed member is detrimental to the best interests of the association."

All sorts of trucking abuses were taking place. Local cartage concerns were advertising "long haulage" in telephone book yellow pages, although they had no licence for such work. Trucks were being so seriously overloaded that the attorney general ordered police to

A 1941 Smith Transport GMC and Fruehauf semi help the sale of war savings stamps and certificates.

investigate. He said that up to 3000 trucks a day were using the Queen Elizabeth Way, sometimes loaded to the point where four trucks were carrying as much as eight were licensed for.

PCV frauds were still common. In one fraud which was popular, a shipper would give an unlicensed carrier a "bill of sale" so that if he were stopped he could claim the goods he was carrying were his own and so not subject to transport by a PCV-licensed truck. The scheme worked well in most cases, but sometimes the unlicensed trucker would vanish with the goods. In that case the shipper could scarcely press charges for theft since he would then have to admit that he had been in collusion to defraud.

In the Legislature there were still rumblings about irregularities in the trucking industry, more or less as an aftermath to the Chevrier Royal Commission which had commented on them. When the Legislature opened January 10 the Liberal whip, Ian Strachan, K.C., said: "I would urge upon the minister of highways that every consideration be given to the recommendation of the Chevrier Report to set up a transport board in Ontario with powers, duties and jurisdictions with reference to transportation by trucks and buses in Ontario . . ."

Hon. C. D. Howe, in the federal government, continued as a problem for the truckers. He and his colleagues of the cabinet converted—in name at least—the former Board of Railway Commissioners into the Board of

Transport Commissioners. The ATA objected on the grounds that the board was still railway-oriented.

Worse still, Bill 14 was introduced in the House of Commons. Its intent was to empower the new Board of Transport Commissioners to take over the administration of any provincial regulations of bus or truck traffic with the agreement of the provincial legislature concerned. Up to this time, carriers making interprovincial or international runs had been subject to regulation in the provinces or states into which they traveled. Now the federal government proposed to move into the field and place power in the hands of a board that was, as the ATA had pointed out, historically and philosophically "railway-oriented". It could be the beginning of even wider federal control aimed at protecting the profits of the railways.

But Bill 14, like the Chevrier Report, was also to be shelved when, on April 9, 1940, the war erupted with the Nazis invasion of Norway. On May 10 they stormed into Belgium, Holland and Luxembourg. On that day British Prime Minister Neville Chamberlain, who had tried so hard to appease the Nazis, resigned, to be replaced by that doughty warrior, Winston Churchill. The change was too late to stop the Nazi blitzkrieg that shattered the French line on May 15 and swept on to the Channel, forcing evacuation of the Allies via Dunkirk early in June.

At last everyone realized the Germans were dangerous. Britain was on food rationing and blackouts. The enormous loss of vehicles of every kind at Dunkirk meant a breakneck tooling-up for production of military equipment everywhere, including Canada. Canadian war plants had orders for more than 4000 planes and C. D. Howe announced a major ship-building program. There was no time for bickering with truckers or worrying about railway losses.

The importance of trucks in the war effort soon became apparent. World War II was literally a "war on wheels"... soldiers carried in trucks... wheeled or tracked artillery... no total reliance on railways to transport war materials, but trucks pouring directly to the front, wherever it was. And far behind the lines, trucks supplying materials to build war factories, bringing in the raw materials for the new factories to work on, and finally transporting the finished war material to waiting ships.

By 1941 there were 278,771 trucks registered in Canada representing, with associated plant and equipment, an industry value of $500 million and employing more than 450,000 people—more than all other forms of pow-

ered transportation put together. Many communities in Ontario were served only by truck.

Trucks began to be used virtually as traveling billboards, a means of communicating the war message as well as transporting goods for it. Their signs advertised war savings stamps and recruitment. Canada's first Victory Bond campaign was introduced early in 1941 and was oversubscribed within a few months as Canadians united behind the war effort.

But though the Nazi successes united the country for war, there was confusion, which was inevitable. The government still had not fully realized the vital part trucks would play. Truck drivers were recruited into the armed services; they could also earn more money in war plants than by driving civilian trucks. Truck owners soon found themselves facing a major labor shortage, exactly at the time when they and the country needed the trucks rolling.

The industry appealed to the federal government to declare it "essential to the successful prosecution of the war" and the government complied, which meant that at least a trucker could not be conscripted. This by no

A 1940 Ford Three Ton hauling a Fruehauf semitrailer bearing the handiwork of O. M. Tinkess Signs. McAnally & Son Ltd. was taken over by Dominion Freightways, now part of Dominion-Consolidated Truck Lines Ltd.

means solved the labor problem, which remained acute to the end of the war.

There were other problems, too, and they were destined to get much worse. Shortages developed in trucks, parts, gasoline and other essential items needed to keep the trucks rolling.

Two grades of gasoline were introduced during 1941, standard and premium, the latter containing tetraethyl lead. The trouble with the standard gasoline was that it tended to damage engines. One trucker reported pistons seizing up and breaking; another that five engines had thrown connecting rods through the blocks within a few weeks. Manifolds plugged up with carbon causing excessive back pressure. Other truckers complained of reduced fuel mileage from the standard gasoline, ranging up to 33 percent.

Although theoretically the allies controlled plenty of oil, it was not readily accessible without risk. Only the

rubber, most of which came from British-owned Malaya. The destruction of the American fleet at Pearl Harbor upset the balance of power in the Pacific and Britain, hard-pressed at home, could not remedy the situation. Malaya fell and the end result was a serious shortage of tires.

These various shortages meant that the federal government was forced to take greater control of the trucking industry and this time there were no objections. But there were debates about the means of doing this. An inquiry, headed by a former railroader, recommended to cabinet that truck transport be limited to a radius of 75 miles from home base. This was not thought by the industry to be in the interests of the war effort.

Walter Little, MP, a truck owner from Kirkland Lake, took Joe Goodman to see the Hon. C. D. Howe personally about the matter. Howe had become minister of munitions and supply—the No. 1 man in government

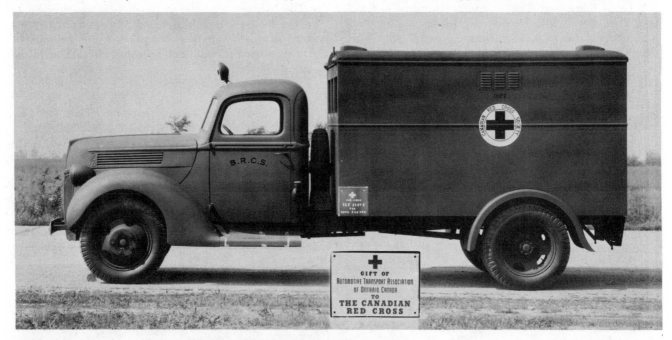

Members of The (then) Automotive Transport Association of Ontario supported the war effort in many ways. One tangible way was the gift of this fully equipped ambulance to The Canadian Red Cross in July of 1942. Presentation was made at the 14th annual meeting of the association at the Boulevard Club, Toronto. At that time the ATA also presented substantial cheques to the Mayor of Toronto War Fund and the Sports Service League. The following year an electric organ was presented by the ATA to the RSASC, Camp Borden.

United States, not yet in the war, had oil to spare, though Britain had huge supplies in her Middle East sphere of protectorates and possessions. Italy's entry into the war and the German presence in the Mediterranean made it impossible to bring oil by that short route and necessitated the long journey around Africa . . . a hazardous trip because of the U-boats.

It was equally dangerous to carry oil across the Atlantic from the U.S. or Venezuela. Oil, therefore, was a precious commodity and gasoline rationing was soon inevitable.

But more problems were to come. When Japan attacked the United States on December 7, 1941, rubber supplies were affected. Tires were made from natural

after Prime Minister Mackenzie King.

Goodman has recorded what happened at the meeting with Howe:

"Walter said to Howe: 'Clarence, Mr. Goodman here tells me that you're considering limiting trucks to 75 miles. I operate between Toronto and Kirkland Lake and I am hauling a lot of supplies up there. This would put me out of business and it would affect all the trucking industries in these isolated places. I don't think you realize how important the trucks are to the economy.' "

Little warned Howe that because of the rumors of expected restrictions, truckers were afraid to enter into contracts, to make commitments to buy equipment or

The ATA was active in encouraging first-aid training.

to set up warehouses. This uncertainty was creating problems not only for the industry but for the war effort.

Goodman says they talked for about 20 minutes and then Howe made a statement which, coming from a member of the federal cabinet, must be considered historic:

"I want to assure you that it is not our intention to limit trucks to 75 miles and I will see that the trucking industry, because of its essential nature, gets all the fuel necessary, because the railways can't do the whole job."

This was the first time a cabinet minister had conceded that long-haul trucking was truly essential and that the railways "could not do the whole job."

Because of the suspicion with which truckers looked upon the philosophies of the federal government, Goodman knew that they would need more than a mere report from him of a conversation with Mr. Howe.

"I went back to my hotel and wrote a report of what Mr. Howe had said, quoting him. Later that afternoon I showed it to Walter Little and asked if we could get Mr. Howe to initial the statement as factual.

"This was done and Mr. Howe wrote on my report: 'This is an accurate verbatim report of my statement' and signed it personally."

After that the ATA issued a report to the industry that put fears to rest and created a new feeling and rapport with the federal government that enabled

trucking to play its full part in the war effort.

By the time the U.S. was bombed into the war by Japan it was becoming clear that the federal government would eventually exercise total control of trucking in Canada. By February 1942, only three months after the attack on Pearl Harbor, there was estimated to be only eight months' supply of rubber left in Canada, rigidly controlled by a federal government agency, the Fairmount Corporation.

Natural rubber had to be replaced, at least partly, for making tires and the government organized the Polymer Corporation to do this. It opened in Sarnia in 1943.

Synthetic tires were quickly developed, but they had problems. Smith Transport was one of the companies that tested the early synthetics. The tires ran so hot on the road that Smith had to mount barrels of water on each side of its trucks, with spigots dripping water onto the tires as the truck rolled along.

On March 2, 1942, the Ontario government announced restrictions on the issuing of new PCV licences. In future, licences would be issued only to applicants whose trucks were needed for direct war work, or very real public convenience and necessity.

On March 21 the federal government proved its intention to co-operate with the trucking industry, at least for the duration of the war. It appointed Wilfred Male as deputy administrator of services in the Wartime Prices and Trade Board, his duties being to control and regulate the trucking industry throughout Canada. The appointment thoroughly satisfied the industry. Male was no railway supporter. He was a trucking man from way back, as well as being respected for his extraordinary administrative ability. He had the complete support of the industry, even though some of the things he had to do were tough on the truckers.

The truckers were also reassured by the fact that Male's immediate boss was James Stewart of Toronto, a banker by profession, who had no bias against the truckers.

Male opened offices on the sixth floor of 255 Bay Street, Toronto, and announced a policy to enforce pooling of cargoes. This policy had already been suggested by the ATA. He also announced there would be co-ordination of services in some areas, that reserves of parts and tires would be established for each truck operator so that he could be sure of at least 18 months operation, and that dead-end hauling would be drastically curtailed. Restrictions would be imposed on hours of operation, especially those of delivery and pick-up trucks.

Soon afterwards, the government announced that manufacture of trucks and trailers for civilian use would be discontinued after April 1, 1942. Gasoline rationing was introduced. Commercial vehicles were at first issued with two ration books, each good for 320 gallons of gasoline. When a book had been used up, its cover had to be returned to the nearest regional control office and another book was issued.

By 1942 manpower problems in the industry were serious. More than half of its total employees had had to be replaced due to enlistment, or loss to the higher-paying war industries.

Pooling of cargoes not only saved valuable trucks, tires and gasoline, it reduced the need for manpower as well. Privately owned delivery trucks had been restricted to a maximum range of 35 miles from home base. Newspapers, department stores and manufacturers agreed among themselves to deliver each other's goods by pool arrangements. Your Toronto Star might be delivered to your newsboy in a Toronto Telegram truck in one area, while The Telegram was being delivered by The Star in another. Your new winter coat from Eaton's might arrive at your door in a Simpson's van.

Common carrier trucks also were subject to pooling. In areas where there was more than one licensed hauler, arrangements were made to transfer freight so that vehicles were hauling for competing companies but traveling full instead of half empty.

While the war effort received considerable attention, it was not the only activity of the ATA. It continued its work on safety programs, reasoning that the fewer accidents, the less the wear and tear on irreplaceable trucks. In March 1943, Harvey Kaster of Walkerton was given the Legion of Safety trophy by the ATA for driving 930,900 miles without an accident. He had been driving since 1926.

The ATA also set up a Freight Claims Bureau to study causes of losses, to prevent losses and to secure

A 1940 AC502 GMC tractor with its Fruehauf traveling billboard.

cooperation from the shippers in properly packing their goods. During the war damage and loss had risen, due to a number of factors. One of these was the shortage of protective materials for shippers to use in packing. Another was the lack of experienced personnel, both in shipping departments and the trucking industry. A committee was appointed to study the matter under the chairmanship of W. Dennis Day, former president of Metropolitan Transport Ltd., that had merged with Direct-Winters.

By 1944, the industry was experimenting with two-way radio communication in trucks, though this development was not to come about in any big way for a number of years.

Even by this time the ATA was still a small organization, its staff of seven far from adequate for the large job it had to do. It had 700 members, many of whom owned only one or two trucks.

Some fleet owners had vision far ahead of their time. One was John Labatt Ltd., of London. During 1944 and 1945 the Labatt firm realized that a problem could be turned into an opportunity. A problem for trucks had always been that they were so big, so visible, that everyone noticed the inconvenience they sometimes caused when car owners couldn't get around them on narrow roads, or couldn't pass them on hills. Labatt turned the truck's visibility into an asset. Labatt trucks were kept sparkling clean and in top running order. Drivers were trained in first aid and ordered to stop and help private motorists in trouble. An opinion poll conducted at the time showed Labatt trucks were looked upon by the public in a special way: they were the "good guys" on the road.

Labatt's did more than that; they shared their ideas in a practical way. In 1945 they sponsored a course for motor vehicle supervisors. The course, held in Toronto, was limited in attendance to 50 people and the fee was only $10 a person. Conducted by Professor Amos E. Neyhart of Pennsylvania State University, the course introduced new ideas for motor fleet management into Canada.

By early 1945 victory in the war was close and planning for peace began. The Canadian Army newspaper, *The Maple Leaf*, published for men serving overseas (its editor J. D. MacFarlane, later editor of the Globe and Mail and The Telegram and now with the Toronto Sun) reported that there were lots of jobs waiting in the trucking industry. This was confirmed by Joe Goodman who estimated, in an ATA Bulletin, that the industry needed 47,000 people in Ontario alone.

This was a time for the industry to look back with pride. Despite all its problems it had come through the war intact and had made contributions that could scarcely be overestimated. The ATA had not only helped the trucks keep rolling, it had collected and sent to the armed forces more than 2500 phonograph records, 3000 books, 1000 decks of playing cards, 1500 assorted games and 30 tons of magazines, as well as sports equipment. The ATA's war fund also made possible, in July 1942, the donation of an ambulance to the Canadian Red Cross Society. In late 1943 an electric organ was presented to the RCASC at Camp Borden. Wilf Male made the presentation on behalf of the ATA. The association also helped the war effort in other ways, not the least of which was assisting in the organization of collection drives for scrap metal, paper, and other materials of value for recycling.

The truckers had worked long hours. Like everyone else, they had had to make do with inferior equipment and the experienced had suffered the tribulations of working alongside inexperienced people. The industry had shown what could be done in a common cause and when politicians responded realistically to real needs. Feeling was good between Ottawa and the trucking industry. On a larger scale, people everywhere had joined in the cause of winning the war and morale and national unity in Canada had brought the country closer to true nationhood, despite the nit-picking of preceding years.

7

Rebuilding With the Peace

With the approach of peace, uneasiness again began to grow in the trucking industry that the federal government would become less co-operative.

Goodman warned in an ATA Bulletin: "No federal government will do anything to antagonize the railways, but rather will tend to sacrifice other transportation agencies to strengthen the railways' position."

Already railway interests were again beginning to put forth a strong case for federal control of the trucking industry. In 1944 the Affiliated Railwaymen's Organization of Ontario, also known as the Ship-by-Rail Association, presented a brief to the Hon. J. E. Michaud, K.C., the federal minister of transport, suggesting that "your government, with the co-operation of the provinces, give consideration to the control and regulation of highway transport by placing it under federal jurisdiction in a similar manner to that of the railways, thus bringing these two industries on a competitive basis rather than having an unregulated rate structure in the for-hire highway carrier industry, which unregulated rate structure not only adversely affects that industry and its users but also unjustly discriminates against the railways and railway employees . . ."

The ATA had a firm reply.

It pointed out that the railway unions had managed to more than double their wages between 1914 and the outbreak of World War II and "The motor transport industry contends, in view of the facts of the case, that the association seeks restrictions on highway carriers, not for the benefit of the Canadian public, but quite simply to protect the jobs and the relatively high wages of its members."

Although the railwaymen were claiming unfair competition from for-hire truckers, the ATA pointed out that these trucks constituted only ten percent of the trucks in Ontario and, of the communities they served, 57 percent could not be served by rail.

"In point of fact, operations of the for-hire vehicles aid rather than compete with the railways, bringing them a great volume of traffic from points inaccessible by rail and also opening up new areas."

The ATA noted that the for-hire carriers were small companies, averaging two vehicles to a firm.

"No more effective blow could the railways land against highway transport than to have this industry saddled with the same voluminous regulations required for operation of their own billion-dollar companies."

In brief, with the war in Europe coming to an end in 1945, the war between the railways and the trucking industry was beginning all over again, with the federal government in the uneasy position it had held before the war—a position made inevitable by the fact that it owned a railway.

In August 1944 the trucking industry met with the federal government's special committee on reconstruction and re-establishment, among those present being Morley Pape, Wilf Male, Col. R. G. "Curly" Caley and Joe Goodman. Caley had just returned from service with the U.S. Army in construction of the Alaska Highway and was fleet superintendent with the British American Oil Company. One hope of the truckers was for much better equipment after the war. They had made-do for years.

At the ATA annual meeting in 1944, Professor E. A. Allcutt, head of the Mechanical Engineering Department of the University of Toronto, spelled out some of their requirements: Improved safety through reliable steering, brakes, tires and lights; more economy in initial cost and operating costs; manoeuvrability for ease of handling, loading and unloading; more power for flexible operation in traffic and emergencies; a wider choice of gear ratios for the driver; temperature controls for engines, cabs and perishable cargoes; and greater comfort for the driver, including better springs.

"The comfort of the driver is important to prevent fatigue," said Allcut.

Aluminum and similar light metals might be coming in, he predicted, but their price compared to steel was still high and the difficulty of forming and welding were serious handicaps.

On the other hand, he foresaw true refrigerator vehicles becoming a commonplace. These vehicles would provide climate control, cooling the cargo in summer and warming it in winter.

The Ontario government was embarking on a major program to improve highways. Premier George Drew announced a $250 million road-building program over five years. Mr. Drew had no doubt of the importance of the trucking industry. At the ATA annual convention in 1944 he said: "In the rebuilding of the new world beyond victory, highways and trucks are going to be an essential part of our development. Under the pressure of war we have learned many lessons which will find their results in new designs, not only of trucks, but also of highways over which they will travel...and make both commercial and private trucking possible on a scale never known before."

Another factor was beginning to enter the trucking industry. Labor unions were getting ready to play a much bigger part, once war was over. The old tough attitude of the employer that had prevailed during the twenties and even more during the thirties, the hardships that had been inevitable during the war, were all preparing the way for a head-on collision between the trucking industry and the demands of labor.

Labor demands were not limited to the trucking industry, of course, but were a general development of the times. In 1944 the government responded to labor pressures with the 48-hour week and the Vacations With Pay Act. The trucking industry was exempted from the 48-hour week because it was so desperately short of men and was still so vital to the prosecution of the war.

On June 13 of that year the International Brotherhood of Teamsters, Chauffers and Warehousemen and Helpers of America—the Teamsters Union, in short—served notice at a meeting with the board of directors of the ATA that it would be organizing locals in the Ontario trucking industry.

Perhaps inevitably, it was not a happy meeting. Canadians were not accustomed to the belligerency of the American labor unions.

As Joe Goodman remembers the meeting: "The teamsters representative started pounding the table, just about going up on his elbows, telling us what they were going to do to the industry. All friendly feeling went out the window right there."

The president of the ATA was Art Houldsworth who operated Metropolitan Transport, a fine man, refined, church-going and polished, not at all the kind who appreciated the bombast of the teamsters' representative.

From that point, the teamsters had to fight for everything they got, but they were accustomed to fighting and not dismayed by it.

By 1945 thousands of war surplus trucks were on the market and men flooded home for jobs. The trucking industry was poised to expand. The whole country was buying things, or trying to buy them. But, after years of deprivation and although people had lots of money, the factories were not converted from war work quickly enough to meet the demand, so goods were in short supply.

Housing and offices were in equally short supply as manufactured goods. Coincidentally, the ATA found itself in unexpected need of new offices. Three days before the 1945 annual meeting the office building housing the ATA caught fire. For five hours the staff waited anxiously on the street to enter the building and find out what could be saved. They found a stock room completely gutted and even the board of directors' report to the annual meeting ruined. Mechanical equipment—typewriters, adding machines and mimeographing machines were unworkable without complete overhaul. Much of the furniture was damaged. Most serious was the fact that the office could no longer be used.

The ATA Bulletin wailed: "Office space is the scarcest thing in Toronto. We have contacted every real estate, mortgage, investment and other company that might know of, or have space available. It looks as if we may have to buy a building to get space. But as we have not been able to track one down that is within our means, the situation is really desperate."

Temporarily, the staff of eight worked out of what was formerly the dressing room of the old St. Pats hockey team in the Mutual Street Arena. The arena had been converted for roller skating and the manager, Sid Shaw, was a friend of Goodman's. But the situation had disadvantages. It was so cold in the office that the staff had to wear sweaters and overshoes.

After much aggravation, an office was found at Wellington Street and University Avenue. Later on, another move was made to Queen's Quay at the foot of Spadina Avenue, from which the association eventually moved to its own building at 555 Dixon Road, near Highways 27 and 401 in Rexdale.

Although many other businesses were making a great deal of money in 1946-47, with goods so scarce and money so plentiful that almost anything could be sold, the trucking industry was not in equally favorable circumstances. It was exposed to rocketing costs of labor, trucks and parts and was still tied helplessly to prices imposed by the Wartime Prices and Trade Board. Many common carriers were in real danger of going bankrupt.

The ATA wrote to F. E. Fletcher, deputy administrator of services of the WPTB, pointing out the increased costs in the industry and calculating a rise in costs to ten companies over a six-month period had been 24.39 percent. It urged the board's attention to stop increasing losses in the industry. There followed discussions between the WPTB and the ATA, whose representatives asked for a 20 percent increase in rates on less-than-truckload lots.

The board replied with gratifying promptness that "We are satisfied that there is need for relief from the increased costs which you have been experiencing. The proposed general increase of 20 percent in less-than-truckload lots, however, raises a number of complications, particularly in relation to commodities which are still under price ceilings. The board needs more time to make proper consideration. In the meantime, however, the board is prepared to authorize an increase in the minimum charge on single shipments to seventy-five cents". (The minimum charge had been fifty cents).

The board's gesture turned out to be unnecessary; truckers' rates were decontrolled only three weeks later. Yet a sequel to the affair nearly got the ATA into serious trouble.

As soon as restrictions were removed it was obvious that trucking prices would rise even more and Goodman issued a press statement to the effect that, in some areas, they might rise a further 20 percent. The Globe and Mail published a banner headline to the effect that truckers had decided to raise their rates by 20 percent.

"Within twenty-four hours I had a letter from the Combines Commission asking for copies of minutes and other documents pertaining to the decision," says Goodman. The commission suspected collusion among the truckers, which would have been illegal under the Combines Act. "I could see myself being measured for a black-and-white uniform in jail," says Goodman.

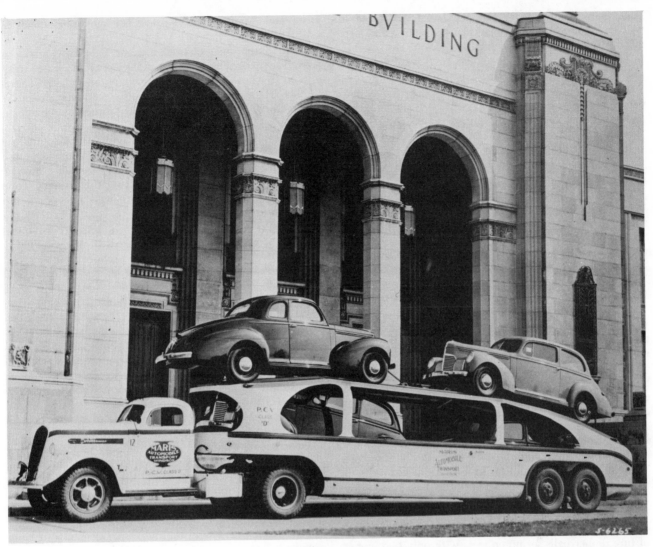

A Studebaker K30 tractor hauls a load of four 1939 Studebaker Champions.
This type of streamlined car trailer was used well into the postwar years.

In fact, the ATA had never had anything to do with setting rates. It had encouraged government regulation, that was all.

Goodman went to Ottawa with the ATA minute book, a copy of the statement that had been issued to the press, which merely said that prices might go up as much as 20 percent in some areas, and a copy of the presentation the ATA had made to the WPTB.

"We never heard any more about it," he says. "I guess they were satisfied."

In 1947 trucks were used for the first time in a new operation that later became important—shipment of rapidly perishable air cargoes to the Niagara Peninsula. In this case a load of tomato plants was shipped by plane out of West Virginia, loaded onto a waiting truck at Buffalo and planted in the ground in Ontario by 7 a.m. the next day.

That same year one of the most important events pioneered by the ATA was the first Canadian Truck Roadeo. It took place in December at the Automotive Building of Toronto's Canadian National Exhibition, with 5000 spectators attending.

It was sponsored by the ATA and there were 66 entrants from 49 companies competing. There were two top prizes, one for tractor-trailer operation, the other for straight trucks. In the tractor-trailer competition the winner was Frank Bell, 33, of Toronto. Bell had served in the war in the Royal Canadian Army Service Corps and was employed by Canadian Breweries. He received the top prize of $425. The $325 first prize for straight-truck driving went to Jules Chartrand, 34, of Port Credit, driver of a tank truck for Trinidad Leasehold (Canada) Ltd. Chartrand had been a merchant seaman before taking up truck driving. Each of the 30 semifinalists won $25.

The roadeo developed out of a trip made by ATA representatives to see a truck roadeo in Madison Square Garden, New York, in 1946. The Americans had started the roadeo idea nine years earlier.

The ATA formed a committee, under the chairmanship of R. J. "Bert" Telford of Reo Trucks, to organize a roadeo with help from American Trucking Associations, Inc. To be eligible a driver had to have an accident-free record for at least 12 months and to have been with the same employer for that year. He had to compete in written and verbal examinations on equipment, safe driving rules, first aid and fire protection. He also had to undergo a personality test. Of a total possible of 340 points, 280 were for actual driving skill.

The sponsors were not sure what response they would get and were gratified when so many drivers competed and spectators carried the winners off on their shoulders.

Roadeomaster of this first Canadian Truck Roadeo was W. Earl Givens, Jr., of the American Trucking Associations.

It was not difficult to decide that the roadeo should be an annual event.

The following year, drivers were entered from the Armed Forces and attendance increased to 6000 persons. While the first roadeo had been held in a single evening, the second was a two-day affair.

Down the years the truck roadeo has become an integral part of the ATA's safety program, a positive and constructive force in rousing enthusiasm among drivers for safety and efficiency. Where most government programs to improve passenger car safety were negative—fines, jail and demerit points—the truck roadeos and other safety programs of the ATA placed emphasis on positive factors, honoring the safe drivers and enabling them to show their skills before large audiences.

Among the new rules were: A driver could not drive his own truck; he had to make a thorough check of the strange truck given him, a truck deliberately tampered with so that faults could be found; additional tests of skill such as parallel parking between two barricades; backing up to a loading platform using only rear-view mirrors and stopping not more than six inches from the dock without touching it; driving through a double row of tiny rubber balls set up on tees, with only two inches clearance for the right-hand wheels—these were tests for real experts, men who had become professionals in the true sense.

The importance of truck roadeos, held provincially as well as nationally, and the other safety programs initiated by the ATA—often in conjunction with the Canadian Highway Safety Conference and its executive director, W. Arch Bryce, could scarcely be overestimated.

They changed the face and image of trucking. As the industry began to attract trained men again after the war, the safety programs kept the emphasis on expertise and driver responsibility, correcting the damage done during the war due to inexperienced personnel and equipment shortcomings.

The ATA played a significant role in the re-establishment of servicemen in civilian life. It worked closely with federal, civil and military authorities concerned with re-establishment. Many had learned to drive and maintain vehicles in the services and these talents were reapplied to the needs of the trucking industry. The ATA also gave counsel and advice to those servicemen without any particular experience, but who were attracted to the trucking industry as a vocation.

But any idea that the industry could settle down to a period of stable growth without stress and challenge was quite wrong. There were so many opportunities, so many changes constantly coming about in equipment, so many pressures from many directions, that only people of imagination who could roll with the punches and come back for more could possibly survive for long.

Unlike many other businesses that could be built up and then find a secure niche, the trucker of the late forties was in intense competition with other truckers, as well as the railways. He was using public highways over which he had no control; he had to satisfy shippers, governments and the increasing demands of labor unions. It wasn't an easy business to be in.

Un demi-siècle au volant!

Half a century in the driver's seat!

PAUL PROVOST CARTAGE MONTREAL

TERMINALS

Long ago, Canada seemed even bigger than it does today.

Distances between settlements were vast. Transporting vital supplies from Eastern Canada to the several thousand pioneers struggling for survival in isolated settlements took months.

The miles have not shrunk with the years, but the time required to transport goods across Canada has. The time now required would seem like the impossible dream to our pioneers.

When you have goods to ship, don't let the enormous size of our country worry you. Call Reimer Express Lines for swift, daily scheduled service between the St. Lawrence and the Pacific.

REIMER EXPRESS LINES LTD.

We've got what it takes to take what you've got

The little old 1924 Ford Model T truck and the modern tractor above, graphically illustrate the changes that have taken place.

Over 100 years of trucking experience

Finch & Sons Transport started trucking in 1918 between Brantford and Toronto. Thibodeau Express started in 1928 between Windsor and Toronto. Their amalgamation represents a combined total of over 100 years of trucking experience and service.

Starting with three trucks and a handful of employees, Thibodeau-Finch Express Ltd., now employs over 900 people and has over 900 tractors and trailers.

The past was rewarding, the present is challenging and the future holds much promise.

THIBODEAU·FINCH EXPRESS LTD.

Head Office:
Box 2430, Windsor, Ontario, Canada
N8Y 4S4, Telephone (519) 966-1222

THINK FAST

WE CAME IN WITH THE CHARLESTON, BUT WE STUCK AROUND.

In 1925, the Charleston was all the rage. And IAC was a small motor vehicle financing company, with an itch to grow.

Today, the Charleston is a fond memory. But IAC has grown into the largest commercial financing and leasing company in Canada.

We know Canadian business. Because we've had more than fifty years experience helping finance its progress. And that's something you can count on when you put money into action in your business.

IAC Money in action.

8

One Crisis After Another

The year 1948 was notable in a number of ways. The British Empire, which had once seemed so indestructible and had controlled a quarter of the earth, began to break up with the granting of independence to Burma and Ceylon, although the latter chose to remain within the Commonwealth. Canada's Mackenzie King became the longest continuously serving prime minister in the history of the Commonwealth, resigning November 15 to be succeeded by Louis St. Laurent. Canada was granted a permanent seat on the Security Council of the United Nations and Newfoundland voted to join Confederation.

Ontario continued to lead in trucking in the country. In 1948 there were 165,137 commercial vehicles registered in the province, compared to 87,954 in Quebec, some 50,000-plus each in British Columbia, Alberta and Saskatchewan, fewer in the other provinces.

The railways continued to be in trouble, a fate they shared with railways in other countries, including the United States and Great Britain. There was no doubt that they were still an essential service and would remain so, but they were enormously expensive to maintain and lacked the flexibility of truck service.

Back in 1937, the federal government had canceled railway loans totalling nearly $600 million, as well as claims for interest of nearly $44 million. Yet CN, despite a profit it had shown during the war, had plunged into the red again. Its deficit was nearly $9 million in 1946, $16 million in 1947 and over $33 million in 1948.

There seemed to be no good answers to the railway problem. It was not simply one of trucking competition. The buses, and to an increasing extent the airlines, took away their passengers. And yet they were stuck with maintenance of their rights-of-way, complex and costly traffic systems, expensive rolling stock and divisional points essential to steam locomotives. They were locked in on the one hand by government regulations, and on the other by powerful unions. Canadians had a fondness for their railways which had done so much to open up the country. Yet there was no doubt that the railways of the late forties were losers and needed a new approach if they were even to operate on reduced deficits.

At the end of 1948 the government set up the Turgeon Royal Commission on Railways. Its terms of reference suggested that the government was not happy with the way the railways were being operated ... "To review the Railway Act with respect to such matters as guidance to the board in general freight rate provisions ... to review the capital structure of the CNR ... to review present-day accounting methods ... of railways in Canada."

The Minister of Transport, Hon. Lionel Chevrier, emphasized to the trucking industry that "the Commission has no specific reference to investigate the trucking industry."

Despite this, as Don Parke pointed out in a speech, later published in leaflet form by the ATA: "Shortly after the commission commenced its hearings in April (1949) it became abundantly clear that the railways and railway labor intended to drag highway transportation into the inquiry. The submissions of the Railway Association of Canada and railway labor groups confined themselves almost entirely to a criticism of highway transportation."

Among the recommendations made in various briefs to the commission were: To amend the BNA Act to give the federal government complete control over highways; to eliminate highway services between railway points; to restrict trucks to hauls between 50 and 100 miles; to eliminate highway subsidies by increasing user taxes.

Parke commented that two thirds of the brief filed by the Railway Association was devoted to highway financing.

Turgeon, former Chief Justice of Saskatchewan, found himself at the centre of a major battle. By November, seven months after the hearings began, he pointed out that highways fell under provincial jurisdiction and that his commission did not intend to "express any opinion or make any finding as to whether or not motor vehicles are now paying their proper share of the costs."

Many people were angered by the fact that the railway representatives seemed to be trying to prevent people from hauling their own goods. The railways wanted to restrict all trucks, yet for-hire trucks represented a small minority, about 5 percent of all trucks. Some 20 percent of trucks were owned by farmers for their own use. By this time all milk consumed in Ontario cities was being hauled directly from farm to dairy. Two out of three head of cattle sold by Ontario farmers were taken by truck directly to packing plants and public stockyards, mostly in the farmers' own trucks.

The remaining 75 percent of trucks in use were privately owned, or in local cartage. Among the owners were department stores, oil companies, construction companies, newspapers and the like.

While Turgeon's commission was unwilling to get into the battle over highways, federal Transport Minister Chevrier was not. Even as the government's own commission was hearing evidence, he made a speech to the Toronto Board of Trade in which he said: "I think that the present-day development of highway trucking is a very serious threat to the well-being of our railway system. If it is left unchecked it will undoubtedly impair the efficiency of our railroads and destroy the economic advantages which we all enjoy . . . I am convinced that trucking has gone beyond the economic value of its operation, so much so that it has contributed in no small measure to the thorny transportation problems which face Canada today."

It was this kind of speech that kept truckers constantly in fear of the intentions of the federal government and made them feel that the government was oriented in favor of the railways.

Others felt the same way and were uneasy about federal government involvement in the trucking industry. As T. H. Mahony of Hamilton, the long-time secretary of the Ontario Good Roads Association put it: "The record of the federal government in controlling other forms of transportation has not been successful." The association passed a resolution in February 1950 as being "unalterably opposed to any measure of highway regulation by the federal government."

The Ontario government, which had undertaken a $500 million road-building program, the most ambitious in its history, wasn't sold on Mr. Chevrier's opinion either.

No one doubted that the railway industry was essential, or that it needed help. But there was considerable opposition to the idea that the railways should be assisted at the expense of the trucking industry and the public it served.

That it was wise to ensure a strong trucking industry was apparent in 1950 when the nation's first mass strike of the railway unions occurred. Negotiations had dragged on for months and the matter came to a head in mid-August. The railway representatives of management and labor closeted themselves in Montreal hotel rooms to try to avert what most Canadians thought would be a major catastrophe—a nation-wide railway strike. Would the country come completely to a standstill? Could the big cities even be fed?

On Sunday, August 21, the impending strike was the biggest news in the nation. The negotiators remained in close conference in a large room at one of Montreal's oldest and plushest hotels. Meals were hustled in and out of the conference room by silent waiters who were promptly pounced upon (fruitlessly) for information by reporters waiting in corridors. Reporters even searched garbage coming out of the meeting room hoping for some scribbled note, accidentally thrown away, that would give some clue to what was going on. No luck. The newsmen remained in the corridors, some of the more blase playing bridge on borrowed tables, others standing silent, afraid even to go to the washroom in case they should miss an all-important announcement.

On the afternoon of August 21, the *Toronto Star's* banner headline on page one announced that the strike would not occur; *The Telegram's* line was that nothing was known; the *Globe and Mail*, a morning paper printing later than the others, carried a headline in its early edition claiming the strike had been averted and, in its later editions, that it had not. The confusion was monumental. No one in the dispute seemed to think the public, which would be most affected, had any right to information of any kind.

At 6 a.m. the answer became apparent to everyone—the strike was on. The railways came to a standstill and freight yards were silent.

Behind the scenes the ATA had been preparing for just this possibility. It had issued a bulletin to all members pointing out that "A railway strike will throw tremendous responsibility on the shoulders of every truck owner and employee. It will give our industry an opportunity of proving that it can rise to an emergency and provide the citizens of our province with urgent necessities of life and business."

The bulletin outlined an emergency action plan. All PCV operators should be on a 24-hour service for moving essential supplies. Priority should be given to delivery of milk, bread, medical and hospital supplies, perishable farm produce, livestock and commodities of national importance. Pooling of loads was urged. Arrangements were made for PCV operators temporarily to serve points for which their licences did not apply—and the Ontario government gave its blessing.

The ATA announced that every director of the association and affiliated associations had been appointed a chairman of a district co-ordinating committee. Each chairman had the responsibility of securing co-operation of local truck owners to make sure that the best use was made of trucks and to join any municipality's emergency committee operations.

By the hour of the strike, 6 a.m., Tuesday, August 22, the ATA offices on Wellington street were like a battle control centre with operators and staff standing by on a 24-hour basis. Bell Telephone had placed its telephone calls on a priority basis.

The City of Toronto was not quite so quick in getting organized. The city fathers, deeply concerned, organized an emergency transportation service headed by Harold Bradley, to try to get food and essential supplies into the city.

Bradley learned about the ATA organization and arrived at its offices to find the operations in full swing. Surprised and gratified, he announced that there was no need for a special city service and, instead, worked through the ATA.

In the Toronto area alone roughly 45,000 trucks carried on a round-the-clock emergency pool service. Most surprising to the public, and presumably to the governments, was the relatively little dislocation caused by the train stoppage. Businesses remained open and received supplies. Milk arrived regularly on doorsteps. There was plenty of food, even perishable produce, in the stores. The ATA office alone handled 10,000 requests for emergency truck services.

The press was surprised too as it had warned gloomily that the railway strike would have far-reaching effects on every home, public institution and business. It had no such thing. The trucks took up the major problem of transporting supplies while the buses, airlines,

This two-way trailer was designed by Bory Dlin and built by Northwest Industries of Edmonton, immediately after the railway strike of 1950. Trans-Canada Auto Transport, an Edmonton-based carrier, used it to haul cars from Windsor and, in the opposite direction, meat from Alberta packers. It didn't work too well as a refrigerated trailer because of temperature control problems.

and private cars made the absence of passenger travel by rail scarcely discernible.

So often antagonostic to the trucking industry, the press now had nothing but praise. *The Telegram*, which had grumbled about trucks for years, said: "... There is no denying that the railways have campaigned and lobbied against truck transport. A good many citizens have recalled ironically within the last few strike-bound days, the railways earnestly prosecuted ship-by-rail campaign. Such appeals do not rhyme at all well with the word 'strike'.

"The trucking associations have rendered excellent service in the crisis and have done much to prevent a greater breakdown in the country's operation. For this their good work will be remembered in their favor, in the event of any further pressure being put on the government to unduly restrict or hamper automotive transportation."

The *Toronto Star* said: "An outstanding feature of the railway strike was the fine service provided by the rubber-tired transportation in the effort to ameliorate the hardships which the strike involved. It may well be, indeed, that the demonstration of the trucks' capacity to handle business which had belonged to the railways will result in the permanent alienation of some of it to vehicles that run on rubber instead of rails ...

"... The Star has always dissented from the contention sometimes put forward that restrictive measures should be applied to truck transportation, whether within provinces or on long hauls across provincial boundaries. The railways, which themselves failed to branch out into rubber-tired business as pioneers, now seek trucking restrictions on interprovincial routes. The Star does not believe that this form of competition should be throttled in any way."

The City of Toronto issued a special commendation to the ATA over the signature of Mayor Hiram E. McCallum which read, in part:

"The Council of the Corporation of the City of Toronto ... desires to commend most heartily the association on the miraculous manner the trucking industry kept the delivery of essential cargo moving on a nationwide basis during the catastrophic nine days of the railroad strike in Canada ...

"To George M. Parke and Joseph O. Goodman, president and general manager respectively of The Automotive Transport Association of Ontario, must go a major share of the credit for the precision and promptness in initiating a successful priority for truck freight in Ontario ...

"Amazement has been shown on all sides at the stupendous efforts put forth by the ATA in keeping essential goods moving ... It is fitting therefore that we, on behalf of the Corporation, should issue this testimonial in public recognition of the inestimable service rendered by the ATA, not alone to this city but the peoples of Canada ..."

Arthur Hailey, then the editor of *Bus and Truck Transport*, said of the rail strike: "Until then, the Canadian trucking industry was not really recognized as a national entity, but it was recognized then in a hurry, and remained so ever since."

Hailey, even after he became famous as a television playwright (*Time* magazine called him "one of the six best TV playwrights in the world") and novelist ("Hotel", "Airport", "In High Places", "Final Diagnosis", "The Money Changers"), remained an intimate and loyal friend of the ATA.

The Turgeon Report, when it emerged in 1951, cannot have been much solace to the railways. As he had warned, Turgeon had avoided the question of trucking or highway transportation. He did, however, admonish the Canadian National Railway to simplify its operations.

These setbacks in no way stopped the railway campaign against the trucks, or the increasing determination of the federal government to gain control of certain aspects of the industry. It is unfortunate in so many ways that these incidents must be recorded in the light of much more constructive actions of both railways and government in later years. Nevertheless, they are part of the history of trucking in Ontario, and a critical part of it.

During the 1950s the railway unions went so far as to keep men in the spectators' gallery at the Legislature—men carefully dressed in railway caps—to remind legislators that "Big Brother was watching".

The federal government penalized mill owners who shipped wheat to their own mills by truck, rather than rail, by denying them certain financial benefits they could obtain only on rail-shipped commodities. This action definitely hurt those truckers involved in that aspect of the business.

During the 1950s too, a court case—the Winner case as it came to be called—was taken all the way to the Privy Council in England and finally gave the federal government what it had wanted all along—the decisive right to regulate extraprovincial motor transport. However, at the time, the federal government contented itself with a moral victory. It announced that it would allow the provinces to be its representatives in the field and, in 1954, Parliament passed legislation to that effect.

The railway strike had one important benefit. It directed the trucking industry's attention more closely than ever toward public service. During the strike the industry had demonstrated again, as it had done during the war, that it could operate as a co-ordinated whole. It had been set up into regions on a voluntary basis during the strike, each with a co-ordinator. This setup was maintained and refined in case of future emergencies and was incorporated into the Emergency Measures Organization established during the scare period of the fifties, when it seemed nuclear war might erupt at any time.

Trucks participated in many emergency operations, sometimes organized through the ATA, sometimes by individual trucking firms. The trucks were always ready to roll without asking where the payment was to come from. Sometimes their owners were eventually paid, sometimes not.

In June 1952 the *Owen Sound Sun-Times* credited a trucking company with saving a man's life. The man was being operated on in an Owen Sound hospital when complications arose. An emergency call for help brought a truck at top speed from Toronto with an iron lung to keep the man breathing.

"We feel sure this is not the first time a man's life has been saved by the existence of the speedy and flexible services provided by modern highway transportation," said the Sun-Times.

After the Emergency Measures Organization was closed by the government, the truckers continued to maintain an informal arrangement for helping out in disasters. Still later, they organized a system of assisting police to locate stolen trucks (not cars), descriptions and licence numbers of stolen trucks being rapidly circulated to truck drivers by company radios.

The truckers, once ill-educated and operating more or less in isolation, were advancing even beyond the stage of being owners and highly professional drivers. They were integrating themselves through co-operation with many organizations, of which police, safety groups and the EMO are only examples, in constructive assistance to the communities they served and the province at large.

One of the last Montreal-built Sicards, the advanced "Compact" shown here with a mixer unit. These vehicles were produced by Sicard Ltd. and many latterly were sold for regular on-highway service. This 1962 "Compact" has a novel tipping plastic hood, an advanced feature for the time. Assembled from well known components, Sicards sold well in Eastern Canada; the firm largely specialized in custom vehicles, including some of the largest trucks produced in Canada.

9

Enter The Teamsters

Labor problems were shortly to beset the Ontario trucking industry, not so dramatic as those that had overtaken the railways, nor on nearly so big a scale, but still traumatic enough. Truckers were set against truckers, sometimes with violence, a thing that had never happened before in Ontario's history.

The Teamsters' Union, based in the United States, had been steadily organizing the Ontario industry for years. Its American boss was the colorful and forceful Jimmy Hoffa, later to be jailed in the U.S. and still later to disappear, presumed murdered. His ways were not those that had prevailed in Canadian labor up to that point. He went everywhere with bodyguards and, in the U.S., was accustomed to high-pressure methods and strong-arm tactics.

In 1951 the Teamsters' Union stepped up its activities and organized a number of trucking companies in Ontario. The ATA issued the following bulletin: "There are at present nine applications for certification in front of the Labor Relations Board. We draw your attention to the fact that The Automotive Transport Association of Ontario has established a Motor Transport Industrial Relations Bureau to negotiate and maintain a master contract for all companies so unionized and who subscribed to the Motor Transport Industrial Relations Bureau. Experience has proven that it is to your advantage to maintain a uniform labor contract through master negotiations.

"We believe that a number of companies, whose employees have been approached recently by the union, are not aware of the existence of the Motor Transport Industrial Relations Bureau. Should the union show interest in your employees, we urge you to contact the bureau immediately and have the bureau represent you, not only during the application for certification but also in negotiations for the labor contract which may result."

The bureau, part of the ATA structure at this time, later became a separate entity, though it still occupies space in the ATA building.

The ATA, by 1951, had grown at a pace that may not have matched the industry as a whole, but it had nevertheless grown considerably. It had 12 full-time employees and was governed by 27 directors elected at the annual meeting. It represented 1200 PCV operators with 4000 power units on the road.

In 1953 the Private Carriers Division of the ATA was established. Wilf Male was chairman of a meeting in February to organize this division, at which he pointed out that the ATA constitution had been amended at the annual meeting to permit formation of the new division. The change, of course, meant a great potential increase in membership since the majority of trucks on the road were private carriers. ATA general manager Joe Goodman was frank in saying that the ATA's main concern was intercity trucking and that private carriers involved in local deliveries would still have to take care of most of their own problems, although the division's association with the ATA would help in solving problems of common concern. The association had much to offer the private carriers in information and services. Where local bylaws seemed likely to hamper intercity trucks as well as local delivery vehicles, the ATA would work closely with the local private carriers.

Private carriers were segregated for convenience within the division into industry groups representing breweries, publishers, chain and department stores, petroleum, fuel and ice, building materials and foodstuffs.

The joining of the private carriers with the ATA greatly strengthened both groups.

Truck use was still developing in new ways. In 1953 Ideal Dairies of Oshawa moved the first fluid milk by tank truck in the province. Movement of livestock by truck was increasing steadily, from 74.7 percent of all livestock transported in the province in 1951, to 78.7 percent in 1952.

That same year, without much fanfare, came one of the significant introductions into the railway industry—piggybacking. This concept was not really new. A hundred years earlier gentlemen in England had shipped their carriages by rail to Scotland for the hunting season. Commercially, piggybacking had been introduced as early as 1926 by the Chicago, North Shore and Milwaukee Railroad, a small electric railway. But in 1952 the railways introduced it, initially for their own use only. They began hauling their own trailers by road to the railway, loading them onto flatcars in Western Canada and hauling them east by rail, to be picked up by tractors in Eastern Canada and taken to their destination by road.

It was to be another five years before the railways extended this service to the trucking industry at large.

The ATA promotes safety and the professionalism of truck drivers at this CNE display in the fifties.

Truck roadeos gained momentum during the fifties.

Not only was piggybacking an enlightened move, it was a constructive one that enabled the railways to regain business competitively. It began to mend the rift between the railways and the trucking industry because now they could work together.

In 1953 a dump truck association was formed as an affiliate of the ATA. Dump trucks comprised the largest single operating class of for-hire vehicles in Ontario, with an estimated 15,000 trucks engaged in the work. The enormous postwar growth of the dump-truck industry had brought many problems. Even by 1953 many did not hold PCV licences and 60 percent had no vehicle insurance. Membership in the new association was limited to PCV licence holders and one of the first objectives was to have legislation passed requiring all dump-truck operators working for-hire to have a Class "F" PCV licence. But it was not in the dump-truck area that labor troubles arose.

The for-hire industry had changed drastically since its

strike," says Goodman. "He was the only one who could control the men. He did it with an iron hand."

Hoffa arrived from the U.S. with his usual bodyguards and went into meetings with truckers and government representatives. An agreement was hammered out in the offices of Hon. Charles Daley, Ontario minister of labor, but the Canadian teamsters' local representative said he doubted he could sell it to his men.

"If you can't sell it, I will," Hoffa said. "I'll do it right on the picket lines if I have to."

But, true to form, Hoffa was almost at once embroiled in an incident, one of many in his colorful career. Goodman says that during the meeting he had to be whisked out the back door because police were coming in the front. It appeared that he had, typically, ignored a border-crossing formality which the police were in no mood to overlook.

Nevertheless, the strike was settled abruptly and although it had had little effect on the economy, being

A 1955 Autocar heavy-duty conventional tractor hooked up to a Fruehauf open-top tandem semitrailer. This Autocar, with Cummins NHB diesel power, has the characteristic set-back front axle and a wheelbase of 177 in.

early days. Where once most ATA members owning for-hire trucks had only one truck, possibly two, now there were large fleets. It was this very fact that made labor union activity attractive.

In 1953 the Hamilton local of the Teamsters' Union went on strike; the Toronto local did not. This created an ugly situation because some of the Toronto members had to pass through Hamilton territory. The Hamilton members objected so strenuously that Burlington Beach became virtually a battleground with striking truckers lining up on both sides of the road and hurling bricks at fellow truckers from Toronto, as they drove through.

Attempts at conciliation proved futile.

"It was really Jimmy Hoffa himself who settled the

confined to a small area, it had one bad result.

"We had been developing a feeling in the truck driver and an image with the public that he was 'a gentleman of the road'," says Goodman. "That all went out the window overnight. We got very bad press and the truck driver's reputation sank a long way. It took years to recover from the black eye we received during the strike."

Robert Erskine, editor of *Truck Transportation*, said in an editorial: "James R. Hoffa negotiated the Western Ontario truck strike settlement with Ontario Labor Minister Hon. Charles Daley's office . . . it was not a pretty picture we saw of Hoffa and his Detroit ilk. A special committee of the U.S. House investigating labor

A 1952 White WC series Super Power tractor with tandem Strick trailer. White introduced the W series about 1939 and continued it in production, with variations, for nearly 20 years. Most were powered with White-built L-head gasoline engines.

The International RC-180 was a general-purpose cab-forward truck produced from 1952 to 1957.

rackets in the Detroit area reports a giant wicked conspiracy involving extortion, gangsterism and dictatorship by the AFL teamsters' leaders in Detroit. The report states that operating under the guise of being labor leaders, officials of the teamsters' have managed to extort and collect millions of dollars with no benefits to members.... Ontario had had good labor leadership within the ranks of the Teamsters' Union. Let's keep it that way."

But if the strike had hurt the industry's public image, there were still many people who thought highly of truckers. Fred Gardiner, first chairman of Metro Toronto—"Big Daddy"—after whom the Gardiner Expressway has been named, dismissed proposals to restrict trucks in the city with the caustic remark: "What's wrong with trucks? Every time the wheels turn, the cash register rings some place. That's healthy."

And, of course, that was profoundly true for a truck is essentially a load of somebody's prosperity going some place.

In January 1954 trucks carried out a spectacular feat. They moved an entire industrial plant from Windsor to Barrie, the first time that trucks had attempted such a thing in Ontario. The move required 300 tractor-trailer loads in low-bed floats, open semitrailers and van-type trailers. The operation was carried out without a hitch.

During 1954 the trucks again showed they were equal to sudden emergencies. Hurricane Hazel devastated low-lying residential areas of Metro Toronto and some 30 people lost their lives, with many others being left homeless.

Brand-new tankers were rushed in with fresh water for drinking. Other trucks with winches were used to haul away debris. Wilf Male of Direct-Winters worked round the clock organizing his own and other people's trucks.

In 1955 the first "in-bond" cargo, picked up by truck in Vancouver from the Orient, arrived at the Midcontinent Truck Terminals, Toronto. The truckload, without having to wait for customs clearance in Vancouver, had left that city Thursday night and arrived in Toronto at 11 a.m. Monday, where it cleared customs. This in-bond transit made it unnecessary to unload goods in Vancouver for customs inspection, as well as possible further unloadings at U.S. border points, if the trucks used U.S. routes to Toronto.

Two-way radios were being introduced at last into trucks, especially for pick-up and delivery locally. The ATA was pressing the Department of Transport in Ottawa to allocate frequencies for trucks and had set up a special committee for this purpose, consisting of Alex Smith of Direct-Winters Transport, Bus Howe of Trans-Canada Express and Norman Young of Canada Cartage. Obviously, city pick-up and delivery could be rendered more efficient with two-way truck radios and in due course the department approved frequencies, opening the way for this further advance of the industry.

Later, highway trucks were to use Citizens' Band radio and while one attraction of the CBs was that trucks could warn each other of radar traps, they had far more significance than that. By the time the CBs came into use most major trucking companies enforced speed limits within their fleets anyway. The big advantage of the CB was that it could warn a driver of detours or accidents ahead, dangerous road conditions in winter and traffic congestion, so that he might choose an alternate route.

In 1955, the Hon. Mr. Turgeon was back in the news with another report. He had been named head of a royal commission nearly a year earlier to inquire into agreed charges freight rates. His report was, as *Truck Transportation* remarked, the "strangest royal commission of them all". It read like a public relations document in favor of the trucking industry.

Turgeon noted that for-hire trucks across Canada numbered about 65,000, owned by some 15,000 operators and representing a capital investment of about $250 to $300 million.

"Some of these trucking companies have developed into what might be called huge-scale carriers. One of them, for instance, is recorded as having 1482 units, comprised of 310 trucks, 350 tractors, 800 trailers and 22 service vehicles," he said. "The figures I have quoted show that the trucking business is now one of Canada's great industries. Insofar as the evidence goes, it is more prosperous than the railway industry. It has experienced some reverse through the recent decline in general business activity, but nothing like the reverse suffered by the railways.

"I was interested in hearing the evidence and the argument put forward by the trucking industry in support of their opposition to the submission of the railways. I was mainly impressed by the fact that this industry has attained great vigor and seems to be bound towards further advances.

"... with its speed, convenience in loading and unloading, less stringent packing requirements and other features, the highway vehicle has become a most effective means of transportation for all but the lowest value bulk commodities, wherever distances and conditions of the highways are favorable.

"I think the most striking development to be noted during the last few years is growth in the size, the efficiency and the prosperity of the trucking industry on the one hand and, on the other hand, the great deterioration to be seen in the financial position of the railways despite all they have achieved in the way of improving their property and their services.

"I am impressed with the belief that the motor (transport) industry has become a factor of permanent value in Canada's economic life and that no legislation concerning railways... can cause it vital damage."

As though this eulogy, this plain speaking by the Hon. Mr. Turgeon had brought the railways face to face with reality, a change began to come about in their own thinking, not all at once, but gradually. This in its turn led to co-operation between the industries and a far more satisfactory situation throughout Canada.

The Canadian Pacific Railway led the way out of the negative thinking, which had been the pattern of the railway approach for years, and began to look on the trucking industry as an opportunity rather than a threat. It is unfortunate that this way of thinking had not come when the railways were offered first chance at PCV licences in 1926, but it is understandable that they had not done so.

Only an individualist—a person of rough, tough, independent spirit—wanted to get into trucking in 1926 when roads were appalling, trucks undependable, well-trained help hard to come by, government regulation nonexistent (or nearly so) and cutthroat competition rampant. It simply wasn't an industry calculated to appeal to the railways, which were well organized in 1926 and performing an excellent service.

By 1958 things had changed drastically and it was much easier for the railways to see that trucking not only could be a valuable asset, but that it could be carried out in an organized way with dependable and responsible help.

And so, in 1958, the CPR began buying up trucking companies. Over the years that followed, the CPR organized its own network of truck lines operating independently of its railway system. Best known of the CP truck operations is the biggest, Smith Transport, which historically went back to Phil Smith, a founder of the ATA, who had carried loads of pianos from Oshawa to Toronto and automotive parts back to Oshawa, starting with a single truck.

Canadian Pacific considerably expanded its own CP Express which, while not truly a trucking company, is truck oriented just as CN Express is today. The express companies handle large loads on an intercity as well as a delivery basis, but load handling is designed to suit small shipments.

CP also bought trucking companies outside Ontario, especially in the West, and operates CP Transport between Winnipeg and Vancouver.

Canadian National soon followed suit in buying trucking companies, best known of which is Husband Transport. Empire Freightways, East-West Transport, Midland Superior Express, Sydney Transfer and Storage, Eastern Transport, Toronto-Peterborough Transport and Hoar Transport were among the companies bought by CN.

Years later, Donald Gordon, president of the CNR, was to say: "...road transport is a better agency for the collection and distribution of much traffic and is more economical and faster for short-distance service... CN proposes to use both its rail and road services for long-haul traffic. In implementing this policy, CN has been proceeding cautiously...to enlarge its trucking facilities through a very selective purchase of existing highway carriers...to acquire a trucking pattern so as to obtain for its own operations the benefit of co-ordination with railway facilities, or even replacement of them in those cases in which the truck is the better tool."

From the public's point of view this enlightened attitude was beneficial, but in the late 1950s when the railways began buying trucking companies, truckers feared that this was just another ploy to infiltrate and destroy their industry.

As it turned out, a change was coming in the thinking of railway executives which led to benefit for both industries. As Joe Goodman put it: "They operated their trucking lines efficiently and in competition with their railways. Their truck lines joined ATA and worked alongside everyone else for the good of the whole industry. I don't think we have any better members or better truck lines."

The battle between railways and trucking was not really over; the difference was that railways, since they owned trucking lines, were obliged to compete in a healthy way by seeking methods of providing more efficient rail service and this is what they did. The verbal attacks on the trucking industry ended; there were no more "Big Brothers" looking down on legislatures from spectators' galleries. Instead, the railways became, after some soul-searching and innovating, more flexible in their operations...they turned to diesel locomotives, far more efficient than the old steam types...computerized their operations and closed down many that were unprofitable or unnecessary.

In following the railway story, we have moved a little ahead of another event which was of great importance to the trucking industry. It occurred in 1955. In that year the Ontario government removed the powers of the Ontario Municipal Board to grant PCV licences and finally set up the Ontario Highway Transport Board—a recommendation originally made by the Chevrier Royal Commission in 1939, was shelved during the Second World War and never implemented afterwards, although the ATA had repeatedly pressed for it.

First reading of the new bill was in March. The legislation was designed to give the new board powers to fix fees for licences, to collect the fees, approve tolls charged by truckers, approve routes and to enforce a wide range of regulations. The board chairman was S. H. S. Hughes, Q.C., (later a justice of the Supreme Court of Ontario) and the vice-chairman E. J. Shoniker, who later became its chairman. It began operations November 1, with a backlog of some 300 PCV licence applications to be heard.

The end of the fifties is a good time to glance back at what had been achieved since the end of World War II. It had been remarkable; the industry had grown all over Canada with well over a million trucks in service, one in every three serving Ontario. In the ten-year period between 1947 and 1957 the operating revenue of the Ontario industry had increased four fold, while the number of employees had doubled. Salaries and wages had risen to five times their 1947 levels.

Shown prior to the first hearings of the newly created Ontario Highway Transport Board are S. H. S. Hughes, Q.C. of Welland (left), chairman, and E. J. Shoniker of Toronto, vice-chairman. Mr. Hughes later became a justice of the Supreme Court of Ontario and was succeeded as OHTB chairman by Mr. Shoniker on July 1, 1958.

Manitoulin

The years between 1960 and 1977 are years of growth and expansion for Manitoulin Transport. The purchase of the first Class "A" licence in 1960 provided the basic route from Manitoulin Island to Toronto; thus began a small business which has become a major factor in Northern Ontario transportation and a respected name throughout the province.

From beginnings which included President Doug Smith as Manager-Driver, Manitoulin Transport has grown to a modern, well-equipped organization with seven locations in the Province.

The energy and growth of Canada's trucking is typified in organizations like OTA and its member companies. Looking back gives us pride in our achievements and helps us to look to the future with renewed enthusiasm.

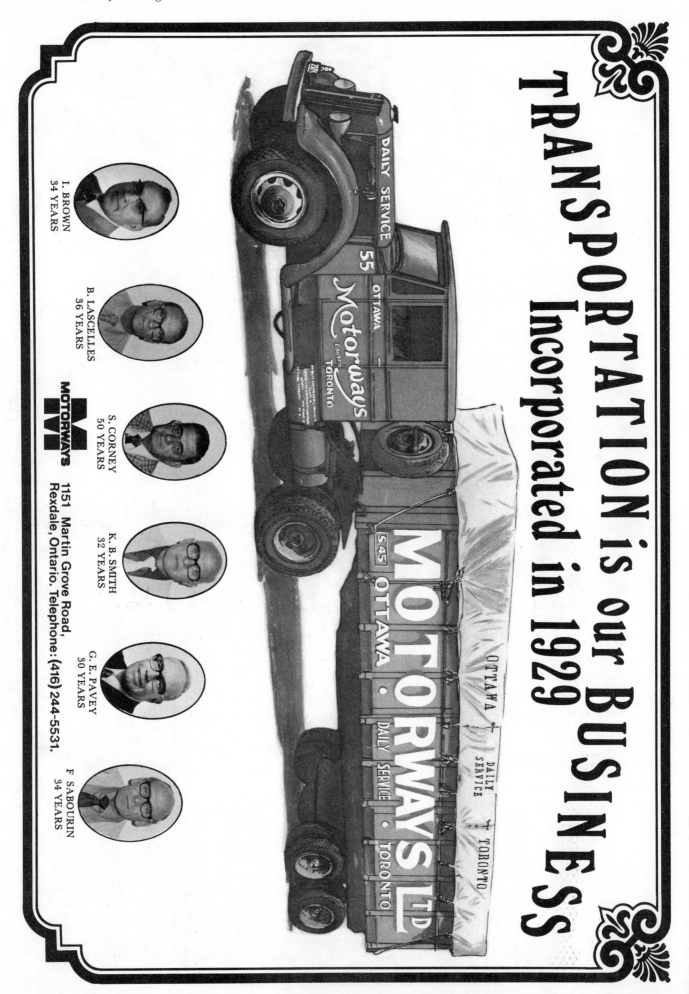

40 Growing Years of Border Brokers Ltd. 1936-1976

It all began in 1936 in Niagara Falls, Ontario

We started with one small office to handle the customs clearance of the growing number of truck shipments from the U.S. That was just ten years after the founding of the Ontario Trucking Association (then, The Automotive Transport Association of Ontario).

As the Association grew, Border Brokers grew with it. Today we are the largest Customs House Brokers and Transportation Service company in Canada.

Now the Ontario Trucking Association is 50 years old. We are proud to have been associated with its members and we look forward with confidence to the next 50 years.

Border Brokers Ltd.
40 University Avenue,
Toronto, Ontario

10

Trucks Remake Ontario

By 1960 Ontario was by far the wealthiest province in Canada and industry in general was fighting to gain a foothold in it. Served by a superb highway system still marked for further improvement, industry could be diversified into relatively low-cost suburban sites in attractive green belts. Fruits, vegetables and other perishables that once had been available only seasonally, were now in the stores in fresh condition all year round. If farmers were not as prosperous as they deserved to be, it was not the fault of the trucking industry.

Small industries located in towns far from railways had sprung up. If the big cities continued to draw off rural populations, they did it to a lesser extent because truck transport kept small-town industry alive and healthy.

Trucks were instrumental in bringing about the better roads that everyone enjoyed in Ontario, although they were paying far more than their share for use of the roads.

The world was changing drastically. The Russians had sent their Sputnik into orbit in 1957. With the arrival of the space age the tempo of life seemed to speed up and the trucking industry met the challenge.

Trucks became bigger, more reliable, more sophisticated and lasted longer. At one time a truck was considered worn out after 100,000 miles. Now a truck could be kept in operation for 400,000 miles or more. Sophisticated techniques of management were developing to keep the trucks rolling with a minimum of downtime. Road breakdowns were becoming more infrequent. It was cheaper to practise preventive maintenance than to have a costly truck laid up for repairs or, worse still, break down on the road, have to be towed in and then repaired. More specialized kinds of trucks were taking to the road, requiring more sophisticated knowledge about their correct application and maintenance.

One of the most versatile of specialized vehicles was the tank truck which had developed amazingly over the years. As far back as 1914 tank trucks had been carrying gasoline but, by the fifties, various tanker types were transporting asphalt, tallow, lard, solvents, jet fuel and suphuric acid. Still later, tank trucks were improved to carry everything from wine to molten sulphur, liquid chocolate, cement, bulk grease, glues, resins, plastic pellets and even sugar.

Chocolate, once shipped in solid slabs was carried by tanker in a molten state and emptied directly into the vats of manufacturers, requiring less time in handling. Cement, once transported in bags, was poured into a tanker at one terminal and out into the user's silos.

Milk is a tank truck operation with stringent government controls on handling and transportation, placing it somewhat apart from other commodities transported by tanker.

Along with this kind of diversification, of which the tank truck is only one example, came many complications too . . . the need to develop better cleaning techniques . . . the necessity that cleaning water and materials be decontaminated before being emptied into a sewer system. Today, big tank truck operations require equipment, experts and financial investments that would have been nearly incomprehensible to the pioneers of fifty years ago.

By the late fifties and early sixties many new truck terminals were being opened to accommodate the growing number of trucking fleets.

In 1957 the ATA organized its Pioneers' Club to honor those who had served the industry a minimum of 25 years. The 514th member was inducted into this select group at the 50th annual convention.

In the same year, the ATA expanded and moved its offices to 439 Queen's Quay at the foot of Spadina Avenue. The building also housed the Motor Transport Industrial Relations Bureau, the Toronto Milk Transport Association, the Ontario Produce Haulers Association and the Hamilton Milk Transport Association.

Perhaps the most significant activity of the ATA in 1958 was to establish the ATA Trucking Industry Educational Foundation Inc., with R. D. Grant of Overland-Express Ltd. as chairman, and C. V. Hoar of Hoar Transport as vice-chairman. Incorporation was applied for October 29 and received November 14. Foundation funds came from donations from carrier members of the new organization, primarily through an agreement to stop giving Christmas gifts to clients and donate them to the foundation instead. Membership was voluntary.

Initially, the foundation program was to provide bursaries for needy Grade XIII students to enter university and who were not eligible for government aid. Between 1959 and 1966 bursaries ranged from $175 to $500 a

GMC's tilt-cab series, introduced in 1960, ranged from medium duty to the heaviest GMCs with gasoline and diesel power. The cab tips mechanically with counterbalancing springs. The two 20 ft semitrailers were built by Trailmobile.

student, depending on need. Some might be living away from home, others not.

Once a student had been granted a bursary for his or her first year, a similar grant was assured in subsequent years of study, provided the student secured passing marks and could prove continuing need. In addition to grants made in this manner to students, funds were made available to universities and colleges.

Later, in 1967, the foundation set up a grant to York University to study the need for an "Institute of Transportation Studies" and a means to implement it. It was the intention to establish the institute at a Canadian university and additional grants to carry out the project were later made.

Grants were also given to the Canadian Institute of Traffic and Transportation for special research; York University Transport Centre was set up with the R. D. Grant Reading Room established later by the foundation.

From 1972 on, more money had to be found to supply help to the community colleges.

In addition to all these things, financial assistance was given to students enrolled in the Ontario Good Roads Association's Civil Technology-Municipal Roads and Services program at Georgian College in Barrie.

In the first 16 years of operation of the foundation, 3000 students were aided through bursaries, at a cost of $650,000.

While the industry was getting the foundation under way in 1958, it was still having troubles of its own, particularly with the Teamsters' Union. A royal commission headed by Mr. Justice Roach revealed that in the preceding two years intimidation, contrary to the Criminal Code of Canada, had been practised in a dispute between truck drivers and gravel pit owners.

Charges could not be laid because the Statute of Limitations made it impossible to charge a person with this particular crime if six months had elapsed since the offence—and it had.

Mr. Roach accused the union of knowingly trying to organize self-employed truck owners whom its officials knew were not eligible for union membership under the Ontario Labor Relations Act.

Despite these problems with labor, the industry was still progressing. It was forming new divisions. In 1958 Tank Truck and Heavy-Specialized Carriers divisions were established in the ATA.

And the industry was still quick to render public service in emergencies, whether paid or not. In Orangeville a big storm on Sunday, December 27, 1959, plunged the town into darkness and hydro repairmen could not cope with the problem quickly enough. It was wintry weather and speed was essential to restore heat.

Four Toronto organizations joined forces—the ATA, the Toronto Telegram, International Quality Controls of Toronto, and Northern Transport. International Quality Controls had war surplus generators and its president, George Newby, phoned The Telegram to ask if there was any way of getting them to Orangeville. The Tely phoned the ATA which, in minutes, had Northern Transport standing by. The day after the storm the first generator arrived.

It was an appropriate moment for Northern Transport to appear in the news. Its secretary-treasurer, Mrs. P. A. Crossley of Owen Sound, had just been named the first woman recipient of ATA's "Man Behind the Wheel" trophy, the Oscar of the Ontario trucking industry. She had been in the industry 35 years and, though 80 years old, still worked part time.

In 1960 the ATA launched a campaign against air pollution, long before government gave serious thought to such programs. The association formed an Air Pollution Committee to work on ways of preventing pollution of the atmosphere by commercial vehicles, especially diesel trucks.

Mike Harper, chairman of the committee, pointed out that the diesel engine need not pollute: "All passenger cars, commercial vehicle and stationary engines contribute to air pollution because of varying degrees of incomplete combustion. The diesel engine, however, comes closest to complete combustion when it is well maintained and has a proper air-fuel ratio. It shouldn't smoke."

Working with manufacturers, the ATA committee contributed to an effort that in later years paid off, just about the time governments and the public were beginning to crack down on air pollution. A diesel engine was produced which, with proper maintenance, reduced

A double-bottom hookup in 1963 with a converter dolly for the rear trailer. Trailers are 20 ft Trailmobiles. The tractor is a 1962 White Compact with short BBC dimension and tipping cab.

exhaust emissions to the point where it was difficult to see any evidence of emissions. Also important was the fact that trucks with the improved engines obtained better fuel mileage, thereby reducing operating costs. It is interesting to note that at the time the ATA launched its air pollution control campaign in 1960, it was believed by most people, including governments, that there was no particular need to conserve fuel from a supply standpoint.

In February 1961, yet another of the multitude of government inquiries and commissions on transportation —this time the MacPherson Royal Commission—made its report. The MacPherson Commission had been appointed in May 1959, with the Hon. C. P. McTague as chairman, to be succeeded later by M. A. MacPherson after Mr. McTague became ill.

The commission conducted hearings across Canada and published a three-volume report, the first volume in 1961.

The MacPherson report acknowledged that "the trucking industry has provided the kind of flexible transport service which Canada's growing secondary industry is requiring." It urged free competition among all modes of transportation and that this should become national policy. But it seemed somewhat confused on the point because it admitted later on in the report that unrestricted free competition leads to trouble.

In earlier days, lack of any form of regulation had nearly led the railways to ruin. Similarly, the failure of governments to control fly-by-night pirate truck operators was continuing to make it difficult for responsible truck owners to pay adequate wages, to maintain vehicles in good condition and to provide adequate service.

Criticizing the MacPherson report, Dr. A. W. Currie, professor of commerce at the University of Toronto, said in a CBC-TV program: "I can sympathize with the MacPherson Commission in its dislike of regulation ... but anyone who has read the history of transportation in Canada and elsewhere knows the evils of so-called free competition. Regulation may be bad, but lack of regulation is worse."

This was, generally, the view of the ATA. It was not against reasonable government regulation but it fought against over-regulation, particularly against unfair regulation and duplication of regulations. This unnecessarily increased costs and made it difficult for the small trucker to stay in business.

In 1962 there was further trouble with the Teamsters'

Canadian-built Hayes Clipper was introduced about 1954 and remained in production until the Vancouver-based company ceased operations in September 1975. The Hayes was a well-built truck of high quality, with a variety of diesel power options. The semitrailer is a Brown.

Union, another strike and more violence. Near Peterborough a tractor-trailer was set afire with a Molotov-cocktail type of incendiary bomb, tires were slashed, brakelines cut and truckers were harassed by carloads of goons driving recklessly.

The Hamilton Spectator reported on July 7: "Police are investigating three separate incidents of violence against non-striking members of the International Brotherhood of Teamsters."

On a more happy note, the long-awaited Trans-Canada Highway was opened during the year, although it was not truly completed until 1967 by which time it had cost about $1 billion and spanned 4860 miles. The idea of the highway had originated in 1910 in a recommendation of the Canadian Highway Association, which had been started by motorists in Western Canada. The association lasted only two years but its idea came to fruition.

On January 30, 1964 the ATA presented a major brief to the minister of transport in Ontario on motor vehicle taxation. The brief noted that the cost of Ontario highways and roads between 1958 and 1977 was likely to be $7.2 billion. However, the ATA estimated that all but about one billion dollars of this sum would be recovered from motor vehicle revenue. This billion-dollar deficit spread over the nine-year period would be less than the amount the government was spending on "development" roads—those rural roads in the north intended to open up new country.

The brief urged: That there be no increase in motor vehicle taxes to meet short-term highway revenue needs; that the cost of development roads be deducted before assessing motorists who didn't need them and in any event, their purpose was to the benefit of all taxpayers; that no policy be adopted to increase the share of the cost of highways already being paid by motor vehicle owners; that there be no diversion of revenue from motor vehicle taxes to any other purposes; that no change be made in taxes being paid by trucks without a scientifically valid study to prove whether they were paying too little or too much; that changes be made in the PCV Act to make its fees more fair to all.

This double-bottom tanker was the last word in combinations in 1961. Carrying capacity was 7800 imperial gallons for a total GCW of 74,000 lb. The full load could be discharged in 35 minutes. All-aluminum tanks were built by King Engineering. Truck is a White with plastic cab.

The brief urged the province to pay road subsidies to municipalities only if their roads were available without undue restriction to all vehicles, including trucks. It asked that tolls on provincially owned ferries and bridges be abolished and that the province should bring pressure on the federal government to pay its share toward roads of national importance, such as the Trans-Canada Highway.

In Ontario the industry was still showing a healthy growth. In the two years, 1963-64, there was a substantial increase in trucking. In 1963 the province had 326,556 commercial vehicles. Ontario had about 30 percent of all the commercial vehicles in Canada, so it was continuing to hold the lead it has established so early in the history of trucking.

By comparison, Quebec which had immense potential wealth—mines, agriculture, forests, secondary industry and ready access to the sea and overseas markets—had not, by a combination of circumstances, been able to develop its trucking equally. As a result it had not been able to build highways and roads to reach its hinterlands, to build up smaller communities and develop its resources nearly as effectively as had Ontario. While it would be an exaggeration to say that trucking alone made Ontario a wealthy province and the lack of it kept Quebec a "have-not" province, there is little doubt that trucking was one of the important factors.

In 1966 there was another strike against the Ontario trucking industry, largely because of the untimely introduction of a new Canadian Labor Standards Code at a time when there was a shortage of labor in the industry.

Harold Whiting, general manager of Northern Transport Ltd., commented: "We had all the trouble because of the unfortunate timing of the introduction of the Canada Labor Standards Code, which has no place in the economy when there is a labor shortage...In one breath politicians say they cannot interfere in negotiations between employer and union and, in the next, they are pushing through federal or provincial legislation that cripples proper and free negotiation of labor matters."

The strike revealed one interesting fact: there were no particular short-term problems caused by lack of rail service. The railways, to a large extent, carried raw materials which could be backed up for a while if need be. During a strike in 1957 against the CPR, dire consequences had been predicted for Ontario towns served primarily by that railway. In fact, the trucks had moved in and no town went short of essentials. But, when there was a trucking strike it was different. They were hauling goods and materials needed immediately and manufacturers and small businesses suffered severely. Therefore, trucks provided a service at least as essential as the railways and, in the short term, more essential.

Whereas in the railway strike of 1950 the Toronto press has been glowing in its praise of the way in which the trucks had kept Toronto supplied, and the city had issued a plaque of commendation, the city found itself in very real trouble when a strike stopped the trucks in 1966.

On April 23, the *Toronto Star* printed an article headed: "Strike is murder to Metro's small businesses". *Independent Business* recounted the woes of small businessmen who could not get, or make deliveries. The railways could move goods to the yards, but nobody could get them to their destinations. The cash registers that the trucks had kept ringing began to fall silent throughout the city and the consternation was real indeed.

Even as the strike was hurting the relationship of the trucking industry with its clients and the public—and there is no doubt that it did hurt as all strikes must—a happier event was going on in Listowel. In that small Ontario town about 30 miles north of Stratford, E. M. "Moe" Bennett was being honored by his employees for his forty years in the industry.

More than 475 employees, former employees and invited guests turned up at the Listowel Arena to give Moe a standing ovation as the founder of Listowel Transport Lines Ltd. in 1928. A unique feature of the anniversary was that it was thought up by the employees themselves who donated $2 each as the initial working capital, while the welfare association and the union donated $400 each.

Aside from the big party, there was a parade of old cars and trucks resurrected from farmers' barns and renovated, and the LTL head office was spruced up and opened to visitors.

Trucks were highly visible in parades during Canada's Centennial Year.

Although Listowel Transport Lines was relatively big and destined to grow bigger, there was something warm and nostalgic of the old days in all the celebrations... the days when a man could start a trucking line with a single truck, grow a little bigger and yet still remain small enough to operate without complex equipment and a large staff.

At the ATA's 43rd annual meeting in 1969, E. J. Shoniker, the Ontario Highway Transport Board chairman, told delegates he thought the days of the small trucker were coming rapidly to an end, though he urged that the trend be stopped.

"I suggest to you it is vitally important that we keep the smaller trucker in the trucking industry," he said. "The smaller shipper likes personal service."

But there could be no doubt that trucking operations were becoming more expensive, the capital needed considerable, government regulations beyond the scope of the unsophisticated, and the competition from large firms intense. For the small trucker it would be a difficult road ahead, even more difficult than the bumpy roads of the twenties, though for entirely different reasons.

A Kenworth tandem tractor with sleeper cab and tandem Trailmobile semi. This combination was registered in 1964 for a maximum GCW of up to 72,000 lb.

Announced in December, 1969, this Ford L-9000 highway tractor is representative of the "Louisville" line of heavy-duty trucks. It is shown here with a Fruehauf tandem van trailer.

Canada's 1967 Centennial Year celebrations were enhanced by nine caravans of eight tractor-trailers. Each of the 72 units was 73 ft long and 10 ft wide, manned by drivers from every province recruited by ATA. There were 659 exhibit stops in the ten provinces from April to November, 1967.

Pioneers, Then & Now.

In 1935, V.B. King founded Truck Engineering. His engineered products pioneered the heavy duty over the road equipment in North America. Our slogan then, as it is now —

KING — A NAME THAT CARRIES WEIGHT

Truck Engineering is continuing to pioneer on International crossroads with its special brand of engineered transportation.

50-Ton Lowbed Semitrailer as made for the Jupp Construction Company in 1948

TRUCK ENGINEERING LIMITED

P.O. Box 518, Woodstock, Ontario N4S 7Z3

KING TRUCK EQUIPMENT LTD.

Market Harborough, Leics. LE16 7PX England

Calgary
Toronto

Montreal
Quebec

*F*ifty years ago when this picture was taken, the roads were snow bound. The shipment on the dog sled consisting of critically needed medical supplies, was delivered from Ottawa to Renfrew, a distance of seventy miles by dog team. Taggart, for over fifty years, have retained an enviable reputation for reliable service.

TAGGART SERVICE LIMITED incorporated in 1924 is one of the oldest Trucking Firms in Ontario. In the early days, Taggart's licence authority was mainly confined to Eastern Ontario and Montreal.

Purchased in 1944 by Joe Perkins, Taggart employed some 35 employees and had approximately 25 units. Since that time, Taggart has expanded rapidly through a program of acquisition and providing good dependable service to the shipping public, and is presently one of the largest Trucking firms in the Ontario Trucking industry.

Traffic jam at the registration desk.

Traditional antics at the 50th anniversary of the OTA with Stan Corney (1926) and the attractive Miss 1976. Enjoying the proceedings are Hon. James Snow, minister of transportation and communications, and Max Haggarty, OTA president.

At Toronto's International Centre, the exhibition part of the OTA's Fiftieth Anniversary Convention.

11

Challenge of The Seventies

The International Centre on Dixon Road is a huge place designed for convention exhibitions. In November, 1976, it was crammed with exhibits pertaining to the trucking industry as the Ontario Trucking Association (which had changed its name from the ATA) held its first major trucking exhibition. Down the road, at the nearby Sky-line Hotel, the association's annual meeting was taking place.

There were huge modern tractors on display, with every sophistication built into them; small gleaming pickup trucks; exhibits by instrument companies; transmissions looking as finely produced as a Swiss watch though considerably larger; displays of clutches, trailer units, truck wash services.... Listowel Transport Lines had a flat-bed with a huge working model of road transport and railroad systems, built by LTL employees in their spare time (appropriate that trucks and trains at last were moving side by side).

In places of honor, refurbished and gleaming and not a bit out of place were the old trucks.... a Packard owned by St. Lawrence Starch Co. Ltd., with a four-cylinder engine, magneto ignition and four-speed transmission, that carried three tons at a speed of 14 miles an hour.... a 1922 Model T Ford truck owned by Teeswa-ter Creamery Ltd., with a four-cylinder engine, two forward gears and one reverse, its brakes mounted on the drive shaft and working only on the rear wheels.... there was Bigham the Mover's 1916 Ford with coal oil lamps and solid rubber tires.... and a 1934 White tank truck owned by Hutchinson Industries. It had a six-cylinder engine, air brakes, and a 1200-gallon-capacity tank.

Over all the glittering display hung the triumphant banner of the convention: "50 Golden Years of Trucking".

Most important of all at both convention and exhibition, were the people...the young men with dreams, the middle-aged with experience and some of the old-timers who had made the industry great. One who would have liked to be there but wasn't, because of a recent operation, was George Tuck of Hamilton. George was 81 years old and still drove his own car. He got into the trucking business in 1919 in a curious way.

His brother-in-law had owned a truck that became stuck on a winter road. He froze his toes and they had

to be amputated, so he wisely decided to get out of the business. George, with what he cheerfully admits was "more courage than brains", bought the 1918 Republic truck with solid tires and built a business. His first load was jam and coconut from the E. B. Thompson plant in Hamilton, to Toronto.

That first year, being young and impatient, he got a speeding ticket. He'd been doing 15 miles an hour and the limit, as he was sternly reminded, was 12 miles an hour.

"They weren't easy years," George says, "but I wouldn't change any of them. I used to work a 14-hour day and even later, when I went with Commercial Transport Co. Ltd., I used to drive from New York to Montreal and that was hard work. We didn't get overtime. Now, with time and a half they love overtime, but I think we enjoyed the life more because it was a challenge."

George went to Harold Leather's company after Commercial Transport sold out in 1964 and he didn't retire until 1969.

That year marked another turning point for Canada. In the early 70s tax reform laws came into effect, making it more difficult than ever for small trucking and other business to cope with mountains of puzzling paper work. Relations between railways and trucks were better but this did not really help the small trucker. It was a time in which only big trucking companies could deal with the increasingly complex regulations, the union demands, the competition of the railways in the trucking field, wild swings of the economy and the uncertainties of fuel supply. Containerization, wisely pioneered by the railways, also hurt the truckers, especially the small ones.

Just as it was a time for big governments, big corporations and big unions, so it was an era of big trucking companies; the small operations with their color and individual character were fading into a history that would never be repeated.

All of which was pretty much what E. J. Shoniker had said at the ATA's annual meeting. In 1970 Shoniker spoke again, at the Heavy Specialized Carriers Division of the ATA, and urged members to bury differences and work together. Even major companies were having financial troubles, he warned, and deplored the tendency of old family trucking firms to fall into American hands. His prediction proved all too true; at the 1976 "Golden Years" annual meeting, only Bigham the Mover of Woodstock remained of the 24 carriers under family ownership which had been in the ATA's first membership directory, published in April 1927.

In 1971 Harold W. F. Whiting, a director of the ATA, warned that spiraling labor costs were driving segments of the industry into bankruptcy. For-hire truckers were being forced to compete with railway express, private carriers, lease operators, pseudo-lease operators and "D" operators who paid wages in some cases 16 percent lower than the for-hire truckers. In 1970 for-hire truckers with Teamsters' Union contracts spent 51.6 percent of their total revenues on salaries and wages.

Whiting bluntly told the teamsters to "be realistic . . . or you will wind up with the highest-paid unemployed truck drivers in the business."

In 1970 the federal government jumped on the trucking industry with both feet, part of a steady move toward socialization of the country that was farther advanced than most Canadians realized. It had formed a Canadian Transport Commission in 1967 to replace the old Board of Transport Commissioners, a move at first greeted by truckers with satisfaction. They had always felt that the old board was against them. The new commission had wider powers over many forms of transport and it was expected to be less biased. But by 1970 federal interference in the trucking industry was not viewed with enthusiasm.

The government had introduced legislation to give it power to regulate truckers operating between provinces although, as was reasonably asked by some, did this give the federal civil service jurisdiction over a trucker who operated mainly in his own province and transported only a single load to another province?

The federal government also introduced its own safety standards for trucks, although it had never done so for the railways.

In mid-1970 an accident occurred that again drew attention to the public service the trucking industry was so ready to perform. On July 5 an Air Canada DC-8 bound from Montreal to Los Angeles, and stopping in Toronto, crashed on landing at Malton, killing all 108 people aboard. It was a Sunday morning and Bill Mathers of McAnally Freightways was sitting with guests in his back garden in Toronto.

"The phone rang," says Bill. "It was the airport manager, asking for refrigerator trucks to carry away the dead."

It was not easy to find refrigerator trucks on such short notice; companies with such equipment tried to keep it rolling. Yet, with the co-operation of ATA, within an hour and a half three refrigerator trucks were on the scene, one from Toronto, the other two from St. Catharines. The Woodbridge arena was turned into a temporary morgue and a hospital at Bramalea was the autopsy centre. Two refrigerator trailers were kept at the hospital.

As the 1970s advanced, more problems for truckers arose. The dump truck operators, who had been asking for legislation were still without it and therefore exposed to cutthroat competition. Their industry had actually been deregulated by the Ontario government in 1968, and is a glaring example of the result of such action. There was poor service, dangerous equipment, overloading and an inability of the owners to do much about these failings. Dump truck operators were giving the trucking industry a bad name, though it was not altogether their fault. They could stay in business only by using methods of the jungle. It was rather as though the government had endorsed cockfighting—allowing any number of birds into the ring and letting them fight it out.

In 1968 *Truck Transportation* had pointed out the need for careful inspection procedures for dump trucks. This had also been recommended by a coroner's jury in Ottawa, after a dump truck with defective brakes flipped over and killed a man and his wife on Highway 17.

"Overloaded and mechanically unsafe dump trucks continue to plague our public highways, leaving a trail of death and carnage behind them, and nothing is being done about it.

"Earlier this year the Ontario minister of transport, Irwin Haskett, brought in amendments to the PCV Act . . . in which a mechanical fitness test will be necessary for vehicles holding PCV licences. Unfortunately, this legislation only covers dump trucks which have such a licence. And even then, the minister and legislators questioned the value of a PCV licence for dump truckers. This legislation covers only about 40 percent of the dump trucks registered in the province," said *Truck Transportation*.

Prior to passage of the amendment, the ATA had urged that every dump truck have a certificate of mechanical fitness. The dump truck owners would have benefited if all had been subject to the same regulations.

Both the Chevrier and Roach Commissions had called for more regulation in the dump truck field.

In 1975 Andrew K. Fraser, president of Bulk Carriers Ltd., speaking at the second annual Dump Truck Owners Seminar and Trade Show, remarked that "The government's deregulatory action in 1968 has created a glaring example of the general effects . . . which demonstrates the counter-argument of all who would deregulate transportation . . . economic stability can only be brought about through reintroduction of control of entry and the enforcement of existing laws governing your activities. Our problem is that the operators must become aware of their responsibilities to the public, and at the same time to educate the public to the importance of the dump-truck industry."

Among the public criticism that had been leveled at the dump trucks following deregulation had been speeding, overloading, having untarped loads and leaving mud and debris on highways.

It was to be 1976 before the Ontario government set up a select committee to look into the matter and, of course, the OTA presented a powerful brief in favor of regulation.

Meanwhile, in 1971, the Ontario government made a basic change in its own structure, establishing the Ministry of Transportation and Communications which merged the former separate departments of highways and transport. The new ministry would have authority over a wide range of transport, including the proposed new GO-train service.

But in the 70s it seemed that the trucking industry was plagued by bad publicity, although in fact it had never been more responsible or more service-minded. In

March 1973, twelve people were killed on Highway 400 south of Barrie. What really happened was that there was an automobile accident; a truck approached the scene and stopped safely, then a bus collided with the truck. Yet the odd thing was that much publicity was given to the fact that he should not have been on the road on a Sunday, also that there were some defects found in his equipment. Because of this, thousands of people today are still convinced that it was all the truck driver's fault.

Another bad thing for the industry was that Premier William Davis, who had taken office in February 1971, seemed at first far less aware of the importance of the trucking industry than his predecessors had been.

As an instance, he stopped construction on the Spadina Expressway, leaving Toronto without ready access to its core from the northwest, where there had been tremendous building in the suburbs. Without easy access, speedy and efficient truck service to and from the city core became increasingly more difficult.

Meanwhile, the ATA had been acting to strengthen itself. At the annual meeting in 1971 a restructuring of the association was approved in principle and, on October 12, 1972, the board adopted proposals for this restructuring. The board itself became more representative of the various types of operations in the association. It became a body of 55 members, 26 elected by active carrier members, 13 more representing special interest divisions or classes, five past presidents, seven representatives of major councils, two elected from allied trade members, (one representing manufacturing, the other sales and/or service), and the immediate past president.

Monthly meetings were to be held and there was to be an executive committee of six officers elected by the board of directors.

The ATA also changed its name to the OTA—the Ontario Trucking Association.

In January 1973 Joe Goodman was named executive vice-president, with an enlarged staff, and a public relations firm was retained.

It was a time for action. The desire of the truckers to be regulated had been met by government over-regulation in many areas. The industry was in danger of being strangled in red tape imposed by governments at all levels. Trucks were subjected to little less than harassment if they traveled across several provinces and into the United States, for laws respecting matters such as axle loadings could vary from one jurisdiction to another.

The business was becoming a nightmare.

Andy Fraser remarked in January 1973 that "the operation of motor vehicles has probably given rise to more legislation than any other single human activity."

He said: "Apart from the normal constraints of civil law, criminal law, tax laws and accounting, the size, weight, speed and design of the production unit, even the buildings from which they operate, are controlled by statute...The equipment specifications evolving from this type of controlled legislation are incredibly detailed, to the point where a light bulb required by one jurisdiction would be illegal or unacceptable in another. Quite apart from the detailed controls on production equipment, there are also complex and conflicting controls on use of labor in the various jurisdictions.

An inordinate amount of a trucking organization's planning effort is devoted to maintaining productivity through a tightly interwoven mesh of legislation. Thus, a trucking operator employing as few as two or three people and involved in the most simple move, say from Toronto to Hamilton, will come under a plethora of regulating agencies.

"This includes the federal and provincial transport departments on the weight, and the registrar of motor vehicles on licensing and equipment. He would be involved with the provincial revenue department on payment of sales and fuel taxes. He would be involved with the federal and provincial labor departments in dealing with two complex and conflicting sets of labor regulations. On the 44-mile trip he would be monitored by provincial police, municipal police and, depending on his cargo, by the RCMP."

The hapless trucking industry, having just emerged from its long struggle with the railways, was involved in an entirely different kind of battle, which had begun through another set of circumstances. In every jurisdiction there had been growing up an enormous army of civil servants—federally and provincially in Canada and, in the United States, federally and in the state governments. The public demanded more regulation of business in general and the civil servants were in no way loathe to give it to them.

Even the average businessman of the seventies found himself enmeshed in government regulations. How much worse it was for the trucking industry, having to cross so many jurisdictions which, without necessarily consulting one another, were passing laws and introducing regulations that applied as a truck left one jurisdiction and entered another.

The politicians, awash with civil servant advice and paper, seemed to have lost touch with the people, much as a truck driver caught in a whiteout in winter, might lose sight of the road.

While the dump truck operators were calling for reasonable regulation of their industry, the highway carriers were engulfed in regulations.

These all added to costs; as an example of how labor costs alone had changed, a highway driver by 1974, covering about 2000 miles a week, was earning roughly $20,000 a year, including fringe benefits.

The industry needed rate increases, which inevitably raised the cost of all goods and contributed to the inflation that harassed the country. But there was nothing that could be done about it. If there was one small consolation, it was that the rising cost of truck transport and the inflation it helped provoke proved once more how important trucking really was.

But the industry received few concessions from governments.

When the energy crisis occurred and the Arab embargo on oil began the steep spiral of fuel prices, Ontario Minister of Energy D'Arcy McKeough was quick to claim that a switch from truck to rail would be desirable, when possible. He asserted that studies had shown that a train required less energy per ton-mile. Yet it wasn't as simple as that. Did the energy mentioned for railway hauling include the shunting operations in yards along the way? Did it include an allowance for the fact that boxcars might not be fully loaded, or less fully loaded than trucks...or that trucks would have to be used anyway to get goods to and from the railway? Did it include the total energy use in all railway operations and compare it to total fuel used in truck operations for comparative shipments?

Did it take into account the fact that so many communities depended exclusively on trucks for their needs, or that hundreds of industries were no longer near railway tracks? Did it allow for the energy and cost that would be required to extend railway lines to serve the areas being taken care of by trucks?

For many reasons, the trucking industry was still fighting for its existence. But it was used to that. And it had plenty of supporters; shippers, merchants, farmers, contractors, and many others. It was a pity that governments and the public were less quick to realize that you can't turn the clock back, and that the economy of the country and the prosperity of Ontario would inevitably wither without the trucks.

It was not noted that the trucking industry was a big employer at a time when unemployment was a serious problem. The industry continued to employ far more people than any other segment of transportation in Canada.

In January 1975 R. M. Haggarty, president of the OTA and of Lafferty-Smith Express Lines Ltd., pointed out in a speech at Belleville that 60 percent of all goods and supplies in Ontario were moved by truck, more than the combined traffic of railways, buses, pipelines, ships and aircraft, and that the industry generated annual revenues of close to $2.8 billion in the province.

The dislocation that would be caused, the economic chaos, the drop in what the Ontario government had called the "quality of life" if trucking were severely curtailed, would be beyond the scope of most people's imagination.

If energy had to be curtailed, the trucking industry, with the co-operation of governments, would rise to the occasion as it had to every other challenge. Manufacturers would develop more efficient, longer-lasting vehicles, better engines, more sophisticated dispatching equipment. Little doubt that the OTA, restructured and more efficient than ever, would be at the hub of the effort.

To grasp the size and ramifications of the OTA in 1977 is not easy. Its members, ranging from owner-drivers to huge fleets, were headquartered in eight provinces and 16 states. As of January 1, 1977, these members operated more than 85,000 vehicles in Canada. In addition, 300 members of allied trades provided input to the association.

The association currently is governed by a 48-man board of directors, 31 elected at the annual meeting, 17 appointed by various divisions. And this is an active board, meeting every second Tuesday. The OTA has a permanent staff of 25.

Its divisions include: the Air Cargo Carriers', "C" Carriers, Dump Truck Owners', Heavy-Specialized Carriers, Livestock Transporters, Ontario Milk Transport Association, Ontario Movers Association, Ontario Unit Masonry Transporters' Association, Private Carriers, Refrigerated Trucking Association of Ontario, Regular-Route Common Carriers, and the Tank Truck Carriers.

It also has councils and bureaus: the Safety Council, the Economics and Finance Council, the Engineering Council, the Freight Claims Bureau, the Industry and Public Relations Council, the Manufacturers' and Suppliers' Council, the Operations Council, the Sales and Marketing Council, and the Security Council.

It has ten standing committees and fifteen subcommittees—and, of course, the subsidiary ATA Trucking Industry Educational Foundation Inc.

It's come a long way since 1926, as has the industry it serves.

Just how vital the trucking industry has become is indicated in the words of an advertisement published by International Harvester and headed: "This is the House That Trucks Built". It went on: "These are the trucks ... that brought the bulldozers ... that dumped the dirt ... that poured the cement ... that delivered the lumber ... that hauled the brick ... that brought the carpenter ... the plumber ... the electrician ... the other trades ... that completed the house that trucks built".

Premier William Davis said in a message to the 50th Annual Meeting: "The important and unique contribution made by the trucking industry to the overall economy of this province cannot be cited too often. A tradition of reliable and responsible service extends even to the traffic on our highways, where Ontario truckers have earned an enviable reputation for safe driving and thoughtful aid to those in trouble."

The few—too few—of those at the annual meeting who could remember back to the beginnings of the association in 1926, had indeed seen fifty golden years.

Burning of the ATA mortgage at the Ascot 27 Hotel, Rexdale, April 10, 1973. Participating at the ceremony were, from left, Joe Goodman, Mel Donnelly, Marsh Davis, Al Hume and Harold Whiting.

The first permanent home of the association, this building was purchased in 1967. It is located on a 3½-acre site on Dixon Road in Rexdale, close to the junction of Highways 401 and 27.

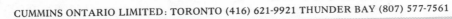

ADDENDUM

Trucking in Ontario comes under intense scrutiny by Select Committee of Legislature

The year 1976, the fiftieth anniversary year of the Ontario Trucking Association, was a notable one for the trucking industry in Ontario for reasons other than those generally associated with such an epoch. It was a year in which the industry was to come under scrutiny as never before by a select committee of the Legislature. The three-party committee was officially designated the Select Committee on Highway Transportation of Goods and it was charged with the responsibility " . . . to examine, investigate, enquire into, study and report on all matters pertaining to the transportation in Ontario of goods on Ontario highways, including all matters affecting or pertaining to the shippers of goods and the transporters of goods whether for gain or not for gain, the regulatory process and the public interest in general . . .".

The 13-member committee, under the chairmanship of Bud Gregory, MPP for Mississauga East, was formally approved by the Legislature on May 25. Under its terms of reference, it was to submit an interim report by September 30, 1976, and a final report by the end of the year. It didn't quite make either deadline and this was understandable since, as the inquiry developed, the scope and complexity of the task almost certainly exceeded by far its original expectations. Before the interim report appeared, the committee heard nearly 200 witnesses in 18 Ontario centres and had studied some 150 written submissions. The committee's existence and purpose had been widely publicized before the hearings started and about 500 trade and other associations had received direct notification by mail.

Apart from its own hearings, the committee attended hearings of the Ontario Highway Transport Board, it visited a truck inspection station, examined a customs compound at Fort Erie, and inspected a road transport terminal. It also met with authorities in the United States, England, Belgium and West Germany. It was a full-time task for the dedicated committee members who examined every conceivable aspect of truck transportation in the province, even reaching back into the 50-year history of regulated trucking to examine, identify and evaluate the important and significant events that had shaped the industry.

The question arises: What had brought this about? Certainly the trucking industry in Ontario had been under fire throughout its long history for a variety of real, sometimes imagined reasons. A highly visible industry, it had finally emerged in the past decade or so as a viable and dynamic force in the economy of the province as, indeed, it had in other parts of the world.

The reasons appear to lie not so much with the trucking industry per se, but with the regulatory process under which it operates. A somewhat parallel situation had arisen in the U.S. during the past few years, where the main battle lines had been drawn around the issue of regulation vs deregulation of the trucking industry. More succinctly, the question is: Should there be control of entry into the trucking business under a system of operating authorities, or should it be thrown wide open to anyone with a little capital, a little courage and a competitive spirit?

In its simplest terms, this would appear to be a confrontation between a regulated and organized trucking industry on the one hand, and the forces of deregulation, as represented by illegal carriers and a segment of the shipping public, on the other. It's reasonable to believe that much of the argument and counterargument surrounding this issue was exported to Canada where the problems of illegal trucking also existed and were of great concern to the authorities and the regulated trucking industry.

But it would be an oversimplification to suggest that the origin of the select committee lay in this direction alone. As Hon. James Snow, minister of transportation and communications noted in the Legislature on April 20: "Various members of the general public, the Legislature, the highway transport industry, the shipping public and the news media have raised many questions over the operation of the public commercial vehicles system—specifically as such operations concern the Public Commercial Vehicles Act . . . no satisfactory response has been developed or offered to address the criticisms which have been directed at the system."

The minister was speaking just five weeks after Bill 4, An Act to Amend the PCV Act, which was aimed at curtailing one-way leases, had been introduced in the Legislature and subsequently referred to the Standing Committee on Resources Development. The Legislature simply could not deal with such basic legislation without the detailed information that a select committee might gather and the recommendations that might flow from it.

Mr. Snow also told the House: "Recommendations from this Select Committee should yield extremely valuable insights into the regulatory process. Public concerns could be allayed where they are unfounded. And should any adjustment to the present system be desirable, such recommendations would stem from an impartial group."

Thus Bill 4 was returned to the House, to stand on the order paper and await the Select Committee's final report. Meanwhile, the committee proceeded with its demanding task.

The government gave some guidance to the Select Committee by providing a background paper that summarized the principles and theory of regulation, a history of the PCV Act and its evolution, a brief description of private, for-hire and unlicensed trucking as they are practised today, and a statement of issues of concern to various public interests.

In stating the issues, the government not only established its concerns but also provided some detailed terms of reference for the committee. First, it posed the question: "What are the objectives of government regulation of trucking." Then it asked: "Does the PCV Act, originally written in 1927 and amended continually since then, meet the required objectives? Specifically, does the act provide adequate powers for the Ontario Highway Transport Board and the ministry to fully arbitrate the shippers, carriers and general public interest in such matters as efficiency of operation, public necessity and convenience, changes in the industry's internal structure, rate-setting, enforcement, and other statutes that affect for-hire and private trucking in the province.

Under its first question, relating to objectives, the government noted some of the areas that should be looked into, including consumer and producer protection, the encouragement of free enterprise and competition, the conservation of energy, minimization of government control, the fullest utilization of all trucks, efficient highway utilization, and the overall economic efficiency in the movement of goods.

These were heady matters to start with, establishing as they did the all-embracing nature and extent of the probe, while encouraging the committee to seek out any unmapped areas that might prove fruitful.

The 150-page Interim Report, when tabled in the Legislature on October 28, had some heartening news for Ontario's regulated trucking industry. Prominent among its recommendations was one that would retain control of entry to the industry. Said Select Committee Chairman Bud Gregory: "We believe that it is prudent to retain economic regulatory controls over the movement of goods on Ontario highways. To retain capability for that movement is an absolute necessity; to retain influence and control over the shape and nature of that movement is clearly in the public interest."

Gregory also told the House that his committee had met with the U.S. Department of Transport, a body that supports the principle of deregulation and is, in fact,

reviewing the Select Committee's testimony and documentation. Other meetings were held with the U.S. In-met with the U.S. Department of Transport, a body that supports the principle of deregulation and is, in fact, reviewing the Select Committee's testimony and documentation. Other meetings were held with the U.S. Interstate Commerce Commission and the American Trucking Associations, both of whom favor retention of a regulated trucking industry in that country. Other experts from Australia and England testified before the committee, offering views opposed to those who claim benefits for deregulation in their respective countries.

The committee report listed a number of negative effects that would result from deregulation, each contributing to deterioration of the industry and the shipper/carrier relationship.

The committee recommended that any operation, which is for-hire in its nature, must be licensed; that private carriage remain exempt; and that safeguards be applied to leasing arrangements. Thus leasing would be prohibited where the arrangement provides for drive control by the truck owner rather than the shipper. Trip leasing would be permissible only between licensed carriers, not between shippers and carriers. Buy and sell arrangements between an unlicensed carrier and a shipper would be illegal, recognizing the for-hire nature of such services.

The Interim Report covered many other areas but those mentioned comprised the major thrust of the committee's recommendations. If written into law they would put many unlicensed carriers out of business; they would also have the effect of making shippers, as well as unlicensed carriers, liable for violations, with substantially increased penalties for both.

The Select Committee's final report was tabled in the dying moments of the 4th Session of the 30th Parliament, on April 29, 1977. A massive document of 1235 pages, including exhibits, it was the result of the most far-reaching examination of the trucking industry ever undertaken in Ontario or, indeed, in all of Canada.

The government will face the task of deciding what legislative changes will be made as a result of the committee's work. It will have plenty of material to work with in the 323 recommendations.

If the government acts on its recommendations, it will enlarge the powers of the Ontario Highway Transport Board, authorizing it to issue carrier licences, enforce the licensing regulations, and arbitrate carrier rates upon demand. Passenger cars transporting parcels on a for-hire basis will be brought under the PCV Act, or its successor.

The successor, in this case, is a recommendation that the PCV Act be replaced by The Ontario Transportation Act and, in the words of the final recommendations, "...to indicate more properly the concepts, policies, terms and conditions with which it deals. This change would focus the true purpose of the act and encourage the government and the public to regard transportation in the comprehensive fashion that is necessary."

Officers and some of the newly elected directors of the Ontario Trucking Association at the 50th Anniversary Convention in November, 1976, at the Skyline Hotel, Rexdale, (Metro Toronto).

PART II

LEADERS, HONORS AND AWARDS

Some of the industry's outstanding people

OTA OFFICERS AND DIRECTORS—1926-1977

Some 272 persons have given unstintingly of their time as officers and directors of the association throughout its 50-year history. They are listed here with the year first elected or appointed and location of corporate headquarters of their companies.

Adams, H.E., Chatham	1940
Agnew, J. R., Toronto	1954
Anderson, A., London	1940
Anderson, D., Stouffville	1975
Andrews, R. M., Toronto	1932
Apps, R. J., Toronto	1967
Arthur, E., Otterville	1942
Ash, L. K., Toronto	1974
Atwell, J. M., Toronto	1955
Austin, D. G., Toronto	1976
Bacon, S. A., Brantford	1941
Baird, P. C., Hamilton	1977
Baldrey, F. G., Preston	1926
Ball, G. F., Toronto	1959
Barnstead, R. C., Toronto	1968
Bartlett, H., Dunnville	1971
Barlow, W. W., Cambridge	1976
Bater, G., Rexdale	1964
Binkley, C. E., Waterdown	1949
Blackwell, E. F., Brantford	1927
Bouk, M., Fonthill	1950
Boxall, P., Oakville	1976
Brader, W., Brantford	1954
Brown, A., Simcoe	1938
Brown, D., Leamington	1943
Brown, S., Windsor	1951
Cain, W. R., Barrie	1976
Campbell, G., Toronto	1961
Campbell, K. M., Ottawa	1968
Carruth, J. C., Rexdale	1966
Cathcart, J. M., Peterborough	1954
Chalk, G. R., Aylmer	1940
Chandler, K., Toronto	1964
Cleland, H., Niagara Falls	1926
Coleman, E. M., Galt	1944
Connors, J. P., Hamilton	1975
Cooke, L. E., Barrie	1968
Cooper, R. E., Sudbury	1971
Cope, H. G. H., Toronto	1943
Crawford, W. W., Hamilton	1939
Crossett, C., Toronto	1957
Crossley, J. C., Jr., Toronto	1938
Crowther, P. F., Mississauga	1975
Cumberland, I., Toronto	1951
Davey, M. H., Toronto	1975
Davis, M. D., Toronto	1957
Davison, R. C., Toronto	1972
Dean, R. S., Hamilton	1927
Delongchamp, G., Sudbury	1937
Dick, P. A., Chatham	1957
Dirksen, M., Kingston	1972
Doerr, C. J., Waterloo	1942
Donnelly, M. W., Clarkson	1960
Drury, N. V., Toronto	1969
Duff, D., New Lowell	1939
Duncan, J. N., Malton	1940
Dunlop, J., Petrolia	1977
Dwhytie, K. I., Mississauga	1972
Emblem, N. J., Montreal, Que.	1937
Earle, C. F. A., Brockville	1971
Emslie, R., St. Anne's	1948
Endert, C. J., Hamilton	1964
Erdman, H. H., Toronto	1975
Erwin, T., Toronto	1926
Fabello, L., St. Catharines	1975
Fabian, L. G., Toronto	1929
Finch, A., Brantford	1927
Findlay, F., Chatham	1939
Fink, I. C., Preston	1938
Fleming, W. R., Hamilton	1976
Follwell, W. E., Markham	1975
Foy, F. C., Toronto	1926
Fraser, C. A., Jr., Oma	1959
Fraser, A. K., Cooksville	1968
Fraser, D. M., Toronto	1940
Fraser, R. M., Weston	1970
Furness, G. L., Hamilton	1969
Giles, F. S., Hamilton	1928
Goodale, E. G., Hamilton	1926
Goodine, F., Sault Ste. Marie	1972
Goodman, J. O., Toronto	1934
Goodwin, T., Regina, Sask.	1953
Grant, R. D., Woodstock	1951
Gray, M. J., Stratford	1928
Haggarty, R. M., Belleville	1968
Hall, J. S., Ottawa	1935
Hall, R., Ayr	1969
Hampson, W., Mississauga	1974
Harland, L. C., Montreal, Que.	1944
Harper, M. R., Toronto	1961
Harper, R., Toronto	1971
Haslam, H., Hamilton	1949
Hayhurst, T., Toronto	1931
Hazell, R. T., Toronto	1944
Hendrie, G. C., Sr., Hamilton	1945
Hendrie, G. M., Toronto	1970
Hepburn, R. D., Port Stanley	1941
Higgins, E. E., Oshawa	1956
Hill, R. M., Toronto	1945
Hines, W. J., Montreal, Que.	1953
Hinton, C., Windsor	1953
Hipwell, V. O., Toronto	1939
Hoar, C. V., Toronto	1955
Hoar, E. V., Toronto	1927
Hoar, H. T., Toronto	1930
Hofland, E., Hamilton	1977
Houldsworth, A. T., Toronto	1931
Hume, A. T., Toronto	1958
Husband, T., London	1945
Hutton, G., Lakeside	1944
Hyndman, H. J., Gorrie	1956
Irving, M. C., Bradford	1964
Johnston, M. E., Chesterville	1972
Johnston, R. A., Toronto	1940
Kembel, L. O., Rexdale	1972
Kennedy, N. A., Toronto	1960
Kidd, K. W., Toronto	1951
Kieffer, V., Guelph	1961
Kipfer, L., Milverton	1969
Kostek, J., Toronto	1958
Kron, R. E., Kenora	1938
Kron, J. W., Toronto	1977
Larke, W. S., Oshawa	1928
Lawrence, A., Toronto	1966
Leather, H. H., OBE, Hamilton	1933
Leslie, R. E., Toronto	1942
Levy, E., Toronto	1960
Levy, P., Toronto	1974
Lincoln, A., St. Catharines	1960
Little, J. K., Kirkland Lake	1953
Little, W., MP, Kirkland Lake	1938
Logan, D., Toronto	1965
Lyon, A. E., Ottawa	1939
Lyon, G., Kingsville	1937
MacGillivray, C. J., Toronto	1942
Mackan, D. G., Hamilton	1968

MacKinnon, W., Guelph	1972
MacQuarrie, D. R., C.A., Toronto	1926
Male, W. H., Toronto	1932
Maris, T. C., Windsor	1933
Martin, H., Floradale	1976
Martin, A. E., Toronto	1966
Martin, A. J., Edmonton, Alta.	1955
Martin, S. V., Toronto	1933
Mason, H. R., St. Catharines	1952
Mason, J. A., Timmins	1966
McCallum, F. N., Oshawa	1940
McCreary, W. R., Belleville	1931
McGiffin, J. W., Montreal, Que.	1949
McGregor, A. D., Toronto	1948
McKay, C., Weston	1976
McKeen, W. C., Comber	1973
McKinlay, M., Dixie	1956
McManus, H. J., London	1949
McNab, R. D., Toronto	1965
McNaughton, C., Walkerton	1946
McWhirter, W. J., Cooksville	1969
Medhurst, J. H., Toronto	1967
Mellway, A. P., Toronto	1926
Merrick, W., Edmonton, Alta.	1966
Middleton, C. W., Toronto	1928
Middup, R. T., Toronto	1957
Minnes, E. D., Don Mills	1971
Monette, R. J., Timmins	1975
Morris, R. L., London	1953
Naylor, B., Toronto	1977
Nichols, P. W., Toronto	1970
Nickel, H. G., Listowel	1964
Noble, C. S., Ottawa	1942
Nussey, A. M., Tilbury	1972
Oatley, K. C. H., Hamilton	1968
O'Neil, J. W., Mississauga	1975
Owen, H. E., Sault Ste. Marie	1963
Palangio, J., North Bay	1936
Pape, M. J., Toronto	1933
Parke, G. E., Toronto	1926
Parke, G. M., Toronto	1937
Paxton, D. A., Peterborough	1958
Payne, E., Toronto	1956
Perkins, J. A., Jr., Ottawa	1956
Pickard, W., Toronto	1941
Pink, J. W., Scarborough	1970
Poll, B. J., Toronto	1975
Pressey, T. E., Sarnia	1936
Pugh, H., Chatham	1931
Ransom, R. C., Hamilton	1969
Rea, E. P., Streetsville	1973
Reid, J. S., Point Edward	1962
Reimer, D. S., Winnipeg	1960
Reynolds, P., Bondhead	1948
Richards, E., London	1933
Richards, R. W., New Toronto	1938
Richardson, J. J., Walkerton	1955
Robertson, C., Fort Frances	1940
Robertson, V., Hamilton	1957
Robinson, D., Hamilton	1976
Rodanz, G., Toronto	1935
Rodger, T., Ottawa	1972
Rogerson, J. H., Dutton	1933
Roper, P. K., Toronto	1962
Roth, C. L., New Hamburg	1961
Rowan, D., Jr., Toronto	1951
Rumble, J. L., Toronto	1943
Rumley, R. V., New Toronto	1974
Russell, W. J., Toronto	1941
St. Denis, G., Guelph	1974
Sauers, L. P., Hamilton	1974
Sayle, F. N., Brantford	1939
Sayle, T. W., Brantford	1927
Scace, J., Riverview	1941
Schell, N. C., Woodstock	1937
Schilling, G., Kitchener	1929
Scobie, L., Jr., Niagara Falls	1957
Scott, M. D., Oakville	1969
Sentineal, R., Oakville	1967
Shanahan, W. M., Long Branch	1945
Sinclair, J. W., Malton	1976
Slater, D. G., Toronto	1963
Slote, R., Hagersville	1971
Smith, A., Toronto	1964
Smith, D. A., Gore Bay	1969
Smith, G. M., Unionville	1971
Smith, H. W., Port Arthur	1961
Smith, K. H., Toronto	1943
Smith, P., Oshawa	1926
Smith, T. G., Toronto	1968
Smith, W. C., Toronto	1949
Snyder, D. N., Baden	1949
Stacey, J., Hamilton	1926
Stack, Mrs. M. B., Sault Ste. Marie	1975
Stalvey, W. B., Toronto	1977
Stauffer, D. G., Jr., Bright	1971
Strachan, H. B., Woodbridge	1968
Sumner, J. R., OBE, Toronto	1953
Swain, G. S., Toronto	1965
Sweezey, R. J., Toronto	1962
Syer, R. M., Scarborough	1960
Taggart, F. S., Ottawa	1938
Tanner, C. W., Toronto	1946
Taylor, G. K., Markham	1956
Teakle, L. G., Woodstock	1943
Telford, R. J., Toronto	1946
Thibodeau, C. A., Windsor	1942
Thibodeau, L. J., Windsor	1964
Thibodeau, L. W., Windsor	1936
Thomson, R., Streetsville	1977
Thompson, J., Owen Sound	1975
Thompson, V. J., Toronto	1974
Tuckey, B. W., Exeter	1965
Tudhope, G. C., Parry Sound	1962
Van Esterick, J., Toronto	1938
Wahl, K. N., Toronto	1972
Ware, C. L., Ottawa	1956
Waring, R. A., London	1977
Warren, J. R., Toronto	1951
Watson, A. J., Toronto	1970
Wells, R. G., Woodstock	1968
White, H. C., Toronto	1958
White, H. G., Hamilton	1950
White, W. T., Toronto	1977
Whiting, H. W. F., Toronto	1961
Widdicombe, A. A., St. Catharines	1944
Williams, W. R., Rexdale	1972
Wilson, C. H., Toronto	1950
Woods, J., London	1970
Woods, H., London	1962
Wright, A., Seaforth	1960
Wyllie, W. R., Downsview	1977
Young, J. N., Toronto	1955
Zavitz, H., Wainfleet	1953
Zavitz, K., Wainfleet	1963

PAST PRESIDENTS 1926 TO 1952

Fred C. Foy
1926-1927

Charles W. Middleton
1928-1929

Harold T. Hoar
1930-1931

Wilfred H. Male
1932
1953-1954

L. Gordan Fabian
1933

E. G. Goodale
1933

Arthur T. Houldsworth
1934

Milton J. Gray
1935

George E. Parke
1936

George Rodanz
1937-1940

Walter W. Crawford
1941-1944

Harry E. Adams
1945-1947

Rodger E. Leslie
1948-1949

George M. (Don) Parke
1950-51

C. J. (Doddie) Doerr
1952

PAST PRESIDENTS 1955 TO 1977

Frank N. McCallum
1955-1956

W. J. (Jim) Hines
1957-1958

Robert D. Grant
1959-1960

Charles V. Hoar
1961

Harold G. White
1962

Proctor A. Dick
1963-64

Marshall D. Davis
1965-1966

Harold W. F. Whiting
1967-1968

Benson W. Tuckey
1969-1970

Halley G. Nickel
1971-1972

M. W. (Mel) Donnelly
1973-1974

R. M. (Max) Haggarty
1975-1976

George M. Hendrie
1977

Donald R. MacQuarrie
(Founding Secretary)
Treasurer
1926-1934

J. O. (Joe) Goodman
Assistant Secretary
1934

In 1957 Nelson A. Boylen, a Weston, Ont. milk transporter, completed 50 years in the industry. He was selected to receive the Pioneers Club engraved tie clip on behalf of the 33 others entering membership in that year. R. D. "Bob" Grant, left, ATA first vice-president, made the presentation.

OTA PIONEERS CLUB

Members of the Ontario Trucking Association who have been engaged continuously in the trucking industry for at least 25 years are listed herein, with the year of starting in the industry. The Pioneers Club was organized in 1956 and only those active in the industry from that time on are included.

PIONEER CLUB MEMBERS   Year commenced in trucking business

Adams, G., Markdale	1947
Adams, H. E., Chatham	1930
Alger, E. J., Hamilton	1921
Allan, J., Hamilton	1929
Allworth, W. B., Windsor	1940
Alteman, M. G., Brampton	1931
Anderson, A. J., London	1929
Anderson, N. T., Don Mills	1940
Andrews, G. H., Toronto	1946
Apps, R. J., Toronto	1938
Arbuck, M. M., Toronto	1947
Arbuck, S., Toronto	1934
Armstrong, E., Guelph	1928
Armstrong, G., Port Arthur	1924
Ashton, C., Scarborough	1939
Ashton, O. C., Enniskillen	1928
Barker, J. V., Erindale	1930
Barr, J. S., Stratford	1929
Barrand, F. G., Toronto	1929
Bartlett, H., V., Dunnville	1936
Bartlett, H. E., Dunnville	1930
Bauman, E. H., Rexdale	1939
Bauman, O. F., Kitchener	1930
Beaney, C. H., Brockport, N.Y.	1931
Bell, B. J., Desboro	1928
Bell, R. A., Port Arthur	1932
Benedetti, P. F., Hamilton	1929
Bennett, D. E., Listowel	1944
Bennett, E. M., Listowel	1928
Bennett, J. G., Bowmanville	1928
Bennett, R. J., Listowell	1946
Bigham, F. G., Woodstock	1920
Bigham, G. L., Woodstock	1931
Binkley, C. E., Waterdown	1928
Blakely, L. C., Greenbank	1939
Beauregard, C., LaSalle, P.Q.	1948
Boal, J. R., Toronto	1936
Bondy, H., Windsor	1937
Bonnetta, H. W., Whitby	1947
Booth, C. E., Simcoe	1934
Bowen, M. F., Chatham	1945
Boxma, J. P., Ottawa	1934
Boyd, B. C., Meaford	1951
Boylen, N. A., Weston	1908
Bradley, F. J., Brockville	1928
Brady, J., Windsor	1945
Brady, R., Windsor	1944
Braund, E. F., Jarvis	1934
Brindley, C., Goderich	1940
Brock, K. M., Thorndale	1934
Brohman, F. A., Waterloo	1940
Brohman, J. J., Waterloo	1940
Brooking, A. D., Bowmanville	1946
Brooks, L. C., Rexdale	1939
Brown, S., Windsor	1930
Brownlee, M., Richmond	1929
Bruce, G. R., Barrie	1944
Bryan, T., Sunderland	1934
Bryans, R. J., Campbellford	1951
Buckham, B., Peterborough	1947
Buell, E. L., Toronto	1928
Bulmer, R., Fenelon Falls	1927
Burns, R. D., Georgetown	1944
Bushell, A. E., Toronto	1926
Butterworth, G., Hamilton	1936
Cadby, R. W., Toronto	1923
Cameron, W. R., St. Catharines	1934
Campbell, A. C., Dalkeith	1934
Campbell, A. E., St. Thomas	1945
Campbell, D. W., Durham	1935
Campbell, R. E., Exeter	1944
Campbell, W. D., St. Thomas	1946
Casey, A. M., Toronto	1932
Casey, J. L., Ottawa	1937

Cathcart, H. A., Peterborough	1946
Cathcart, M. J., Peterborough	1941
Cavers, R. S., Wellandport	1925
Cerson, C., Kincardine	1947
Charlton, W., Oshawa	1927
Charron, A., Chatham	1929
Chittick, J. C., Lakefield	1951
Church, J. C., Bradford	1934
Church, T. J., Bradford	1934
Clarke, N. L., Orillia	1931
Clifford, B. H., Ruthven	1933
Clifford, J., Agincourt	1939
Clifford, R. W., Agincourt	1946
Cohoe, G. B., Hamilton	1948
Collins, R. W., Stoney Creek	1945
Collins, T. A., Hamilton	1919
Cook, C., Port Perry	1932
Cook, L. S., Petrolia	1947
Cooke, L. E., Barrie	1938
Cope, H. G. H., Toronto	1928
Copeland, R., Newton Robinson	1925
Corney, G. T. S., Rexdale	1926
Coyle, F. S., Lakefield	1936
Cronin, F., Dublin	1934
Cronin, J. G., Dublin	1947
Cronkwright, M., Simcoe	1929
Crossley, J. C., Jr., Rexdale	1925
Crowther, W., Mississauga	1929
Cullen, E. J., Scarborough	1932
Culver, B. L., Waterford	1946
Curry, J. C., Ottawa	1929
Davey, G. R., Verona	1938
Davey, K. A., London	1941
Davison, R. C., Toronto	1940
Dean, R. S., Hamilton	1925
Delongchamp, G., Sudbury	1912
Desrosiers, A. O., London	1947
Dick, P. A., Chatham	1936
Dickey, R. O., Stayner	1930
Dickson, W. W., Ottawa	1935
Dietz, T., Mildmay	1935
Dixon, F. L., London	1947
Dobson, K., Brampton	1927
Doerr, C. J., Hespeler	1923
Drimmie, N., Elora	1931
Duck, R. C., Cooksville	1931
Duncan, J. N., Malton	1930
Duncan, J. R., Ottawa	1929
Duncan, K. L., Ottawa	1932
Dunford, F., Peterborough	1948
Edwards, H. S., Frankville	1931
Einwechter, H. C., New Dundee	1926
Emblem, N. J., Cornwall	1920
English, C. W., Midland	1939
Enright, E. J., Mississauga	1948
Erwin, T., Toronto	1926
Falla, F., Hamilton	1945
Feasby, C. S., Stouffville	1928
Ferris, H., Grimsby	1933
Fess, G., Selkirk	1931
Fife, W. R. H., Omemee	1937
Finch, A. C., Brantford	1921
Finley, J. E., Sr., Dresden	1949
Flanagan, J. P., London	1941
Fraser, C. A., Jr., Toronto	1939
Fraser, C. A., Sr., Toronto	1909
Fraser, R. M., Toronto	1933
Frohlich, E., Kitchener	1936
Galipeau, J. E., McGregor	1925
Garbutt, A., Cooksville	1925
Gardiner, I. D., Carleton Place	1946
Gardner, J., Toronto	1921
Gareau, W. A., Rexdale	1941
Gibson, W., Alliston	1946

PIONEERS (cont).

Glesta, J. R., Oakville	1951
Godin, E., Rexdale	1940
Goldstone, C., Uxbridge	1944
Gordon, J., Toronto	1921
Gouin, D., Tecumseh	1929
Gould, J. A., Mississauga	1947
Goy, J. H., Acton	1946
Graham, M. A., Blackstock	1930
Graham, N. K., Toronto	1929
Grant, H. M., Ottawa	1936
Grant, P., Toronto	1911
Grant, R. D., Mississauga	1935
Gravelle, L. A., Sudbury	1946
Gray, E., Toronto	1929
Green, G. A., Arnprior	1939
Greer, S. L., Kars	1929
Guest, A. R., Arthur	1946
Haggarty, H. D., Belleville	1946
Haggarty, M. W., Brantford	1930
Haggarty, N. N., Wooler	1930
Haggarty, S., Brantford	1928
Hanson, C. H. W., Montreal, Que.	1926
Hanson, C. S., Ottawa	1947
Harris, E. W., Hamilton	1929
Harris, G. R., Whitby	1945
Hartwick, C. M., Kincardine	1951
Hatton, C. F., Montreal, Que.	1940
Haviland, W. B., Kirkland Lake	1927
Hawkins, C. C., Peterborough	1951
Hayball, D., Lambeth	1934
Hayball, W. F., Oshawa	1949
Henderson, S., Fort William	1938
Henry, A., Weston	1933
Hepburn, R. G., Port Stanley	1921
Herniman, W., Cottam	1935
Hilson, N., Milton	1939
Hines, W. J., Rexdale	1949
Hinton, C., Windsor	1927
Hirons, G. A., Toronto	1922
Hoar, C. V., Scarborough	1937
Hoar, E., Toronto	1923
Hodge, W. J., Maple	1929
Holland, M. E., Hamilton	1919
Holland, M. F., Cottam	1949
Hopp, K., Mississauga	1948
Hotchkiss, J. Wm., Straffordville	1938
Howe, C. F., Mississauga	1934
Howe, E. H., Jerseyville	1941
Hume, A. T., Toronto	1927
Hume, G. W., Toronto	1929
Hume, M. C., Toronto	1934
Hunter, W. A., Hanover	1946
Hurdman, W. P., Ottawa	1931
Hutton, G., Lakeside	1933
Hutton, L., Tiverton	1945
Hutton, W., Lakeside	1933
Hyndman, A. W., Gorrie	1937
Hyndman, H. J., Gorrie	1937
Ireland, W. H., Sault Ste. Marie	1904
Jeffers, Mrs. R., Toronto	1935
Jensen, P., Toronto	1930
Jerome, L., Mount Hope	1924
Jessop, C. W., Schomberg	1948
Johnston, C., Glanworth	1929
Johnston, P. J., Agincourt	1936
Johnston, M. E., Chesterville	1934
Jones, D. S., Scarborough	1938
Jones, F. E., Newbury	1936
Jones, M. F., St. Thomas	1932
Jordan, W. H., Kerrwood	1939
Jubenville, L. B., Chatham	1947
Kaysmith, C. R., Toronto	1923
Kembel, L. O., Rexdale	1950
Kendall, J. W., Los Angeles, Cal.	1925
Kennedy, W., Mount Elgin	1942
Kennelly, L. J., Hamilton	1929
Kenwood, P. G., Montreal, Que.	1941
Kenwood, P. R., Montreal, Que.	1946
Kenwood, W. F., Montreal, Que.	1940
Kerr, J. L., Timmins	1930
Kidd, D., Toronto	1930
King, E. C., Owen Sound	1932
Knill, J. S., Paris	1936
Knipfel, C., Kitchener	1929
Kostek, J. W., Toronto	1935
Kraus, L., Sr., Toronto	1933
Kreaden, S., Dorval, Que.	1934
Krick, G. A., Binbrook	1931
Kron, R. E., Kenora	1935
La Flamme, J. A., Asbestos, Que.	1930
Laidlaw, R. A., Hagersville	1924
Lamb, J. P., Thornhill	1932
Lambert, G. W., Courtland	1926
Lambert, J., Brooklin	1941
Lancaster, E. E., Malton	1946
Lancaster, E. W., Windsor	1917
Lane, R. H., Georgetown	1940
Lasby, G. L., Guelph	1925
Lawrence, K. H. D., Milton	1951
Lawrence, R. E., Forest	1925
Lawrence, S., Port Hope	1928
Lawrence, W. J., Brampton	1939
Leather, H. H., Hamilton	1920
Lefebvre, G., Alexandria	1936
Letts, E., Beeton	1934
Lewis, C. H., Lucan	1943
Lewis, W. E., Toronto	1930
Lightfoot, C., Alvinston	1930
Lisson, A. A., Merrickville	1926
Little, F. R., Windsor	1910
Little, J. K., Kirkland Lake	1935
Lobraico, M. A., Scarborough	1935
Lobraico, P. A., Toronto	1919
Lobraico, V. L., Scarborough	1942
Lodwick, C. G., Beaverton	1939
Logan, D., Toronto	1936
Lowes, F., Woodstock	1925
Lowes, G., Woodstock	1936
Luckhart, H. W., Sebringville	1951
MacDonald, E., Dutton	1943
MacKay, W., Toronto	1946
MacKinnon, L., Guelph	1929
MacKinnon, W., Guelph	1942
MacVicar, J. T., Kitchener	1932
Mackie, M. R., Oshawa	1930
Macoun, J. C., Campbellford	1933
Maislin, Abraham, Tonawanda, N.Y.	1947
Maislin, Alex, East Rutherford, N.J.	1947
Maislin, Sam, LaSalle, Que.	1945
Maislin, Saul, East Rutherford, N.J.	1947
Maislin, Syd, LaSalle, Que.	1946
Male, W. H., Toronto	1928
Manary, J. W., Dundas	1922
Marcus, H. A., Bothwell	1946
Marlow, W., Blackstock	1926
Marsh, S., Arkona	1927
Marshall, M., Ridgeville	1931
Marshall, W., Toronto	1906
Martin, A. E., Toronto	1933
Martin, D. S., Toronto	1939
Martin, S. V., Toronto	1918
Martin, T. S., Emo	1926
Martin, Mrs. S. V., Toronto	1918
Mason, C. W., Trenton	1945
Mathers, W. T., Toronto	1951
Mathies, J. J., Etobicoke	1946
McAllister, K. J., Toronto	1942
McCallum, F. N., Oshawa	1931
McCreary, A., Belleville	1931
McCreary, Miss E. J., Belleville	1937
McCreary, H. E., Belleville	1933
McCullough, N. H., Toronto	1929
McDonald, C. V., Harrow	1929
McEachern, P., Toronto	1909
McElhone, F., Tillsonburg	1924
McGarvin, J., Chatham	1922
McGrath, H., Burlington	1925
McGregor, A. D., Toronto	1927
McInnes, K. E., Kenora	1932
McKay, G., Hickson	1927
McKeen, W. C., Comber	1945
McLeod, J., Sr., Fort William	1920
McLeod, J. A., Jr., Fort William	1936
McLeod, K. A., Fort William	1937
Medland, Mrs. M., London	1931
Meharg, I., Glen Meyer	1929
Meiler, L. S., Troy	1927
Meldrum, A., Mrs., Montreal, Que.	1932
Meyers, D. H., Campbellford	1929
Middup, J. T., Toronto	1917
Miller, R., Sundridge	1930
Miskelly, A. T., Aylmer	1944
Mitchell, J. C., Hamilton	1922
Mitchell, J. E., Milliken	1939
Moore, M. W., Shining Tree	1924
Moore, O. W., Loring	1924
Morgason, L. A., Markham	1948
Morrice, W. H., Windsor	1920
Morris, R. L., London	1926
Mulholland, W. E., Toronto	1931
Munro, H., Lakeside	1945
Naylor, H. R., Toronto	1924

Naylor, W. W., Toronto	1927
Nelson, F., Keene	1927
New, J. D., Downsview	1942
New, R. H., Toronto	1909
Newman, C. D., Harriston	1947
Nicholas, C. D., Peterborough	1945
Nicholas, P. W., Toronto	1946
Nickel, H. G., Listowel	1934
Ninnis, W. G., Weston	1921
Nixon, K., Toronto	1948
Noble, J. K., Uxbridge	1928
Noblet, M. M., Grand Rapids, Mich.	1936
Norris, W. C., Montreal, Que.	1922
Nussey, A. W., Tilbury	1939
O'Connor E., Scarborough	1946
Oglanby, B., Brantford	1936
Owen, H. E., Sault Ste. Marie	1935
Paisley, T. H., Stouffville	1930
Palangio, J., North Bay	1923
Palmer, F. G., Detroit, Mich.	1931
Parent, J., Windsor	1935
Parke, G. M., Toronto	1932
Pascoe, K., Parkhill	1937
Peacock, A., Brampton	1926
Pearson, H. C., Rexdale	1928
Peart, C. R., Paris	1947
Peplow, A. E., Kitchener	1948
Perriman, K. J., Paris	1944
Pettinger, J. D., Courtland	1932
Pickard, W., Toronto	1905
Plyley, M. L., Stevensville	1933
Poll, E. R., New Dundee	1947
Prentice, M. L., Minden	1936
Pressey, C., Corinth	1934
Preston, F., Gormley	1946
Preston, M. F., Bowmanville	1951
Provost, P., Montreal, Que.	1927
Purves, L. F., Toronto	1935
Ranklin, C. A., Highgate	1947
Rawlings, H. W., Mississauga	1930
Rawn, A., Wyebridge	1936
Rennie, W. T., Stouffville	1941
Renton, W. A., Dromore	1930
Rich, C. E., Whitby	1947
Richardson, J. J., Toronto	1941
Ridley, J. L., Acton	1946
Rivers, J., Tweed	1936
Robertson, B., Windsor	1947
Robertson, W. A., London	1925
Robinson, L. R., Brampton	1950
Root, E. J. H., Orton	1930
Root, J. H., Orton	1930
Rosewarne, E., Bracebridge	1926
Ross, B. W., Beachburg	1936
Ross, R. J., Oshawa	1946
Ross, R., Burlington	1946
Ross, T. V., Oro Station	1926
Roth, C. L., New Hamburg	1946
Runions, K. S., Cornwall	1939
Russell, G., Oshawa	1936
Russell, T. C., Oshawa	1936
Saarinen, H., Islington	1929
St. John, J. A., Cornwall	1927
Satchwell, D. J., Toronto	1937
Schauber, H., Milverton	1930
Schives, R. G., Chatham	1942
Schutt, R. C., Tonawanda, N.Y.	1927
Scobie, L. F., Toronto	1926
Scott, M. D., Oakville	1951
Scott, O. A., Jr., Toronto	1928
Scott, R. J., Toronto	1922
Sercombe, G. E., Toronto	1910
Sercombe, S. J., Toronto	1910
Sherwin, G. K., Baltimore	1946
Sicotte, D., Montreal, Que.	1920
Sifton, R. A., Windsor	1928
Sim, C., Willowdale	1944
Simmonds, C., Midland	1925
Sinclair, H. H., Ottawa	1941
Sinclair, J. W., Toronto	1945
Skippen, A., Thornbury	1934
Slack, W. R., Caledonia	1946
Slater, D. G., Toronto	1940
Smith, A., Toronto	1941
Smith, C. M., Downsview	1939
Smith, E. W., Agincourt	1945
Smith, H., Montreal, Que.	1932
Smith, P., Toronto	1919
Snook, M. J., Thorold	1936
Snyder, B. M., Mrs., Baden	1929
Snyder, D. N., Baden	1929
Snyder, O. A., Hespeler	1928

Sparks, G. D., Ottawa	1932
Spencer, C. A., Thornton	1925
Spicknell, D. W., London	1935
Stanfield, F., Erindale	1935
Stanfield, J. J., Islington	1906
Stark, H., Sr., London	1933
Stauffer, D., Sr., Bright	1925
Stevenson, M. G., Uxbridge	1947
Stewart, N., Kemptville	1931
Stone, H. C., Toronto	1923
Strachan, H. B., Burgessville	1946
Strauch, M., Toronto	1940
Suske, S. J., Woodstock	1937
Sutor, E., Cayuga	1931
Sutton, F. W., Guelph	1927
Tallman, G., Allanburg	1936
Tanner, C. W., Toronto	1920
Tanner, F. W., Toronto	1924
Taylor, G. K., Markham	1938
Taylor, J. E., Woodstock	1940
Taylor, S. R., Ajax	1940
Teakle, L. G., Brantford	1927
Teed, E. A., Meaford	1928
Tennant, J. W., Pembroke	1908
Thaler, S. D., Kitchener	1924
Thibodeau, C. A., Walkerville	1928
Thibodeau, L. J., Windsor	1940
Thiel, E., Zurich	1930
Thomas, A. A., Windsor	1941
Thomas, F. C., Hamilton	1928
Thompson, F., Newington	1929
Thompson, J. E., Ingleside	1945
Thompson, W. L., Teeswater	1922
Thomson, R., Milton Heights	1930
Thorburn, G., Mrs., Pefferlaw	1932
Thornton, G., Woodslea	1928
Tippet, C. F. B., Toronto	1924
Town, H. W., London	1934
Townsend, V., Mrs., Fergus	1940
Truesdale, W., Toronto	1930
Tuck, G. W., Hamilton	1919
Tuckey, E. W., Exeter	1929
Tudhope, G., C., Parry Sound	1930
Tyler, E. G., Acton	1929
Tyler, G., Mrs., Acton	1931
Tyner, T. B., Marlbank	1931
Tyrrell, J. K., Vancouver, B.C.	1932
Uren, W. B., Orilliam	1928
Veitch, J., Winnipeg, Man.	1923
Walden, W. E., Wingham	1946
Walker, J. J., Deep River	1940
Wallace, A. R., Toronto	1933
Wallace, H. R., Port Colborne	1927
Wallace, Mrs. R., Toronto	1917
Walsh, K. F., Simcoe	1948
Wardrope, C., Weston	1949
Wardrope, D., Weston	1949
Wardrope, H., Toronto	1926
Waring, R. A., London	1947
Warman, C. S., Winnipeg, Man.	1917
Warren, J. R., Toronto	1936
Warwick, S., Mississauga	1940
Waugh, H., Windsor	1943
Weigel, N., Toronto	1928
Weir, E., Dorchester	1940
Wells, E. P., Dunnville	1921
White, C. E., Bancroft	1937
White, H. G., Hamilton	1933
White, W. J., Listowel	1934
Whitehead, E. E., Teeswater	1945
Whiting, H. W. F., Rexdale	1932
Wilke, O. W., Kitchener	1938
Wills, G. G., Burgessville	1928
Winterhalt, E. C., Cambridge	1947
Witty, F., Ingersoll	1929
Witzu, S. A., Toronto	1942
Wladyka, N., Toronto	1929
Wood, W. G., Pakenham	1933
Woods, H., London	1931
Woods, P. J., Hespeler	1935
Wright, A. J., Seaforth	1945
Wright, G. D., Toronto	1917
Wright, H. R., Toronto	1925
Wright, H. T., Toronto	1927
Young, T., Toronto	1930
Yuill, J., New Toronto	1923
Yuill, T. K., Toronto	1929
Yuill, R. G., Toronto	1938
Zavitz, H. C., Wainfleet	1934
Zavitz, K., Wainfleet	1947
Zigelstein, A., Toronto	1930

The Ontario Trucking Association has initiated or supported many community and industry causes throughout its 50-year history, as well as those with broader provincial or national implications. Most of these have been described in general terms in the preceding pages.

However, certain events in the trucking industry recognize outstanding performance by individuals, particularly in such areas as road safety, in operational, administrative and association activity, and for acts of heroism beyond the call of duty by professional truck drivers.

This history of the association would not be complete without due recognition of industry people in Ontario who have excelled in truck roadeos, of those who have been honored with the "Service to Industry" Award, and to that special group of professionals who have received the "National Truck Hero Award".

Their names are recorded in the following pages.

The 1973 Ontario Roadeo champions are shown here at a Directors' Luncheon of the Canadian National Exhibition Association. From left, Stew Hymers, Premier William Davis, Harold Marsh, Allan Donaldson, and Metro Toronto Chairman Paul Godfrey.

Truck Roadeos in Ontario

The Truck Roadeo was introduced to Canada in 1947 by the (then) Automotive Transport Association of Ontario. Its primary objective was to give recognition to skillful drivers and to encourage them and their employers to take a greater interest in road safety and courtesy.

While the Ontario Trucking Association and the Transportation Safety Association of Ontario actively support truck roadeos, co-ordinating responsibility since 1974 has been taken over by the Etobicoke Centre Jaycees. The National Roadeo, reinstated in 1967, is held in various provinces.

Competitions have been held each year in Ontario since 1947, although suspended in 1962 and 1966 due to strikes in the industry. In 1972 there was joint Ontario-national competition. Divisions have been added and discontinued at various times, as indicated by the years shown in the following schedule of winners.

(*indicates national champion)

STRAIGHT TRUCK DIVISION

Year	Name	City	Company
1947/49	* Jules Chartrand	Port Credit	Trinidad Leaseholds
1948	* Bernard E. Jones	London	John Labatt Ltd.
1950	Wallace Postill	London	Harry Woods Transport
1951	Beaumont Lehigh	Cobourg	Imperial Oil Ltd.
1952	* C. G. Brown	Sudbury	Imperial Oil Ltd.
1953	Douglas Coomber	Hamilton	B-A Oil Co. Ltd.
1954	* David LaRose	Malton	Imperial Oil Ltd.
1955	Wm. A. Jodrell	Toronto	John Labatt Ltd.
1956	R. E. Cumming	Dundas	Imperial Oil Ltd.
1957/58	J. D. Chapman	Sudbury	Imperial Oil Ltd.
1959	H. N. Everett	Sudbury	CN Express
1960	P. R. Babcock	Kingston	Imperial Oil Ltd.
1961	M. Berberick	Kitchener	Argosy Carriers
1963	R. Hartnup	Burlington	Shell Canada Ltd.
1964	A. Murray	Denfield	Consolidated Truck Lines
1965	A. Goldhawk	Watford	Consolidated Truck Lines
1967/69	* Earl Hawthorne	Kitchener	Kingsway Transports
1968	Herb Foden	Toronto	Taggart Service
1970	Patrick F. Kelly	Old Chelsea, Que.	Kingsway Transports
1971/73	G. A. Donaldson	Georgetown	Peel Express (Brampton)
1974	Len Hunt	Beeton	Canada Cartage System
1975	* George Virgoe	Weston	Kingsway Transports
1976	G. A. Donaldson	Georgetown	Armbro Transport
1977	Tom Campbell	Downsview	Imperial Oil Ltd.

SINGLE TRACTOR-TANDEM SEMI DIVISION

Year	Name	City	Company
1953/54	Robt. H. Brownlee	London	John Labatt Ltd.
1955	Roy J. Perin	Port Credit	Regent Refining (Canada)
1956/58	* John W. Murphy	Elmvale	B-A Oil Co. Ltd.
1957	* G. F. Cumming	Dundas	Imperial Oil Ltd.
1959/67	* Patrick Hennessy	London	Inter-City Truck Lines
1960	R. E. Thibert	Sandwich East	Chrysler Corp. of Canada
1961	T. Roach	Concord	Scott Transport
1963	Chas. Goudreau	Sudbury	Motorways (Ontario)
1964	Wm. Austin	Kitchener	Consolidated Truck Lines
1965	J. Ed Elliott	New Hamburg	Kingsway Transports
1968/70	John Wilkinson	Hamilton	Allan Industries
1969	Ken Wright	Perth	Taggart Service
1971	Orval A. Smith	Dundas	Gulf Oil Canada Ltd.
1973	H. G. Marsh	Forest	Imperial Oil Ltd.
1974	Roy McKend	Toronto	Kingsway Transports
1975	Ralph Hilborn	Grand Valley	Armbro Transport
1976	* Alex Tait	Toronto	Listowel Transport Lines
1977	Tom Williams	Niagara Falls	Overland Western

TANDEM TRACTOR-TANDEM SEMI DIVISION

1959	G. L. Herron	Hamilton	Shell Oil Co. of Can.
1960	* M. E. Hawman	Port Credit	Regent Refining Ltd.
1961	R. Carter	Hamilton	Hanson Transport
1963	S. Heier	Waterloo	Consolidated Truck Lines
1964	S. Sadlak	Welland	Consolidated Truck Lines
1965	Lloyd Scott	Ancaster	Hanson Transport
1967/69	* Wm. C. Hicks	London	M. Loeb (London) Ltd.
1968	Gary Nauss	Toronto	Richard's Delivery Service
1970	John Hellingman	Carlisle	Imperial Oil Ltd.
1971	* Henry J. Huys	Burlington	Scott Transport
1973	* W. S. Hymers	Atwood	Listowel Transport Lines
1974	John Giffin	Islington	Kingsway Transports
1975	John MacDonald	Brampton	Miracle Food Mart
1976	Glen Campbell	Mississauga	Carling-O'Keefe Transport
1977	Glen Campbell	Mississauga	Carling O'Keefe Transport

SINGLE TRACTOR-TANDEM TANKER DIVISION

1961	M. Holcomb	Winona	Imperial Oil Ltd.
1963/65	O. Smith	Dundas	B-A Oil Co. Ltd.
1964	G. L. Herron	Grimsby	Shell Canada Ltd.

TANDEM TRACTOR-TANDEM TANKER DIVISION

1961	A.A. Allen	Scarborough	Shell Canada Ltd.
1963	W. Hickey	Toronto	B-A Oil Co. Ltd.
1964	L. M. Bowerman	Brampton	B-A Oil Co. Ltd.
1965	L. Maki	Sudbury	Imperial Oil Ltd.
1966	T. A. Wilcox	Pickering	Shell Canada Ltd.
1968	Harold Marsh	Forest	Imperial Oil Ltd.

TANDEM TANK TRUCK-THREE-AXLE FULL TRAILER DIVISION

1966	K. Bigelow	Ottawa	Imperial Oil Ltd.
1968	Ivan Gamble	North Bay	Shell Canada Ltd.

SINGLE TRACTOR-SINGLE SEMI DIVISION

1947	* Frank Bell	Toronto	Canadian Breweries Transport
1948	Norman Tomlinson	Burlington	A. S. Nicholson & Son Ltd.
1949	F. W. Leach	Toronto	Imperial Oil Ltd.
1950	Clayton Reesor	Toronto	Smith Transport Ltd.
1951	George Cumming	London	John Labatt Ltd.
1952	* Alan Shepherd	Burlington	A. S. Nicholson & Son Ltd.
1953	Donald Semmens	Toronto	HEPC of Ontario
1954	Ralph G. Doerr	Toronto	Canadian Breweries Transport
1955/56/58	* Thomas Roach	Toronto	Robinson Cotton Mills
1957	* J. E. Elliott	New Hamburg	Kingsway Transports Ltd.
1959	K. A. Anderson	Hamilton	Shell Oil Co. of Canada Ltd.
1960	T. W. Stephens	Toronto	HEPC of Ontario

CAR TRANSPORTER DIVISION

1961	A. Boothby	Oshawa	Charlton Transport Ltd.

"Service to Industry" Award

The OTA-Canadian Trailmobile "Service to Industry" Award, first presented in 1958, is open to any member of the Ontario Trucking Association or any official of a member company. It recognizes outstanding service to the welfare and development of the trucking industry in Ontario in the fields of accident prevention, education, freight claims prevention, general or specific industry activities, industrial relations, legislation, new techniques, public relations and shipper-carrier co-operation. Nominations are submitted to a committee of three for evaluation. Following is a list of recipients:

1958	W. J. Hines	1968	H. W. F. Whiting
1959	F. N. McCallum	1969	A. K. Fraser
1960	* W. H. Male	1970	Wm. McKay
1961	A. D. McGregor	1971	B. J. Poll
1962	R. D. Grant	1972	M. D. Davis
1963	* L. G. Teakle	1973	H. G. Nickel
1964	* C. Crossett	1974	B. R. Naylor
1965	P. A. Dick	1975	G. M. Parke
1966	M. W. Donnelly	1976	G. M. Hendrie
1967	H. G. White		

* Deceased

First winner of the Trailmobile "Service to Industry" Award was Jim Hines, right, shown here being congratulated by R. M. "Bob" Syer, then president, Canadian Trailmobile Ltd.

On March 30th, 1974, when a fuel tanker and a freight truck collided and burst into flames at Vegreville, Alberta, Kenneth Bishop of Lloydminster, Saskatchewan, withstood severe burns to his body to save the life of George McAdie, who lay helpless in the midst of flames and explosions. On impact, Mr. McAdie was flung from his truck and suffered a serious injury. Some 7,000 gallons of gasoline from his ruptured tanker ignited and surrounded the driver within walls of fire. No one but Kenneth Bishop dared attempt to save the victim and as he approached the inferno, the rescuer was thrown several feet by an explosion. His clothes caught fire but he refused to turn away. Already severely burnt, Mr. Bishop protected his face from the blistering heat and snaked his way to Mr. McAdie. Taking a firm grip of the man, under the arms, he dragged him safely away from the conflagration. Although aware that his deed might cost him his own life, Kenneth Bishop exhibited the finest example of selfless courage and humanitarian concern to save a complete stranger.

(The Canada Gazette, April 10, 1976)

One of the outstanding trucking professionals to receive the Dunlop (Dayton) National Truck Hero Award was Kenneth Wilfred Bishop of Lloydminster, Sask., who received the award in 1974. Further recognition of his bravery came in 1976 when he received the Cross of Valour, Canada's highest civilian award, from the Governor General, the Rt. Hon. Jules Leger. Ken Bishop's citation, as it appeared in The Canada Gazette of April 10, 1976 is shown above.

Dayton Tire National Truck Hero Award

Known for many years as the Dunlop National Truck Hero Award, this is a significant annual award honoring the truck hero of the year. Instituted by Dunlop in 1956, it involves the entire Canadian trucking industry and the Canada Safety Council in a search for the professional truck driver who has performed an act of heroism beyond the call of duty. Nominations from across the country are submitted to an Award Committee and the winner is announced at the annual convention in November of the Ontario Trucking Association, where he is presented with $1000 in cash, a watch, a trophy, and is a guest of Dayton at a VIP weekend for two in Toronto.

The OTA is pleased to give this further recognition to the gallant professional truck drivers who have received the award since its inception.

1956	Richard Lanthier	Reliable Transport Co. Ltd.	Montreal, Que.
1957	Lonas Fraser	John W. McKay Refrigerated Transfer	New Glasgow, N.S.
1958	Wilmer Nuhn	Hyndman Transport	Gorrie, Ont.
1959	Glenn Austin	Dunnville Packers	Dunnville, Ont.
1960	David Walker	Municipal Tank Lines Ltd.	Brampton, Ont.
1961	James Hampton	Toronto-Peterborough Transport	West Hill, Ont.
1962	Gerald Christie	Maislin Transport Co. Ltd.	Fort Erie, Ont.
1963	Bill Pirlot	Soo Security Motorways Ltd.	Regina, Sask.
1964	Arthur Hewson	Direct Winters Transport Ltd.	Brockville, Ont.
1965	Richard Laverdiere	La Compagnie Citadelle Gax Propane	Quebec City, Que.
1966	Anthony Thornton	Shell Canada Ltd.	Willowdale, Ont.
1967	Ronald Stewart Young	C.P. Merchandise Services	Nanaimo, B.C.
1968	Raymond Merrill Day	Self-employed (Joint award)	Maugerville, N.B.
	Kenney John Bartlett	Self-employed	Maugerville, N.B.
1969	* Donald Gordon Myers	Gulf Oil Canada Limited	Ottawa, Ont.
1970	Perry Waite	Ontario Dept. of Highways	Brighton, Ont.
1971	Ted Daubreville	Canada Cartage Systems Ltd.	Toronto, Ont.
1972	Ray Hamblin	Vail & Sheppard Cartage	Scarborough, Ont.
1973	Gerry Smith	Doman-Marpole Transport Ltd.	Richmond, B.C.
1974	Ken Bishop	Self-employed	Lloydminster, Sask.
1975	Frank Preis	Porter Trucking	Golden, B.C.
1976	Fred Reber	Self-employed	St. Catharines, Ont.

* Posthumous

Since 1928 G.M.C. Truck Centre have been serving the Transportation industry

GMC TRUCK CENTRE

The Truck People from General Motors

1650 The Queensway at Hwy. 427, Toronto, Ontario M8Z 1X1   Phone: (416) 255 - 9145

GM

1917.

"Looks as if that air-filled tire will be the coming thing."

Back in 1917, a Packard truck blazed a rutted trail from Akron to Boston and back, proving to the world that the trucking business and the Goodyear pneumatic tire was the "coming thing."

The journey of the "Wingfoot Express" used up 28 days and 28 tires for the round trip.

Today however, it is not unusual for a trucker to expect 150,000 miles from a Goodyear tire.

Through its history, Goodyear has precipitated an enviable list of firsts.

Like the "quick detachable" straight side tire, and the use of an open-weave ply to prevent the tread and carcass from separating at higher speeds.

Then came the concept of flexibility in tire construction, and a special cord tire that wouldn't chafe against an inflexible rim. Quickly followed by the idea of adding plies to Goodyear's tough cord fabric for pneumatic truck tires.

Goodyear also developed the extraordinary moon tire that helped man travel the lunar surface.

All of which is simply another way of saying, Goodyear has pioneered the "coming thing" in the tire industry for three quarters of a century, and intends to retain that leadership in the years ahead.

Goodyear Canada Inc. Toronto, Ontario.

PART III

AXLES, PISTONS, TIRES AND TEARS

A tale of truck technology

by Rolland Jerry

Rolland Jerry's lifelong interest in commercial vehicles goes back to the twenties and, over the years, he has assembled one of the finest collections of truck historical data and photographs on the continent. Throughout his working career he has been editor of a trucking publication and contributor to trucking periodicals in Canada, the United States and the United Kingdom. More recently, his articles in *Old Cars*, a widely circulated American paper devoted to automotive history, have been credited with much of the rising interest in vintage commercial vehicles. This has been further stimulated by his writings on the same subject for other publications in North America and elsewhere.

The first commercial vehicle manufactured in Canada, an electric wagon built by the Still Motor Company, Toronto, in 1899. Drive was by belt to the rear wheels from the mid-mounted motor. Ackerman-type steering was used.

The first commercial delivery wagon used in Canada. This 1898 electric was built by Fischer Equipment Company, Chicago. Owned by the Robert Simpson Company, Toronto, it appears to have greater carrying capacity than the Parker wagon.

It was a good start, but instead of a bang it was a series of click, click, clicks from an electric controller gear. The onset of trucking in Ontario was heralded by a noise no louder than the ticking of a grandfather clock with, perhaps, a muted whine from straight-cut gears.

What matters is that Ontario's first commercial vehicles were away and down the road.

The "trucks" were battery-powered electrics—two four-wheelers and an electric tricycle that carried a box for a payload that might have amounted to 200 pounds. The year was 1898 and it all happened in Toronto.

An industry had started, too; it wasn't apparent even as a dot on a distant horizon, but it was there. This is an account of some of the vehicles and technical advances that helped transform that dot into what it is today—the trucking industry.

Two well-known Toronto firms, Parker's Dye Works and the Robert Simpson Co. Ltd., bought electric vans that year. The electric tricycle—hardly a truck with its very light load—had appeared earlier, in 1896. It was Canada's first "commercial vehicle", according to the authoritative "Cars of Canada".

The electric tricycle wasn't a success and it disappeared, although gasoline-powered light tricycles attracted many pioneers in Europe and the United States. The weight and bulk of an electric motor and its batteries were insurmountable disadvantages in so small a vehicle.

Technically, it conformed with cycle practice of the era; today as well. The frame was heavy-wall tubing with ends reinforced and brazed the way it's done now. Like a bicycle, chain drive was used; the motor and batteries were grouped under the seat at the bottom of the frame. The "body" was a large box mounted between the rear wheels and the weight distribution between the axle and the front wheel would have been in the order of 80/20. Heavy-duty forks, dual handlebars and a bell rounded out the specs.

More is known of the two four-wheelers. These were practical, functioning vehicles that "worked", proving reliable for Ontario's first motorized delivery operations.

Simpson's moved into the automotive age with the purchase of an American-made job, described as the Fischer "Number 2 Coach Delivery Wagon". It was built in Chicago by a manufacturer who achieved some success with electrics from 1898 to 1905, when production ended.

The driver sat up high at the front, an awkward perch and difficult to reach from the ground with the obstacles posed by front wheels and sides of the vehicle.

Farther up Yonge Street, Parker's Dye Works opted for a Canadian-made vehicle. This was about the same size as the Fischer, differing in appearance to the extent that the driver sat lower and under the roof. It was built by a Toronto firm, The Canadian Motor Syndicate. The company was founded to produce vehicles designed by William Still. Later on, some were identified as Still electrics, but Parker's unit was produced by the Canadian Motor Syndicate.

The successors to CMS—Canadian Motors Ltd.—produced a few more, including a handful of vehicles exported to England where they earned an excellent reputation for finish and workmanship. But it wasn't enough to save CML as 1902 proved to be the end of the line for the company.

Both vehicles drew heavily on established carriage-building practice—safe and proven guidelines known to work well with a horse, perhaps with a self-powered vehicle as well.

The body of the Parker vehicle was a high-grade, horse-drawn van, modified and reworked to meet automotive needs. Then as now, bodywork was expensive and a specialized craft; if a manufacturer could convert a horse-drawn vehicle to suit his own needs, so much the better. He would get a first-rate varnish finish generally superior to anything he could do himself in an automobile plant of the day. But high gloss and the "bottomless pool" lustre were short-lived, depending on care and maintenance. Re-varnishing was a certainty within two years if the carriage finish, as opposed to durable but flat enamels for workaday wagons, was to be preserved.

Neither vehicle had a chassis as such; bodies were beefed up to accept the undergear, essentially the motor unit, full elliptic suspension (we'd call them "buggy springs" now) and a front steering axle. The absence of a chassis as such was not advanced automotive thinking. It was simply the way carriages had been built for at least 150 years to meet needs and design requirements of the times.

Starting, stopping, and everything in between was regulated by the electric controller gear. This was a large switch unit which the driver used to regulate speed. It also provided braking through the motor.

Movement of the controller increased voltage to the motor by cutting in more battery cells for extra power. The Fischer's four tray-mounted batteries, connected in series, produced a maximum of 80 volts.

Each click of the controller represented a different speed to a maximum of 14 miles per hour. There was also a reverse, through other controller and motor circuits.

Tire and wheel specs of both vehicles were in line with carriage thinking. The larger rear wheels on the Fischer were 46 in. in diameter, a good 10 in. or so larger than the front wheels. This was a legacy from carriage building with little merit for self-propulsion, though familiar and acceptable to a public conditioned to the appearance of horse-drawn vehicles.

It's safe to assume that the wheels on the Parker van came with the body (as received from the carriage builder) as standard equipment. Then, as now, "specials" and optional equipment boosted prices. Better to take a stock unit from the carriage builder and watch prices.

Both vehicles had straight front axles, good for clearance and simplicity but scarcely an aid in holding down the towering height. The height, and lively undamped characteristics of full-elliptic suspension guaranteed an exciting ride with every corner an adventure in side-sway!

A variation of the idea was the electric (later gasoline-powered) "fore carriage". This was a self-contained "power unit" that slipped under the front end of a cart, wagon or dray. The idea was that draymen could easily convert their horse-drawn vehicles to power. The concept fizzled out, although it had some success in converting early horse-drawn fire apparatus.

The manufacturers of both vehicles used automotive-type steering, similar to what we have now, a fixed axle and wheels pivoting on spindles at the ends. Horse-drawn carriages used "fifth wheel" or platform steering, with the axle turning in whatever direction the horse turned, an early form of power steering. Front wheels had to be smaller than the rear wheels for clearance beneath the vehicle when the axle turned.

Both vehicles suffered from the electric's big failing, short battery life. No electric can wander far from the charger and a reviving overnight charge. Simpson's found that the Fischer couldn't make it through the day, although it could travel 35 miles between charges on smooth paved roads. Some of Toronto's streets were anything but, so battery drain was heavy and the unit had to return to the store at noon for recharging.

The CMS and the Fischer had electric lights and they most certainly would have been used sparingly, particularly toward the end of the day when batteries were in need of a charge.

Friction was the arch enemy of the electric with its short-lived and easily spent batteries. The Fischer's "best grade" hub ball bearings helped, as did the thin-section hard rubber tires. Ball bearings were the hallmark of a quality carriage in the 1900s. The Fischer also needed them to reduce rolling resistance. What was good for Old Dobbin also applied to battery power.

The internal combustion engine was a noisy handful in 1898, although European engines were somewhat more advanced than their American counterparts. The gasoline engine of the day ran in a setting of blued, overheated steel and leaking hot oil. Many saw it as an outrage against public order, a reason why Simpson's and Parker's didn't give it a try, preferring to leave it to rabid "automobilists".

Steam power was another not very viable option in 1898. Everyone knew steam was "explosive" and as tricky in its way as the nervous gasoline engine. Steam power was in and out of the mainstream of automotive development for some years, finally losing out completely to the internal combustion engine for commercial vehicles.

Steam never had much of a following in North America although it gained a strong foothold in England. Massive steam lorries were part of the British street scene well into the 1930s. The diesel is about as near as you can come with an internal-combustion engine to matching the characteristics of steam power.

There was scarcely a land office rush to commercial vehicles after the Fischer and CMS. Apart from a number of experimental gasoline-powered tricycles and a few light steam vans, not much happened. There was one development though. Parker's, pleased at the success of its electric for city service, added a small Winton van to its fleet. This went into service in 1901 on country routes.

It wasn't a truck, although it passed for a commercial vehicle in its time. The unit was based on a Winton passenger car chassis and it featured a 2-cylinder flat or horizontally opposed underseat engine, driving through a 2-speed transmission. Winton was the corporate ancestor of a familiar present-day name, Detroit Diesel Allison.

There were many North American automobile manufacturers in 1901. When a firm decided to add a truck to the line it did just what Winton did—simply put a van body on a car chassis. Oldsmobile had one, mounting a small box at the rear of the Olds "one lunger" (1-cylinder) runabout for perhaps as much as a 100-lb. load.

European manufacturers were making good progress with gasoline-powered commercial vehicles. The German Daimler-Phoenix truck of 1898 was a real truck with a platform-type body. This job had a 2-cylinder water-cooled engine out in front under a hood, similar to what would be called a conventional-type today. The driver sat behind the engine and he had a steering wheel, not a period-piece tiller bar customary on most horseless carriages of the era.

Drive to the rear wheels was by side chains, a form of final drive that would be in use for years in heavy vehicles. There was no cab but there was a bench-type seat, as much as truck manufacturers would offer until 1910 or so. The Daimler-Phoenix was ahead of its time and it's still running. Anyone seen a Fischer or CMS electric van lately?

If the usage of commercial vehicles didn't amount to much in Canada before 1905, less had been achieved in the manufacture of trucks. Even allowing for advances in Europe, the state of the art wasn't high anywhere and development of the commercial vehicle lagged behind the passenger car. A Canadian project did nothing to change the picture.

Repeat Orders for One to Ten Trucks from more than One Hundred Gramm Owners

The Gramm is built in 1, 2, 3 and 5-ton chasses.   Bodies are furnished to meet the purchaser's requirements

Every inch of 145,000 square feet of floor space taxed to its utmost capacity, with a force of 2000 men working full time and over time—that tells you better than words can where the Gramm stands in the truck world today.

This condition has obtained for months; and the Gramm product has been going out with magnificent regularity into the hands of owners satisfied in advance that the Gramm is *a truck it is absolutely safe to buy.*

While you have been debating in your mind the wisdom of buying a truck, or wavering between several truck reputations; nearly a thousand of the greatest truck-buying concerns in America have long since settled the question of utility—*and made up their minds which truck to choose.*

These thousand-odd Gramm trucks are in daily use all over America.

Contrary to general custom, not one of them is on probation, consignment, or trial.

They are sold—sold outright—without quibble or qualification—and are implicitly accepted by every Gramm buyer—not because of what we say; but because of what the Gramm owner is quick, and ready, and glad, to say of the service he is getting.

No man who has ever seen the great Gramm plant—a small sized industrial city in itself—could hesitate about his choice.

THE **Gramm**

Gramm Trucks are in as great demand, proportionately, in small cities as in large.   Our distribution covers, approximately, all cities of largest size, like New York, Philadelphia, Chicago, San Francisco, etc.   Valuable representation can still be secured by men of the right calibre.

If you are interested in establishing an attractive business of immense possibilities, to which you can devote all your energies, arrange with our sales department, either by letter or wire, for open territory.

No man who has been properly told the Gramm story can fail to see *how secure he is in the Gramm reputation.*

By the Gramm story we mean the building of the first trucks in America by a man who refused to be tempted away from the more permanent possibilities of the commercial field by the allurements of pleasure-car popularity.

We mean ten years crowded with hard, practical, progressive experience; which solved for the Gramm all the worst problems of the commercial truck *before most manufacturers had confronted them.*

The astonishing sales of the Gramm today are not a sudden freak of public demand; but the natural heritage of these ten years of heart-breaking research when no adequate reward was in sight.

The Gramm is selling today because, of all motor trucks, *it most deserves to sell.*   Ten years of devotion to an ideal have culminated in this magnificent plant and are receiving a magnificent expression in the Gramm Truck.

The long and impressive list of Gramm owners, more than one hundred of whom have repeated their orders; the detailed and unsolicited reports from business houses of records made in service and economy—all these offer precisely the sort of conclusive evidence for which the truck buyer has been looking.

We want you to know both the technical and practical features of the Gramm. Write today for full information

THE GRAMM MOTOR CAR COMPANY   **114 South Lima Street, LIMA, OHIO**

Canadian Manufacturers: THE GRAMM MOTOR TRUCK COMPANY OF CANADA, LTD., Walkerville, Ont.

(Circa 1913)

The Canadian Advertising Wagon, shown above closed for traveling and on the opposite page with flaps up and ready for business. The vehicle was a 1905 four-wheel drive with gas-electric propulsion. It lacked power, a good suspensions, in fact everything. It was replaced by a steam-driven Darracq-Serpollet bus chassis in 1907, shown below, although the same exhibits were used.

A reminiscence of Olympia.

This new advertising van, a Darracq-Serpollet, has replaced the Canadian-built vehicle which was sent over by the Dominion Government in 1905.

Canadian Government advertising wagon, with side and end flaps hinged up, revealing interior exhibits of cereals, grasses, fruits and game. The rear panel shows a map of the world.

In 1905 the Canadian Government commissioned the Commercial Motor Vehicle Co. Ltd., Windsor, to produce a gasoline-powered truck. The CMV was an early-day branch-plant operation as the parent firm was located just across the river in Detroit. Seemingly, the Windsor company was hastily formed just to fill this one order and comply with a stipulation calling for an all-Canadian vehicle. The Canadian plant was a short-lived venture, and the U.S. company didn't fare much better in a brief span from 1903 to the end of production in 1905.

The firm was the author of its own mechanical misfortunes with a vehicle it dubbed the "gaso electric". It was an odd one and I'll describe it. But first there's some background; it was a curious scheme.

The Canadian government was interested in attracting British immigration to Canada in 1905. The West was opening up and there was a pressing need for immigrants who knew something about farming and the straight-and-narrow with a plow. British farmers did, so a drive was launched to sell Canada in Britain. We'd call it PR today. Who knows what it was called then?

Ottawa decided to throw a horseless carriage into the act as an attraction in itself. Maybe this was colonial thinking and it might have been a big deal for Canada, but it wasn't quite the case in Britain. Motor-minded Englishmen had been driving cars for years and they weren't sideshow novelties, nor were they called horseless carriages either.

The Windsor-built "truck" was outfitted as a traveling display van. It was a large unit and might be called a COE today. It was 20 ft long on a wheelbase of 156 in. with a track or gauge of 81 in. The height isn't given in the specs but it was a high one.

Big windows in the sides of the body displayed the "fascinating" contents inside—specimens of grain, corn, fruit and vegetables. All were indicative of what the British farmer could expect to raise "out in Canada". Bold lettering proclaimed what Canada had to offer.

"Faithful Labor is Well Rewarded"; "Canada, the Granary of the Empire"; "Cattle Thrive and Fatten Faster in Canada", and "Free Farms for Willing Workers" were a few of the themes pitched at the yeomenry. The sides of the vehicle dropped down to form a platform for walk-through viewing of the displays.

Technically, the unit was a gasoline-electric, one of the many systems favored by early designers for propulsion. Gasoline-electrics never made much headway but the concept appealed to a number of manufacturers (Fischer was one). With gasoline-electrics the engine drives a generator to operate an electric motor, which actually powers the vehicle. One electric motor wasn't enough for this unit—it had four, one for each wheel and the benefits of four-wheel drive. Gasoline-electrics as a class worked well enough and were successfully used with city-type buses in later years.

Some manufacturers favored the gasoline-electric for the absence of gear-changing. In this case there would have been other more important advantages, since the unit had four-wheel drive. Achieving this by a mechanical power train—drivelines and transfer case—would have been very difficult, if not impossible. But you could do it by "wiring", with power supply from the generator to each wheel-mounted motor. The gasoline-electric was in and out of automotive development all

through the 1920s; it's still around in heavy construction equipment in a continuation of the "motorized-wheel" concept.

The van was shipped to England and readied for a trip to include "every town and village in the country". This was unwarranted optimism; it never got out of London! Badly underpowered, it couldn't negotiate the slightest grade and 20 horsepower was all the 5½ x 5 in. 4-cylinder engine could put out. And not for long either, even though cooling needs were looked after by a 40-gallon water tank.

British automotive writers and journalists quickly spotted the bugs and weaknesses in the Canadian vehicle. "Considering the time and the money spent on this vehicle, and the admirable purpose in sending it to the country it is unfortunate that those responsible for its manufacture did not first secure technical advice as to road conditions in Great Britain," sniffed the *Commercial Motor*.

That British truck operators already had a trade paper of their own indicates just how far the industry had progressed in Britain in 1905. Canada's *Bus and Truck Transport* started in 1925, *Motor Truck* in 1934, while the U.S. *Commercial Car Journal* was a bit earlier in 1911.

Commercial Motor, a British journal founded in 1905, worried about all the glass and the fragile exhibits subjected to the jarring effects of solid tires and rough roads, also the poor performance. "We fear it will be impossible to carry out the laudable program projected. The wagon cannot climb a gradient beyond 1 in 25, and the steering is very difficult." CM was right. The Canadian government scrapped the plan and promptly bought a French Darracq-Serpollet steamer chassis and outfitted it with a similar body.

This was a much more sophisticated design with a good suspension to protect "the fine collection of stuffed prairie chickens" and other glass-cased items for the edification of British farmers. There was a new banner, too: "England's Nearest and Greatest Colony". One hopes George Bernard Shaw's "Great British Public" finally got to see the "many specimens of cereals" and the hermetically sealed glass jars which made up the show.

The years between 1906 and 1910 were good ones in the truck world for development and innovation. Now the gasoline-powered truck was clearly a vehicle in its own right; there was less and less relationship with the passenger car. But most automobile manufacturers offered at least a light van and had done so since the inception of the automobile.

European manufacturers favored the conventional type, an engine out in front under a hood with the driver sitting behind. American preference swung the other way, namely the COE or the cab-over-engine truck. The COE offered ample chassis space, but there was a price to pay and the driver paid it—heavy steering. This was unavoidable in the days before power or assisted steering and with some 30 percent of the vehicle's weight on the front axle. Drivers of the conventional type fared better with only 15 to 20 percent of the weight on the front axle. The ride was superior, too, sitting behind and not over the axle.

But heavy front-axle loads weren't seen as a disadvantage with the COE and drivers were a husky lot any-

This 1911 Packard conventional had the engine out front to simplify accessibility for maintenance and to reduce front axle loading for easier steering. The driver is Art Dunham who took a course in Detroit on driving and maintenance of this vehicle. Grant Cartage & Fwdg. Co. was a predecessor company of Inter-City Truck Lines Ltd.

way. They had to be good outdoorsmen, since the cab was no more than an exposed park bench. But, there were few complaints from early drivers. Driving a truck at maybe $12 a week was the best job in town and the envy of every schoolboy.

While this was an American show, many of the new vehicles appeared on the Canadian market. This didn't expand quite as rapidly as the U.S. scene, although there were big changes by 1910 and 1911. Toronto automobile dealers scrambled for the agency rights to a variety of American makes. Customers in search of a heavy-duty truck had a fair selection such as White, Autocar, Mack, Rapid, Peerless, Reliance, Packard, not to mention the U.S.- assembled Saurer of Swiss origin.

As an aside, one of the oldest signs in Toronto touted the merits of the Rapid until the building it was painted on was torn down a few years ago. The Rapid was an oldie to say the least, having come on the American market in 1903, although it's doubtful that any were sold in Canada before 1905. The Rapid and the Reliance, popular makes in Ontario at the time, also the Randolph which wasn't popular, are still around today. They're called the GMC now!

They were great days. Memory holds the door for Horace Harpham, in his nineties now and as interested as ever in a business that was so much a part of his life for years.

"I started selling British-built Commer trucks in Toronto in 1910. There were a few trucks around then but not many," he says. Harpham doesn't know who had the first motor truck but he knows George Hardy, a well-known cartageman, had a few. "George had one or two trucks when I sold him some Commers in 1910 or 1911. After that he bought most of his trucks from me."

The Commer was a quality job and a conventional type. A dominant feature was the Lindley semiautomatic or pre-selective transmission for easy gear changes by a shift mounted on the steering column, as opposed to a floor-mounted lever. A 3-speed unit, the transmission was an integral part of the jackshaft needed for chain-drive.

Sealed chain cases were used, a novelty on American trucks but quite widely used on European makes. Side chains functioned in an oil bath, if at the expense of some complexity and substantially higher manufacturing costs for the chain cases.

The make is uncertain, although it resembles a Reliance in some ways. The year is about 1911 and many of the technical features of the era can be identified: vertical steering column, massive front axle to carry much of the load, underseat engine and the 'dual' rear solid tires. The driver is Billy Payne.

Commer produced a wide range of units in light, medium and heavy-duty capacities. All were powered by 4-cylinder engines, with a big 6-cylinder engine developing 100 horsepower reserved for the fire truck. Speeds "upwards of 45 mph" were claimed for this unit. The ride and the reaction of solid tires at this speed can be imagined. Twenty to 30 hp. was entirely adequate for Commer's trucks.

Harpham believes that the British American Oil Co. Ltd., may have had the first "big" fleet in the Toronto area. "I sold B-A five Commers in 1911 and took in five Rapids as trades," Harpham says. He can't recall what year the Rapids were, but they were old and well-worn, in need of overhaul before he could sell them as used trucks. Presumably these would have been 1906 or 1907 models, perhaps the earliest heavy-duty units in Toronto.

The Rapid was a popular American make that also found a good market in Canada. Earlier units were COEs of course, but Rapid could supply a conventional type by 1910. The COEs were characterized by a low-mounted radiator, chain drive, vertical steering gear, and a suspension using semielliptic springs. Spoke wheels and 4-cylinder engines were other features of the Rapid. The number of models was comprehensive, with capacities ranging from one to five tons.

Rapid did well with buses. These were open sightseeing units based on stock Rapid chassis, so passenger step height was considerable with the high truck frames of the era. The firm also believed in advertising, promoting its trucks widely in a selection of consumer and trade publications.

Coville Cartage, another old-established Toronto cartage company, was a customer of Harpham's. "The firm liked Commers and I sold a good many over the years. But after 1916 Commers went to France, not to Canada, and I didn't have anything to sell for a time."

Harpham's brother, Cecil, was a partner in the business, but not before he tried his hand selling a rival make, the Scottish-built Albion. The Albion—"Sure As The Sunrise"—was a conventional type and a heavy-duty truck, again with a 4-cylinder engine. But for all of its Scottish virtues (excellent workmanship was a strong point with the Albion), the unit proved too slow.

Harpham recalls that a milling firm bought an Albion and was so unhappy with the performance that he had no difficulty in making another Commer sale. After that, Cecil Harpham joined forces with his brother to advance the Commer's use in Canada.

Both men had a good deal of experience with several makes. "When the supply of Commers dried up with the war, we switched to the American-built Republic trucks", Horace adds. "It proved to be a very good seller and we did well with it." Harpham could sell as many as he could deliver, in fact right on into the 1920s as the industry boomed.

Then he made another change, dropping the Republic for the Stewart, which was built in Buffalo and proved to be a popular truck with Ontario operators for years. But the Republic and the Stewart were rather different trucks than the Commer. Horace explains: "Both were assembled jobs using stock engines, transmissions and axles, whereas the Commer people built the whole vehicle themselves, using their own engines and other major components." Harpham says this led to fierce rivalries between competing salesmen. "Packard, White and Mack weren't assembled jobs and they felt their trucks were superior on this count, but they were expensive units and not every operator could afford them." Harpham says there was lots of room in the market for assemblers.

"If a Packard salesman convinced a customer that his truck was better because it had a Packard-built engine, I'd ask who supplied the tires, the battery and the magneto on the Packard." Horace says Packard didn't make these items and they were purchased from specialists in the same way that Stewart and Republic bought engines, transmissions and other components.

"I sold a good many trucks using this argument because then the Packard man would have to admit that the Packard truck was assembled to some extent. Besides, my prices were usually better," he says.

Curiously perhaps, Packard had swank showrooms on the edges of Rosedale, Toronto's most exclusive residential area. Packard cars were expensive as were the firm's trucks, and anyone who could afford either, or both, lived there.

Harpham also remembers the Great Axle Debate. "Back in those days many customers bought an axle, not a truck. The type of axle the vehicle had was a great selling point and we salesmen made the most of it." He points out that the years between 1910 and 1919 saw radical change in axles and final drives used in heavy-duty vehicles. "Pierce-Arrow made a big thing of its worm-gear axle, Mack its chain drive, and White and Autocar their double-reduction axles."

Harpham had a foot in each camp. "Some Commers were chain drive, others featured a worm-gear axle, while the Republic and the Stewart were strong on what was called the internal-gear back axle." Harpham could offer whatever the customer wanted in an axle. "I can't imagine what was merely a technical detail making quite so much impression today, but certainly in those days the type of axle on your truck counted for a lot."

The T. Eaton Co. got into truck operations early with this 1910 Packard COE with stake body. Fancy striping was much in evidence, a carry-over from carriage days as were some other features, notably the rear suspension.

In passing, the Stewart continued to make good progress in the Ontario truck market. In later years its distribution was taken over by another man well known in the truck business, George Anstee. At one point Stewart sold more vehicles per capita in Canada than in the United States.

Harpham made still another move in the early 1920s, this time into the tire business with the Toronto distribution of Firestone tires. But trucks were more important than ever: "We converted hundreds of vehicles on solid tires to pneumatics and there was a big demand for these conversions all through the twenties."

The horse was still part of the picture: "Dairies and bread companies liked the idea of rubber tires on their horse-drawn wagons as well as their trucks, so we put Firestones on them along with the trucks." Harpham says it was a tidy source of extra business and a good sideline for years.

While Harpham was doing well with his Commers, Republics and Stewarts, as were rival salesmen with their Macks, Whites, Packards and Pierce-Arrows, a few Canadian manufacturers ventured into truck production. None lasted for long and most were merely American makes assembled in Canada. Their plants were scattered throughout Southern Ontario and handy to the border for close contact with parent American companies.

The Gramm was one, described by Harpham as "no competition". This was an American job assembled in Walkerville between 1911 and 1914. A number of Canadian sales were made in Toronto and Montreal and the Canadian Army took a few to France.

Gramm's format was familiar and acceptable for the times—COEs in a range from 1 to 5 ton, powered by 4-cylinder engines, plus mandatory solid tires and chain drive. Frames were rolled structural steel with the flanges facing out, a technique popular then to simplify cross-member connections and the attachment of reinforcing gussets. It also meant that spring hangers had to be located below the side rails with the interference posed by frame-member flanges.

Gramm was early into mechanically operated dump trucks and offered these units in 1911, complete with Gramm-built hoists and dump bodies. This was typical; in the early days truck producers had few specialist suppliers to turn to. If one wanted a dump unit and hoist, or even a winch or truck-mounted crane, it usually meant the chassis manufacturer had to produce his own in lieu of vendor sources.

There were exceptions; a big one was the familiar St. Paul hydraulic hoist. It came on the market in 1912 and was immediately adopted by many truck manufacturers for jobs needing a hoist setup.

Truck specifications didn't change much until well into the 1920s. Truck manufacturers were a conservative lot, as were their customers.

The 3-ton truck buyer in 1912 didn't have much choice in anything excepting, perhaps, color. Most manufacturers produced just one model in each category or load capacity. This was also the case with wheelbase, just one choice, although sometimes there was a "long" and a "short".

Customers didn't question the absence of options. Why should they? Most were buying a truck for the first time and few customers knew much about them. The demands of truck users weren't very sophisticated then. It was sufficient if the vehicle carried 3, 4 or 5-tons, whatever, had the power for grades and hills, plus a top speed of about 10 to 12 mph. That was the extent of specifications in 1912.

The engine was a "big bore" (4 to 5 in.) 4-cylinder unit with a peak of around 1000 rpm. The performance curve was flat as a billiard table for good "pull", what we call "low-down" torque now. In general, torque characteristics were constant and steam-like from 250-300 rpm, great for valued pull, less than great for speed. So big horsepower wasn't needed, anything from 30 to 50 hp sufficed with the sort of speeds permitted by solid tires. A speed of 10 mph was about right, perhaps a bit much on some of the rougher streets where spring leaves simply collapsed and gave up the ghost with the hammering from solid tires; there was no need for a governor.

Ignition was universally by magneto and one of the best ones—Bosch—came from Germany. It was reliable but costly and had the advantage that it was self-contained and didn't need a battery or an electrical system. There was another virtue—usually a first-time start when hand-cranking the engine, providing the magneto had a "lively" magnet. Today, with coil ignition, a flat battery calls for a "boost" or a push. Magnetos are still used on many industrial engines.

When a truck manufacturer adopted coil ignition (it provided a good and consistent spark irrespective of engine speed), he needed a battery to energize the coil for starting. He then required a generator to maintain battery charge. And since he now had a generator, it was a relatively simple matter to add electric starting and lighting. Coil ignition was quite general in the early twenties (though not on the Model T Ford) for lighter vehicles, less so among the heavy trucks.

Mack, White, International and a dozen other heavy-duty makes stayed with the self-containment and simplicity of magneto ignition all through the 1920s. Big, low-speed 4-cylinder engines posed no demands for sophisticated ignition systems. Two names, later linked, were prominent in the development of coil ignition, Delco and Remy.

Weighty cast-iron pistons were fitted with three, and often four compression rings. The oil control ring was a later development, triggered by higher compression engines and rising speeds. As a result, early engines smoked from new and streets of the era—even well into the twenties—were perpetually hazy from the smog of smoky exhausts. So much for emission control and what we call a problem today!

Exhaust valves were troublesome in early engines—they burned and needed reseating frequently. All engines used side valves. With fixed heads, valve access was through "cages" or plugs at the top which could be removed for quick valve access. Half-length water jackets and low-grade fuels were hard on exhaust valves. Metallurgy was in its infancy but coming up fast. Steel specs and alloys were basic, but customers knew a truck manufacturer was using top-grade steel if he could claim "Krupp's Best" in his vehicles.

Engine lubricants weren't much better. There were two grades, "light" and "heavy". They were so thick, viscous and full-bodied (a desirable quality then) that a brick could float on them! Both lubricants sealed as much as they lubricated, an essential requirement with the wide clearances prevalent in early engines. Another characteristic was the rapidity with which they converted to carbon. This wasn't the hard, rock-like carbon of modern gasoline engines, but rather a soft, all-pervading paste that coated and plugged everything. It had to come out as frequently as once a month.

"Decarbonizing" could be a spectacular service operation. A quick way was to insert an acetylene torch into each combustion chamber through the plug hole and burn it out. The torch was hotter than the engine's normal combustion process and the carbon ignited. It was a safe enough technique with cast-iron pistons, although most manufacturers preferred that the carbon be scraped out.

Another odd method in ridding the engine of carbon was the chain technique. This was simply a very short length of chain with links of soft copper or brass. The plug was removed from the cylinder and the chain dropped in. Then the engine was run at low speed on three cylinders. Bouncing of the chain knocked most of the carbon loose so that it would blow out with the exhaust when the plug was replaced. But don't try either on a modern engine!

The detachable cylinder head wasn't common in early-day heavy-duty truck engines, although much progress was being made with this feature in the passenger car field. Mack and White, for instance, didn't swing over to detachable heads until well into the 1920s, at least for some models, and it was the same with other manufacturers too.

Instead, cylinders were cast in pairs of two and bolted to an aluminum or a cast-iron crankcase. Cylinders had to be raised when pistons needed reringing. This could be a tricky operation with a high mortality rate in broken rings, pinched thumbs and broken nails.

Lowering a pair of heavy cylinders down over the pistons and their rings called for the patience of a saint, perhaps a doubtful metaphor with the general incidence of profanity. It took two men to do the job, one to lower the cylinders and the other to watch for snags and broken rings.

When the detachable cylinder head did gain acceptance for heavy-duty engines, it did so in stages. Where a truck manufacturer retained separate cylinder blocks (cylinders cast in pairs of two, then three for 6-cylinder engines), the castings were modified for detachable heads. This is still a popular arrangement for big diesel engines.

The next development was the casting of all of the cylinders in one block, which in turn was bolted to the crankcase. Naturally the layout favored a detachable head, which was used. The final stage was the monobloc or one-piece casting combining the upper crankcase and the cylinder block in one unit. There were numerous advantages in this which can only be touched upon briefly, typically a shorter engine, better cooling and, most important, a much more rigid block providing excellent support for the crankshaft.

Ford had offered a monobloc-type engine as early as 1908 with the Model T, although it wasn't the first company to use it. It had the enormous foundry, production and machining facilities to produce monobloc castings and its huge sales justified the move. This wasn't the case with truck manufacturers.

Any small but good foundry could turn out separate cylinder blocks, whereas a big complex monobloc casting would have been out of the question. Much the same applied to the machining of separate cylinder blocks; any machine shop could do the work, in contrast to the costly and sophisticated production equipment required to machine monobloc castings.

It was a matter of economics, really. Automobile production outpaced the production of trucks by nearly thirty to one, so monobloc engines and elaborate manufacturing facilities were justified by the volume. Of course the producers of heavy-duty trucks and their engine suppliers did turn to the monobloc engine by the late 1920s, as by then truck production was on a large scale. But, as mentioned earlier, the monobloc type did not completely oust the earlier configuration as heavy-duty engines with separate cylinder blocks are still being produced.

High-volume production methods had no place in the production of top-grade engines in the early days of the industry, indeed until the onset of the 1920s. The castings for better-grade engines were always allowed to "age" for a year or so before they were machined, the idea being that stresses induced during casting would be normalized. Thus engine plants were often ringed with mountains of "green" cylinder blocks undergoing ageing before machining.

Babbitted bearings of the era performed well enough with low engine speeds, but babbitt was a very soft material with little strength. The bearings were poured from molten metal—cast in place, never an easy task and beyond many mechanics of the day.

The softness of babbitt was an advantage in a negative way. Soft and pliant, these bearings acted as great collectors of dirt from unfiltered lubricating oil. Babbitt could absorb a heavy intake of abrasive grit without scoring crankshaft journals or pins, at least to a point.

There was a casual approach to bearing care, as indeed there was to all phases of vehicle maintenance. An all-too-familiar rap from an excess of "big end" wear was the signal that bearings needed "taking up" by the selective removal of shims. This contracted or closed up the bearing for a tighter, perhaps even the correct fit. Pressure lubrication for main and connecting rod bearings was coming in fast at the time, though "splash" lubrication often sufficed for 1912-style engines.

In later years the industry had a conspicious holdout against full-pressure lubrication—Chevrolet. Chevrolet retained a quaint set of lubrication specs until the 1940s, a combination of splash for the shimmed and babbitted connecting rods and pressure to the camshaft and main bearings.

Chevy's cast-iron pistons might be hard on wrist pins, and babbitted bearings could test the skill of a mechanic who had to fit them, but they worked and obviously contributed to the engine's reputation for durability and longevity. GMC used Buick six-cylinder engines in its trucks in the late twenties and early thirties. It was similar in many respects to the Chev, though full-pressure lubrication was used with these rugged engines.

Like one-piece cylinder blocks and detachable heads, the modern interchangeable insert bearing wouldn't put in an appearance for years. When it did, in the late 1920s, the essential simplicity of the insert bearing

(Above) Pierce-Arrow's 1914 4-cylinder truck engine for its 2-ton model. T-head blocks of two cylinders each were bolted to an aluminum crankcase. Valve springs and tappets were fully exposed. Note magneto mounted behind the water pump, both driven from the timing case at front. Heads were fixed, non-detachable

(Right) The 1914 Pierce-Arrow chassis had a flexible frame with few crossmembers. Torque arm to control rear axle can be seen at centre, supplemented by radius rods below the springs. The 3-speed transmission had a cast aluminum housing and was mounted amidships in the frame, separate from the engine.

This circa 1909 vehicle appears to be based on the Russell passenger car chassis and probably never carried more than a 100-lb payload. The buyer wanted appearance and got it. Canada Cycle & Motor Co. in time became Willys-Overland of Canada Ltd.

One of the few all-Canadian trucks, an early Clinton built by the Clinton Foundry Ltd., Clinton, Ont. and shown here with the foundry staff as its load. About eight were said to have been built in 1910-11, along with a few cars. This one was sold to T. H. Hancock Lumber Co. of Toronto. Specifications included a structural-steel frame, acetylene lighting and braking on the jack-shaft chain-drive sprocket. Length of the hood suggests a 4-cylinder engine. Ninth from the left is the late Gabe Elliott who drove the truck to Toronto and then went to work for Canada Cartage where, at the time of retirement, he was general superintendent.

evaded mechanics who continued to treat it as they would a babbitt bearing. A good many engines were ruined through a simplicity that wasn't understood. Inserts didn't need scraping for final fit nor did bearing caps require filing in the process.

The transmission in our vintage truck would have three-speeds, with coarse straight-cut gears enclosed in a massive cast iron or aluminum split housing. The heat treatment of gears was a hit-and-miss affair. If gears were properly hardened and ground, they'd last for years. Otherwise they howled almost immediately.

One got "good gears" in an expensive quality make, but it was pot luck in the cheaper vehicles. Stripped gears and broken teeth accounted for as many breakdowns as "running out of oil" and engine overheating. Truck operators tried to ward off lubrication problems by providing drivers with cans of oil to refill near-empty crankcases.

Early transmissions were the devil to shift. Each shift was by double-clutching, with timing approaching vir-

tuosity. Big 250-pound flywheels took a long time to slow down for gear changing. A mistimed shift could strip gears and perhaps split a transmission housing. Engines of the period were designed with fairly flat torque curves so that drivers could stay in top gear or "high" most of the time.

Modern gear lubricants were unknown and couldn't have been used anyway with the limitations of felt and leather oil seals. These had a habit of burning out if lubricant levels were too low, or simply emptying the contents of the transmission if the oil level was too high. Leaky oil seals constantly posed problems in the early days.

Heavy-bodied grease worked better in transmissions, particularly when it had warmed and thinned. Gear changing was impossible until there was a semblance of fluidity. The transmission lubricant was never changed, nor engine oil either with the high consumption. The index of 1000 miles to a quart of oil arrived with the oil control ring in the late twenties.

There was no cab, or at the most simply a canopy top slung up over the driver's seat. Chances are our unit would have been a COE but the conventional type was fast coming into fashion by 1912. White, Peerless, Pierce-Arrow and Packard offered the type, as did Commer, Saurer and Albion who had produced conventional units in Europe for years.

Operators were taking a second look at the industry's "standard" in a heavy-duty truck, the COE. Drivers complained of killing steering, the hard ride, plus a cab and/or seat difficult to climb in and out of maybe fifty times a day. Not much has changed; drivers still prefer the conventional type to the COE, and for the same reasons.

There was more to it than that. Heavily loaded front axles on COEs often meant a short life for kingpins and bushings, not to mention bent axles and spindles. Spring failures were rife, too, though springs had the saving grace of quick access for replacement. The COE was less and less an attraction as the benefits of the conventional type became more apparent to customers.

But before we dismiss the COE, many of them were simply badly engineered, if in fact they could claim any real engineering input. Design by rule of thumb was generally adequate but when it wasn't, oh boy, did operators have problems! A good many early COEs fell into this classification.

While the COE went into a decline after 1911, a very good one survived, the Autocar EUS. Autocar never referred to theirs as a COE, it was "Engine Under the Seat" instead. Contractors liked the EUS for its nimbleness on building sites where the short wheelbase was an advantage. Autocar kept the EUS-type in production until 1933, then revised it with the COE's big comeback. FWD built COEs too, although they were more specialized units with four-wheel drive.

Our truck buyer, checking out what manufacturers had to offer in 1912, would have been interested in tires. If there wasn't much choice in mechanical specs and options, there was even less in tires. They were all solids.

Tire manufacturers were experimenting with pneumatic tires for heavy trucks in 1912, but they wouldn't be generally available (or trouble-free) until the 1920s. The coming of the pneumatic tire was a tremendous advance affecting every phase of vehicle design, in fact a real breakthrough. But in 1912 pneumatics were restricted to light-duty trucks and sparingly at that as they were expensive.

By the 1920s some solids were less "solid" than others. The "Swiss Cheese" or air hole type was one. This was merely a solid tire with air holes molded in, the voids, in theory at least, affording some slight cushioning. Another was the sectional solid tire, essentially blocks of rubber secured to a rim around the wheel. Gaps between the blocks provided space for expansion when the rubber was compressed under heavy load.

Wheels had wooden spokes in 1912, but the newer cast-steel wheel and the disc-type were gaining interest. These were far stronger than the artillery or wood-spoke wheel, also heavier. Wheels had to be sturdy to take the pounding from solid tires, also to resist the pressure of press-fit rim bands seating tires on wheel rims.

Cast-steel wheels were machined on massive lathes like rail-car wheels. Wheels, tires and rims made up a very large part of truck technology in 1912, just as they do today.

More massiveness was evident in the vehicle's frame, another structure calling for over-design to absorb hard knocks from rough roads and solid tires. The pressed steel frame had made inroads among the smaller trucks, but structural steel was the popular choice for larger vehicles.

Structural steel was heavy stuff—anything up to thirty pounds a running foot. Some of the structural shapes truck manufacturers used—I beams and channel sections—wouldn't have been out of place in a railway bridge. White used an I-beam for its heavier models; Mack a channel section in structural steel, while the Saurer was a good example of what could be achieved in a pressed-steel frame.

Loose rivets were a problem with frame weave and flex. These were bucked hot like the rivets in a steel-framed building, or the construction of a battleship. But they still popped and fell out with frame distortion. Replacing rivets was a big job; they were awkward to reach and had to be bucked and set while red hot. The rivets in modern truck frames are set cold, less colorful perhaps than hot riveting but cold rivets do a better job and rarely loosen.

The efficiency of the radiator and the cooling system was a vital concern of truck operators in 1912. Early gasoline engines had earned a bad reputation for running hot and memories of the problems stuck. Cooling systems were much less troublesome by 1912, but the potential for problems was there. One way of avoiding them was by acre-sized radiators, often not much smaller in area than they are now.

Early cooling systems still needed plenty of water, well into the 1920s. The 1922 Transport with its 4-cylinder engine of less than 60 hp, needed 11 gallons of water. Today, 11 gallons is sufficient for a 200 hp engine, while one big V-12 diesel only needs 15½ gallons to cool 430 hp!

But lots of water didn't prevent another cooling system defect—leaks. Hard tires, bad roads and stiff springs simply shook apart soldered tubes in the core. If bumps and road shocks failed to open seams and connections; engine vibration did.

Mounting the radiator on springs helped, although it could introduce other problems. Some manufacturers believed spring-mounting increased the bounce. But White didn't; two big spring mounts supported the radiator at the sides. These were so large they formed "ears" and identified the White for years.

What a customer didn't get in truck specs in 1912 is of interest. Absent was electric lighting and starting. Electric lighting was a novelty in the passenger car field and Cadillac has just introduced a practical, workable electric self-starter. But neither yet figured in heavy-duty trucks.

Many years would pass before some manufactuers offered them as standard equipment. Customers who wanted electric lighting and starting on a 1930 Mack AB paid extra for it. It had nothing to do with progress; Mack knew that many customers for ABs such as contractors, hadn't much need for either. Big low compression 4-cylinder truck engines could be balky at times,

The 1915 National, a truck manufactured by the National Steel Car Company Ltd., Hamilton, from 1915 to 1925.

but in the main they started easily by hand-cranking. Other truck manufacturers applied the same reasoning at the time, naming "electrics" as an option on heavy units.

During the early 1920s, starting and lighting provisions were designated as "single" and "two-unit" systems. The former identified systems like those used on Dodge Brothers/Graham Brothers trucks (the two were associated and major truck sellers) in which the starter and the generator were combined in one unit, the "dynamotor".

Dynamotors worked well and reliably, also quietly in terms of starting. But they were expensive and the increasing size (even with 12 volts) was a problem.

With two units, operators got a separate starter and generator. The two-unit system was standard practice in the industry after 1926 when Dodge/Graham also went to it. Six-volt service was used until the mid-1930s when 12-volt systems were developed to accommodate heavier starting loads imposed by larger truck engines.

Chain drive was still very much the fashion for heavy duty trucks in 1912, with a few notable exceptions, namely Pierce-Arrow with its worm-gear axle (introduced the year before) and Autocar with a gear-type double-reduction axle. The worm-gear axle was a British innovation, introduced to North America by Pierce-Arrow, while Autocar seldom used anything else but its own double-reduction unit which was a gear-type.

Then there was the American-built Mais with yet another axle, the internal gear. As a minor make it wasn't a factor on the Ontario truck market. Several other smaller American manufacturers also offered gear-type axles in various forms. And, as we have noted, Ontario customers had a choice of British-built Commers with chain drive and worm-gear axles.

Otherwise it was chain drive and its acceptance amounted to another industry standard. The theory in chain drive was that the large drive sprocket inside the wheel placed the chain's pull out near the tire for maximum leverage. It was a theoretical advantage compared to shaft drive and the advocates of chain drive made the most of it. Suffice to say, shaft drive won, but it took years.

Chain drive afforded a degree of simplicity in that all of its elements—drive and wheel sprockets, jackshaft and radius rods—were in plain view for easy access. This was also a weakness; the exposure to dirt and grit caused rapid chain wear. Enclosed chain cases, like the Commer's, were not popular with American manufacturers because of cost and complexity, although the Avery had them.

Roller-type chains were used; chains in which the connecting pins were enclosed within outer rollers and free to rotate on engagement with the sprocket teeth. Chain life depended on getting lubricant between the inner pins and the outer rollers. A very light oil had to be used to ensure penetration. The trouble was that light oil was flung out of the chain by the high rotational speed; it wouldn't stay there.

A number of metered lubricating devices were available as accessories for chain drive vehicles. These dripped light oil steadily at a controlled rate from a small reservoir, that needed filling daily. There was some reduction in wear this way, although oil and dirt were thrown over much of the vehicle by chain movement.

There was a way to boost the life of drive chains and it was generally advised by chain manufacturers. The facilities required were basic and seemingly had little part in automotive servicing. They were (a) 5 pounds of tallow, (b) a big wash tub, (c) a slow fire, and of course the chains. It wasn't recommended on a hot day, but here's what operators did to preserve their chains:

The chains were cleaned and placed in the wash tub, along with the tallow. As the tallow melted it flowed and coated the vital pins and their rollers. When the tallow cooled, it returned to its normal viscosity—a tacky, stiff, clinging lubricant. But, as it had already reached and coated the vital pins, it stayed there, resisting throw-off. Chains could wear fast; 50,000 miles on a set was considered exceptional and rarely attained.

There was another advantage to tallow, it didn't attract and hold dirt like a heavy-bodied oil. Oil or grease, plus dirt and grit, resulted in a grinding paste ruinous to chains and sprockets, although light oils were less damaging in this respect.

While enclosed worm-, bevel- and internal-gear axles weren't vulnerable to dirt and grit, early examples produced their own problems for operators and maintenance men. Gears stripped and axle shafts snapped, not to mention bent and cracked housings, depending on the type.

Removing a heavy worm-gear differential from the axle housing was a difficult feat, since room above was cramped by the vehicle's frame or floor of the body. Where possible, the bodybuilder provided a trap door directly above the axle to haul it out, but even then it wasn't easy.

Then too, there were early problems with lubricants for the worm gear; some operators claimed castor oil did a good job. In time the oil companies provided new grades and oil specs adapted to worm gear needs. Removing a broken axle shaft was another problem with any gear-type axle. The technique seems to have vanished now but at one time it was a familiar procedure.

When the shaft snapped, the inner stub stayed in its splines in the differential; it had to come out to permit installation of the new shaft. Removal of the stub tested patience and skill. A long loop-like device was inserted into the housing to "fish" for the broken shaft-end. If a mechanic was good at it, the stub would be pulled from its splines on the first try, otherwise it might be an afternoon's job.

Still, axles of this kind looked good to truck manufacturers after 1912 and the trend to shaft drive started; first to the worm gear, then to the spiral bevel and other types of enclosed axles. But two of the biggest names in the industry, Mack and Sterling, weren't convinced and both retained chain drive on some models for many years. In fact, Sterling still offered it as late as 1951 when the firm was taken over by White.

Canada didn't produce any heavy-duty military trucks during World War I, although thousands of Model T Ford light ambulances and tenders were shipped to France. But technical gains in truck design during the war years meant a great deal in the postwar era when Ontario truck operators and manufacturers benefited.

The widespread adoption of SAE (Society of Automotive Engineers) standards from 1918 on was of singular importance in the improvement of commercial vehicles. The new standards made life much easier for truck producers and their customers. After 1918, Ontario truck operators couldn't buy a new vehicle that wasn't designed around SAE standards.

SAE, an American organization, had attempted to arrive at a few basic standards as early as 1909, when the Society was founded. These concerned tires, splines and bearing sizes. Progress was slow initially.

The picture changed overnight when the U.S. entered the war in 1917 and created an immediate need for thousands of military trucks. The quickest way to get them was to design a new and highly standardized job that could be produced by a large number of manufacturers. This was the Class B 5-ton and it was turned out by the thousands by some fifteen different truck producers. It was a creditable feat and impossible without standardization.

The vehicle was a real "committee job" in that many SAE sub-committees contributed to its design. Tires, wheels, frame width and many other technical details reflected SAE standardization. The advantages in SAE standards were clearly apparent after the Class B; they simplified design and emphasized interchangeability, the basis for easy servicing and upkeep in the field.

All this looked pretty good to truck manufacturers after the war; it still does with the universal adoption of SAE standards, not in Canada and the U.S. alone, but internationally.

For instance, every Gotfredson ever built demonstrated what SAE standardization meant. The Gotfredson, known initially as the G. & J., was a Canadian truck built at Walkerville, though backed by American capital. They were built between 1921 and 1933, maybe into 1934 to clean up factory inventory. Gotfredson's success in Canada inspired its backers to undertake production in Detroit for the U.S. market. But American-built Gotfredsons never sold as well as the Canadian unit, although the U.S. branch outlasted the Canadian truck company by many years. Detroit-built Gotfred-

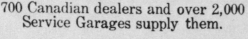

An appeal to farmers in Sept. 1919.

sons were still available as late as 1946, but only as custom-built units with Cummins diesel power.

Gotfredson used Buda engines with SAE bellhousings that matched Brown-Lipe transmissions, similarly designed to SAE specs. They were linked to the Timken worm axle, having SAE splines, by a driveline with flanges conforming to SAE standards. Everything fitted no matter who made the part or component.

The Gotfredson was a good example of an assembled truck. But it was no different with other manufacturers. SAE meant standardization for lower production costs and a new simplicity.

Truck operators gained. For example, an Ontario fleetman who bought, say, an American-built White, knew that Canadian-made tires from Kitchener, or any other source, would fit. If he needed a new magneto, the same convenience applied, as it did if he required nuts, bolts, cotter pins or a replacement bushing—almost anything.

Ontario truck operators had a very wide choice in vehicles by 1918, although the supply was irregular at times because of military demands. The Kelly-Spring-

field truck sold well because the Canadian Army liked them and took many to France. This was an American unit and it resembled the Mack, the International and early Lippard-Stewarts in radiator location, which was behind the engine. Capacities ranged from 1½- to 6-tons.

Rear-mounted radiators had some following at the time. Flywheel-type blowers and accessory-drive fans assured good air flow through the radiator. The vulnerable core was, of course, better protected when mounted behind the engine, away from minor traffic damage.

The Kelly-Springfield also featured a Renault-style hood which lifted from the front and both sides for easy access to the 4-cylinder engine. Solid tires and chain drive were other particulars. These, along with a massive pressed-steel frame made the Kelly-Springfield a good choice for duty behind the lines in France, or bumping down a concession road in Ontario.

The Reo Speed Wagon appealed to many operators in 1918. There were two of them that year, the Model F ½-tonner and the 2-ton Model J. Both were fast vehicles with performance well above average, that is

Introduced in 1919, the Ford Model TT 1-ton truck was the first "true" truck manufactured by Ford. In 1922 an electric starter was added as an option. It is shown here in winter dress with hood muff and rear-wheel chains. Like the Model T car, it was a real tough one, although somewhat frail in appearance.

International's internal gear-type axle of the early twenties. Load-carrying axle beam is behind the differential case with its jackshafts. Noise from worn pinions, oil leaks and speed limitations were drawbacks.

The exposed chain drive got the job done, despite problems of dirt and chain lubrication. Radius rods between jackshafts and axle maintained alignment and permitted chain tensioning. Mack and Sterling were the last to use this type of final drive.

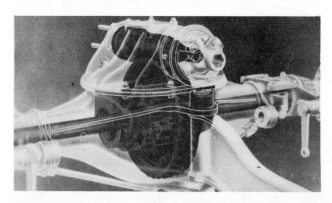

Typical overslung worm gear differential. Buses often had the worm gear below to reduce floor height. Husky torque arm at lower right prevented axle rotation under drive and braking thrusts. Radius rods (not shown) were also part of the setup.

Fleet lineup of the early twenties, from left, two early Ruggles trucks with open crescent cabs, an open Reo Speed Wagon and an unidentified open job. Ruggles and Reo trucks were popular in Ontario.

speeds up to 30 mph. The Reo wasn't an assembled job, Reo built the whole truck, including many of the bodies, particularly on the lighter ¾-ton unit. This was an exception to the rule at the time; usually a customer bought the chassis from one manufacturer, then sought another for the body. Reo had introduced its Speed Wagon during the war and sales boomed in the postwar years.

Reo's success with the Speed Wagon and its high performance moved other manufacturers to produce similar units, collectively described as "speed trucks" and capitalizing in part on Reo's designation for the type. Operators lined up to buy Speed Wagons and speed trucks. Imagine, a truck with the zip and the dash of a passenger car, say a Model T Ford or a 490 Chev!

Figures are lacking, but easily the most popular truck during the war years and well into the 1920s, was the Model T Ford. It was a remarkable feat; Ford didn't produce a truck at the time, only a stripped Model T car chassis for very light duty van bodies. But there was a way and it accounted for much of the Ford's popularity.

Dozens of truckmen got their start in the business by converting a Model T car into a 1-tonner; it was easy via the conversion route.

A sound, used '12 or '13 Model T touring car commanded around $100 in 1918. For about $350 the operator could purchase a kit for conversion of the car into a 1-tonner. Some 25 or 30 manufacturers offered these and the demand amounted to a minor industry in its own right.

New and heavier frame rails fitted over the Model T frame. These ran as far ahead as the driver's seat for good weight distribution, though front axles weren't modified in the process. Extra cross members also beefed up the structure, though one had to watch the weight with the Model T's 20 hp engine and only a 2-speed transmission. Overall, 80 to 90 percent of the weight had to be carried on the heavier back axle, which came with the kit. The overlay frame rails extended the Model T's wheelbase from 100 to 124 in., though there were variations.

Depending on the kit, final drive was by chain drive or a worm-gear axle. Both provided the added reduction needed to carry a 1-ton load. Oversize wheels, tires and brakes completed the conversion kit. An operator could make the switch from Model T to truck himself, but most of this work was done by dealers and conversion specialists.

The front half of the Ford touring car body was retained in most cases as it supplied a ready-made seat. In other instances the body was removed and replaced by a special cab. This wasn't supplied in the kit but was obtainable from any body builder.

Converted Model Ts functioned very well and served as the backbone of Canadian trucking all through the war years and well into the 1920s. A Smith Form-A-Truck or a Dearborn Conversion, two popular conversion kits, produced a do-it-yourself 1-tonner that cost a good deal less than, say, a Maxwell, Olds or an International of equivalent capacity. These were priced around $3000 though one got a brand-new truck, also a better performer.

The Ford Motor Company finally got around to trucks with a new 1-ton unit in 1919. It immediately asserted itself as the industry's best seller. Ford dealers had wanted a 1-tonner for years but the company was much too busy meeting the enormous demand for Model T cars. Now dealers had a truck and it was called the Model TT.

With a wheelbase of 123 in., the new unit featured 30 x 3½ in. tires on the front axle and 32 x 4½ in. on the rear. The engine and the 2-speed planetary transmission were standard units drawn from the Model T, linked via a torque tube to the 7.25:1 worm-gear axle. Performance was a heady 18 mph, just about "all out" for a Model T engine. Prices ranged around $700, plus another $100 for an electric starter and lighting and, say, $150 more for a cab and body. Ford couldn't produce enough of the new TTs to meet the response from truck operators.

Performance of the Model TT 1-ton could be brightened enormously with an overhead valve conversion which almost doubled its 20 hp. But few operators did; the price was a whacking $200 and far too much for Ford owners. A 2-speed axle was another accessory choice, though more particularly for Ford cars and light vans.

The Ford TT was offered in two track widths, 56 in. which was popular in Eastern Canada, and the "Western" track, 60 in. The latter was thought to be better suited to rutted prairie roads.

Curiously, while Chevrolet offered a 1-ton truck in the early twenties, it wasn't much competition for anyone, much less Ford, the leader. Chevrolet was too busy promoting the Chevrolet car during the early twenties to concentrate on truck development. But when Chevrolet did find the time in 1923 and 1924, its truck sales promptly zoomed upwards and stayed there. The line consisted of ½- and 1-tonners until 1929. Early jobs had rolled steel frame side rails, not pressed steel, plus an odd front suspension based on quarter-elliptic springs.

The same period, 1917-19, saw the general introduction of the 4-speed transmission for heavy-duty vehicles, replacing 3-speed units. Some offered more; the 1920 5-ton Schacht had a radical 10 speeds, eight ahead and two speeds for reverse. Experience with military vehicles demonstrated that a 4-speed transmission increased a heavy vehicle's flexibility and versatility.

Pneumatic tires were very much the "in" thing for heavier trucks in 1919. The experience with pneumatics on light and medium-duty vehicles since 1912 had been excellent, impressively so. Heavy trucks were much in need of the same benefits—a vastly improved ride, higher speed and, most important of all, a great reduction in general wear and tear.

But there were problems. A tire suitable for a 3-ton truck was called a "giant pneumatic". The reasons weren't hard to find. For instance, the rear tires on the 1920 Packard 3 tonner were 44 x 10s when pneumatics were specified, big compared with the 36 x 5s if equipped with solid tires. As a result, frame and body hieghts increased when giant pneumatics were used, although it was a relatively small price to pay for the benefits. There was another objection; a big pneumatic tire for a heavy truck cost $250 and one flat could ruin it. Pressures were almost as high as prices, up around 200 psi. When one blew, everyone in town jumped!

Odd "spring wheel" on a 1920 Diamond T, a popular accessory item before pneumatic tires appeared. The expensive extra had rubber-filled inner wheels for added resiliency. They were popular with bottlers to moderate the heavy impact of solid tires through stiff springs.

A 1920 Reo with Hotchkiss drive, using springs to locate the axle, absorb driving and braking thrusts and, incidentally, support the vehicles weight. The cushioning effect was said to protect the drive train but, to exponents of radius rods, this seemed less important than warding off spring failures.

The industry knew that giant pneumatics were too large, but that's the way it had to be in 1919 with the state of the art in heavy-duty truck tires. They had to be large to hold enough air. The Goodyear Tire and Rubber Company devised a novel solution for smaller tires and lower frame heights.

Goodyear produced several vehicles in a new configuration, the 6-wheeler with three axles. Rated at 5 tons, these trucks were fitted with six 40 x 8 in. tires, small for the time. In 1918, a 5-ton truck with only two axles and four wheels needed big 48 x 12 in. giant pneumatics for enough air volume to carry the load.

Mechanically, the trucks had oversize engines with a bore and a stroke of 5 x 6 in., generous 3 x 7¼ in. frames, and two 1½-ton capacity worm-gear axles for the bogie unit. They were heavy-duty units in every way and attracted a great deal of attention. But that was as far as it went in 1919. Truck manufacturers admired the superior traction with twin driving axles, also the excellent weight distribution, but the vehicle was considered too specialized a type.

This would start to change by 1925 with the first production-type 6-wheeler, the Moreland. From then on the 6-wheeler would come into its own. Now, of course, the familiar tandem is the most popular heavy-duty vehicle on the roads of Ontario.

As pneumatic tires needed air and service stations weren't that numerous then, trucks carried their own in the form of a Rex or a Kellogg compressor. Mounted on the engine or chassis (with an SAE flange or adapter) "free air" was available en route and it was usually needed. A compressor was an extra-cost item, anywhere from $50 to $300, but an operator with a big investment in pneumatic tires on his truck knew he couldn't do without the safeguard of an on-board compressor.

The swing to pneumatics forced big changes in the engineering of heavy-duty trucks. Solid tires had held speeds down to about 15 mph; pneumatics afforded a potential of 30 mph with a heavy unit. But this wasn't the case if the original design called for solid tires Higher speeds were possible, briefly, but the toll in burned-out bearings, thrown rods and engine seizures clearly indicated that redesign with more power was needed.

Packard and other truck manufacturers saw the problem and responded with new vehicles, shaped around the needs of the pneumatic. When customers ordered a 3-ton Packard with pneumatics in 1920, they got a different engine than the same truck specified with solid tires. The new engine had a bore and stroke of 5 x 5½ in. for an output of 40 hp at 1600 rpm and a speed of 24 mph. Users got a smaller engine if the unit was specified with solid tires, namely 4½ x 5½ in. bore and stroke, developing only 32 hp at 1000 rpm for a breathtaking 12 mph.

Manufacturers could redesign their vehicles to accommodate pneumatic tires but operators couldn't when older trucks were converted to "ride on air". Old vehicles, upgraded by a switch to pneumatics, sometimes exhibited alarming steering characteristics with camber and toe-in settings that had been fine with solid tires. Much experimentation by tire manufacturers, particularly Firestone and Goodyear, put an end to the problem.

Then there was the high cost of a conversion to pneumatics. This ranged around $1200 for a 5-ton truck, since wheels intended for solid tires had to be cut down and modified for pneumatics. The conversion of older vehicles to pneumatic tires was big business all through the 1920s.

The general adoption of the giant pneumatic was somewhat slower than the progress that had been made with smaller pneumatics on light and medium-duty vehicles. While many heavy trucks had pneumatics on all four wheels, some operators preferred them on the front axle only, retaining solids at the rear where the weight was. This was still the case as late as the early thirties, though admittedly the exception rather than the rule by then.

Although traces of the solid tire lingered on into the thirties, as some operators still preferred them, highway authorities and truck dealers didn't. The former penalized them by higher license fees for trucks on solid tires. Truck dealers automatically discounted used vehicles by a whacking 75 percent if the unit was equipped with solid tires, since by then they were almost unsalable.

The arrival of the heavy-duty pneumatic truck tire triggered interest in another vital area—brakes. Here there was plenty of room for improvement with heavy vehicles now rolling on pneumatics at speeds up to 30 mph. Brakes were complex then, and they still are!

Internal expanding and external contracting brakes had been used from the earliest days, though later than the shoe brake which contacted and grabbed the wheel by the rim. Internal and external brakes had been used in many combinations as well.

A popular early arrangement was the opposite of today's practice. The foot, or service brake, reacted through the driveline, while the emergency consisted of a drum and brake shoes mounted at the wheel. Some varied examples of this practice were the 1910 International Auto-Wagon, the Leyland RAF-type of World War I, also the 1914 Pierce Arrow. Many other manufacturers also used this system. Early Canadian-built Gotfredson trucks had an unusual service braking arrangement. These trucks had worm-gear final drive and braking was via a drum mounted right on the worm shaft at the axle. This provided excellent braking for low-speed operations and eliminated the hazard of loss of braking should a universal joint shear, or the driveline fail for any other reason.

Drivers customarily used their foot brakes and applied the emergency brake (by lever) at the same time with this combination braking.

Braking through the driveline (or the jackshaft if the unit had chain drive) worked well enough at very low speeds. But it was quite a different matter with a heavy vehicle traveling at nearly 30 mph; stress through the driveline could shear universal joints, strip differential gears and break axle shafts.

The result was the adoption of braking systems similar to today's with service braking through drums mounted on the wheels. These were of the external contracting type initially, which was bad with the exposure of linings to dampness. This type disappeared in the late 1920s in favor of drums with internal expanding shoes—much better protected and now universal practice.

With this setup for service braking, the emergency was moved to the driveline in some cases, while in others it was combined with the service brakes, using the same, or separate linkage and shoes. In any event, the brake at the wheel—the foundation brake with its shoes and drum —is a separate component from the actuating part of the system. Actuation was by mechanical means initially (and still is sometimes), then by hydraulic, vacuum or air operation. Actuation is often through a combination of these as it was in the late twenties.

Several Ontario-built trucks appeared on the market between 1915 and 1925, including the Beaver and the National hailing from Hamilton, the London-built Barton & Rumble and, most successful of the lot, the previously mentioned Gotfredson. It was produced in Walkerville. Another was the short-lived Harmer-Knowles, built in Toronto in 1925 and 1926.

One or two Ontario firms had attempted to produce commercial vehicles between 1911 and 1914. These were light-duty units for the most part but only one or two prototypes were built.

Manufacturers who got into truck production later fared better, although none could claim more than cabs, bodywork and associated sheet metal, and possibly the frame, as their own manufacture. Otherwise, these vehicles were assembled from stock American components— engines, axles, transmissions and steering. SAE standards were obviously of enormous help.

Take the National. Five models were offered in 1923 in capacities from 1 to 5 ton. All were powered by Waukeshas, an engine then used by some ten other assemblers. Brown-Lipe and Spicer transmissions and Timken axles were also used in Nationals.

National's 5-ton truck that year was offered in a standard wheelbase of 164 in. with a track of 68-⅜ in. for a chassis shipping weight of 9500 lbs. Tires were 36 x 6 in. solids on the front axle; 40 x 12 on the rear. All told, there wasn't a great deal of difference between the National and, say, a 5-ton Federal, Acme, even a Diamond T. These were popular American makes on the Ontario truck market in 1923. Sources of supply varied from one truck manufacturer to the next, but the formula was always the same—a vehicle assembled from stock components.

Vendors and suppliers outlasted many of their customers among the assemblers. Timken (now Rockwell-Standard), Clark, Fuller, Ross and Shuler, also Erie and Dayton for wheels, are still with us, all larger than ever.

The Gotfredson was a handsome truck and much better looking than the general run of assembled makes. But the firm's earliest units (1921) took no beauty prizes with their heavy cast-iron radiators. Appearance was much improved by 1924 with the provision of a highly polished cast aluminum radiator, which was also good for rapid heat dissipation.

Similarly, the use of shapely pressed steel fenders in 1924 was an improvement over the flat 12-gauge fenders on earlier units. These had been rolled, not die-pressed, and they looked it! Gotfredson produced its own cabs and much of the bodywork. Cabs were excellent and characterized by polished reveals and windshield "ventapanes" which, in fact, were fixed.

Sponsors of the Gotfredson—initially the Gotfredson-Joyce Corp., then the Gotfredson Corporation, finally Truck and Parts Ltd. with the end of production in 1933—followed a similar route among the assemblers. All major components were purchased, including Buda and Hercules engines, Timken and Clark axles, and Brown-Lipe transmissions.

The Gotfredson lineup for 1925 consisted of ten units in capacities from 1 to 5 ton. All were powered by 4-cylinder engines; axles were spiral bevels in the lighter units and Timken worm-gear axles for heavier vehicles. Gotfredsons were sold nationally mostly through company branches rather than dealerships. Buses and fire trucks were a big part of the business, though less so in later years. Gotfredson dropped trucks to produce bodywork on subcontract for Ford.

Ontario truck operators had pneumatic tires on many of their vehicles by 1925. Now they wanted another feature which had proved itself in the passenger car field, the 6-cylinder engine. They had a fair choice of them that year. Six-cylinder truck engines had been used before but not on popular makes or by manufacturers who distributed their trucks in Ontario.

Actually there had been a 6-cylinder truck on the Ontario market as early as 1917 when a Toronto dealer acquired the agency rights to the Stegeman. This American-built truck had other advanced specs, a full-floating worm-gear axle and another novelty at the time, an electric self-starter. But the Stegeman failed to make much of an impression in Ontario or the U.S., and it vanished from the truck scene. Truckers at this point were sceptical of 6-cylinder "pull" and electric starting for a truck was just too advanced to be considered!

Reo offered three Speed Wagons in 1925 powered by 6-cylinder engines. These vehicles were rated at ¾, 1¼ and 2 ton and all used the same Reo-built engine with a bore and a stroke of 3 x 5 in. Reo introduced it the year before but only in its bus chassis. Other trucks in the lineup used Reo's 4-cylinder engines.

The engines were unusual, what's known as an "F-head" or an overhead intake valve and a side exhaust valve, as opposed to an overhead valve (OHV) engine, or a side L-head valve arrangement. An advantage was the somewhat larger valve area possible, compared with some other valve arrangements. The engine developed 50 hp and it was a particularly neat installation with its pressed steel valve cover and clean manifolding. Reo sold a lot of them and the engine earned an excellent reputation for hard wear and easy maintenance.

Stewart also had a 6-cylinder engine. As an assembler (and a very good one) Stewart used a Lycoming in its Model 16X, a "speed truck" for nimble performance in traffic. Rated at 1¼ ton, it found many buyers. Stewart trucks sold widely and well in Ontario all through the 1920s. It covered the market with a good selection of vehicles in 1925, with capacities from 1 to 3½ ton, plus three bus chassis, one of which used a generally similar Lycoming L-head 6-cylinder engine.

While truck operators were interested in 6-cylinder engines, it was the L-head or side-valve type they wanted, not overhead valves. The overhead valve engine made slow progress in the truck field, despite its advantages.

Of the makes of trucks available to Ontario operators in 1925, only International and Chevrolet were offered with OHV engines, two major exceptions indeed with their excellent sales. Reo still had its F-head engine, but otherwise the L-head dominated the power plant scene. It had less potential efficiency but it didn't matter much in the twenties when all outputs were low.

The L-head was a cleaner engine. Early OHVs had a tendency to splash and spew oil all over the engine compartment because of ill-fitting rocker arm covers and exposed pushrods. But overhead valves were more

About midpoint in the evolution of the cab. These 1922 GMCs have enclosed cabs but not the more stylish "coupe cab" which appeared in the late twenties. Cabs were largely of wood, although these appear to have some steel panels in curved areas. Windows were kept small to reduce glass area and minimize breakage from vibration. Note the jack's handy location behind the fender.

Radius rods to absorb driving and braking loads and thus relieve the springs of these functions were widely used on into the thirties. Early operators were afraid of spring failures caused by solid tires and bad roads. This vintage Federal also had a curious overload spring arrangement.

The Mack AC "Bulldog", another quality truck in the early twenties and priced accordingly. Mack supplied the unit complete with all-steel semiopen cab. The radiator was mounted behind the big 4-cylinder engine.

accessible for adjustment, which they often needed. The L-head was considered a quieter engine, a reputation it gained because of the OHV's higher level of valve clatter.

Some manufacturers didn't get around to overhead valve gasoline engines until the 1950s when a new generation of high-compression V-8s appeared. Mack used a few OHV engines in heavier models in the late thirties and the early postwar years, but largely elected to go with L-head sixes. White followed much the same course, using a few OHV engines in heavy-duty units and bus chassis, but in the main stuck to L-head engines. Federal introduced a few sixes in 1930 using the new Continental "R" series OHV engine.

However, International dropped some of its OHV engines in the thirties in favor of the side-valve type. Overall, some makes have had a very long association with the OHV engine, notably Chevrolet and to a lesser extent GMC. Although simple and easy to produce, the L-head engine did not lend itself to the development inherent in the OHV type with the trend to much higher engine outputs in the 1950s.

The big Mack AC, the Bulldog, in capacities from 5 to 15 tons was a very popular choice all through the twenties, with operators who could afford it. It was an expensive unit in Ontario at prices ranging from $8000 to $10,000. The AC's specs were different, using chain drive when other manufacturers had dropped it; a rear-mounted radiator when the front-mounted radiator was popular, and a semi-open cab.

With a 5 x 6 in. 4-cylinder engine and chain drive, the AC had lots of pull, making it a great favorite with contractors and heavy haulers. Solid tires were standard on most ACs, with pneumatics available latterly as an option, though seldom seen on ACs until the 1930s.

The AC's most obvious characteristics, apart from its great bulk and massiveness, was a hood that lifted from the front and an enormous cast-steel front bumper. Anyone who hit a Mack Bulldog with a Whippet or a Model T knew it!

Cabs were improving in 1926 but still had a long way to go. Most were all-wood, others of composite wood and steel construction, while Mack, International and GMC offered semi-open all-steel cabs on their heaviest jobs. Mack's was the famed C-type or crescent cab, so named for the contouring of its open sides. GMC used a Fisher Body cab and International had a particularly rugged all-steel unit.

In an open cab the driver was protected by drop-type rain curtains that could be lowered when necessary. Open cabs were also offered with or without low doors. All-steel cabs were sturdy and durable in their simplicity.

Federals sold well in Ontario and these three posed for the camera about 1920. An assembled truck out of Detroit, they appear to be Federal's Model X which had a 40 hp 4-cylinder engine, radius rods and magneto ignition. These vehicles were owned by C & D Sugar Co. Ltd.

This 1926 GMC "Big Brute" was typical of the times in truck design with solid tires, cast steel wheels, worm-drive axle and semi-open "Cab by Fisher". The engine was a long-stroke, low-revving 4-cylinder unit for heavy-duty service.

American-built trucks sold in Canada and American models produced here often had different cabs than their American counterparts, most of which could be supplied with a stock cab by the manufacturer. But not in Canada. Importation of the cab added to import duties, so it was often built in Canada instead. But the American-pattern cab couldn't always be built in Canada, with differing production facilities in Canadian plants. Canadian-built Fords carried different cabs at times than the American vehicle, although standardization was complete by 1932 when the V-8 truck was introduced.

Similarly, some Canadian-built Dodges and Fargos in the 1930s featured Canadian cabs that differed from U.S. production. It was much the same with other truck manufacturers.

Thus, Brantford Coach & Body, Smith Motor Body, Canada Carriage and one or two other body builders did a big business in supplying production and special-type cabs. The production cab sold for about $150, while a custom cab could go as high as $300.

The enclosed cab offered better protection but it could rattle and maintenance was high. Glass shook and shattered, although 3-point mountings helped to isolate the unit from chassis flexure that tended to twist the cab apart. The all-steel enclosed cab was a rarity, but customers could have it on a Model TT 1-ton Ford in 1926. It was of pressed steel, expensive to tool and warranted only on a vehicle selling in very high volume. The Model AA Ford 1½ ton also had one in 1928.

There were some excellent composite cabs, a type of construction that remained quite general among the heavy-duty makes until 1939, even into the postwar years with some (Sterling). In the heavy-duty field, Diamond T had adopted an all-steel enclosed cab as early as 1926, while International introduced one with the new D line in 1937. Pressed steel permitted a more stylish cab with curves and contours that matched passenger car styling. With the new cabs there was a general adoption of new comfort measures such as adjustable seats, some insulation, and much improved ventilation with cowl vents and air intakes.

Bodies for the vehicle's load were universally of wood, usually massive complexities of tongue-and-groove planking, carriage bolts and united by an abundance of blacksmith "iron" for still more reinforcing. But first-rate lumber was cheap, as was labor, and operators expected to pay between $75 and $150 for a good stake-and-rack body.

Quite a few big van bodies were still made of wood too, although steel paneling was more popular. With a wooden van, the panels had to be painstakingly fitted in grooves routed in the framing, just the way they had been for quality horse-drawn vehicles. Again it was a case of the availability of woodworking skills, also some indifference as to what the body weighed. A well-built wooden body could outlast several chassis.

In the earliest days attempts were made to modify the bodies of horse-drawn wagons and vans to fit a truck chassis, but it usually cost as much as a new body and the truck body soon emerged in its own right.

It was also the era of gold leafing and brush painting. Truck manufacturers had switched over to spray painting but fleet operators and body builders clung to brush methods in their shops. Finishing a truck was a big job with touchy varnishes and enamels that had to be applied with great skill and care. Still-tacky varnish didn't like draughts and dust was always a menace, for obvious reasons. Everyone in the shop spent several anxious hours until the varnish hardened enough to resist these hazards. Wetting the paint shop floor was one way to kill the dust but the varnish could react to the dampness. There were problems aplenty with painting.

The result of all this was a vehicle with a furniture finish, impressive with a glitter and depth of gloss that few modern finishes can match, but impractical for a workaday truck. It could take a month to paint a big unit and the finish was shortlived unless backstopped by unremitting maintenance. A top coat of clear varnish might restore a dull finish, but if not, it meant a new paint job.

Trees, birds and particularly pigeons posed big and obvious hazards from corrosive droppings ruinous to a varnish finish. So were stone and ball-throwing small boys! And if a varnish finish liked water, it was clear, cold tap water for washing purposes, not rain water, which caused heavy spotting. There was lots of room for improvement.

The vehicle's chassis underneath the body wasn't overlooked either. The frame siderails, the spring hangers, in fact all of the visible "hardware", was set off by striping, gold leaf and lining, all skillfully applied by the

This 1921 Barton Rumble, built in London, Ont. by a company of the same name, is shown in front of the old Crystal Palace Building in London's Western Fair grounds. F. B. Dixon built the canvas-sided body with the help of a carpenter. The wooden top was covered with stretched canvas and water-proofed. The closed limousine cab was a new feature at the time. The 4-cylinder engine drove through a Toberson double-reduction sale and the rear tires were described as a "hard cushion type."

The Graham Brothers truck appealed to many customers in the twenties. Dodge dealers sold them and, by the end of the twenties it had become the Dodge Brothers truck. The Grahams had assembled their trucks from Dodge car components, where applicable. As a result, this '26 GB 1½-ton resembles vintage Dodges.

A 1922 Gotfredson & Joyce operated by E. Shelton of Waterdown, Ont. It was the first pneumatic-tired truck to operate in the Hamilton area.

This 1927 Divco was one of the first milk delivery trucks. It's fitted out with decals instead of hand lettering. Steering joysticks can be seen just about the logo, so the driver could stand-drive the unit. Later models had a steering wheel as well. The engine was a 4-cylinder Continental and bolt-on disc wheels were new at the time.

Number 10 was a handsome unit in the late twenties. The chassis was a 1928 model Stewart with a 6-cylinder engine. It was operated by Finch & Sons Transport of Brantford, Ont.

striper with his camel-hair brushes. There was a definite form for this, handed down from carriage painting and decoration, as there was for the style and gold-leaf lettering that spelled out, say, "Smith's Trucking & Draying" on the cab doors. Striping and gold-leafing followed ritualistic styles as defined as the orders in architecture.

Oddly, operators and fleetmen weren't overjoyed with spray painting and fast-drying lacquer finishes when they did start to use them in the mid-twenties. These methods were already established by then, but only in big automobile plants and under ideal conditions. It was quite a different matter with the limitations of a fleet repair shop or a small body-builder's shop.

Spraying was faster than brushwork, once the brushman had broken old habits and learned to handle the gun, never easy. But early lacquer pigments were often unstable; a hood sprayed in red or maroon could turn black in a matter of months from engine heat and atmospheric "fallout". A brushman used to the characteristics of varnish usually put coats on too-heavy, which meant cracking and crazing in short order.

He felt he had to build up a thick coating. Varnish was a heavy and viscous finish with good filling properties to hide imperfections in wood and steel. But thin sprayed-on lacquer wouldn't hide anything and the slightest roughness in the surface became even more pronounced. This meant new standards of surface smoothness before lacquer could be used, also much acrimony between the painter and the body shop foreman as to just how smooth a fender or a body panel needed to be for spray painting.

Actually, lacquer finishes and spray painting were instrumental in banishing wooden bodies in favor of steel construction, since the latter took much less preparation for spray gun methods. Quite often exposed wooden parts were sheathed in steel, since the added cost was offset by reduced preparation time for painting.

The dump-truck body was undergoing a big change in 1925 with acceptance of the new underbody hoist. The vertical chain or hydraulic hoist was on the way out, though the novel "gravity tip" dump body would hang on for a few more years for lighter trucks.

The vertical hoist was just that, a mechanical or hydraulic hoist mounted vertically between the cab and the dump body. Chains running down from the hoist to the dump body lifted it from the front as the hoist raised. There was one drawback; when the laden dump body was elevated, much of the weight was imposed on the vehicle's chassis at the midpoint. Thus frame and side-rail failures were numerous, always hastened by the rough ground around building sites.

The underbody hoist was a different proposition in that it eased loads on the truck's frame, though often at the expense of complexity and higher costs. With this type, lifting stresses were moved back farther in the frame, usually to a point just over or ahead of the rear axle. Sometimes the lifting thrust ran parallel with the frame as when a cam or roller raised the body by leverage against the dump body's hinge points. A variety of mechanical and hydraulic methods were used to power the hoist but the end result was a body that could tip to a steeper angle than the vertical hoist

provided, and with less wear and tear on the truck chassis.

The vertical-type hoist is popular today, even though it was in disfavor for several decades with the trend to the underbody type. Today the vertical type offering single, double, and even triple-stage hydraulic telescopic operation, is widely used for dump trucks and particularly for dump-type semitrailers. The high lift affords steep tipping angles for long dump boxes, and its compactness and low weight are other advantages. Excessive frame stress no longer is the problem it used to be; rugged frames are now designed to accommodate telescopic hoist loads.

Gravity-tip dump bodies were simple and cheap, but only for loads that didn't exceed a cubic yard or so. There was no hoist mechanism; the body was mounted on a cam. When empty, the body sat on the frame through its own weight; when filled, the added weight caused unbalance and the body had to be held down. To dump, the driver released a clamp and the unit automatically tipped with the off-centre weight distribution. When the load was dumped, the body then returned to sit on the frame.

This type could be hard on the frame; when the body tipped under load, chains that limited the tipping tended to bend the frame upwards. Then when the load was dumped and body lowered, the frame was given another heavy whack, this time downwards. A few weeks of this could wreck a light frame and pose maintenance problems.

Overall, the underbody hoist was a big improvement, but it was an expensive feature. A compromise was the hand-cranked underbody hoist that took forever to raise and lower, although it was popular for a time. Actually, the underbody hoist had been around for many years—as far back as pre-World War I—but it took the building boom of the twenties to bring it into widespread use.

Gravity unloading was not an exclusive with ordinary dump trucks; tank trucks used it in an age before pump-unloading. Tanks were mounted on the chassis with the high end at the front to facilitate this, but drivers often had to place wooden ramps under the front wheels to boost the height a little when the level in the tank was low.

In 1926 the only tank vehicle was a gasoline tanker, though experiments were afoot in hauling milk this way. All tanks unloaded from the rear through manifolding no more complex than a few petcocks. The welded tank was well established by then and a big improvement over leak-prone riveted tanks. Such faults as there were usually rested in the vehicle chassis, not the tank.

As always, solid tires pounded tanks like the rest of the vehicle and maintenance was heavy. Another problem was posed by the whippy, flexible truck chassis of the day that could wrench a tank apart through flexure. Thus much attention was directed to a variety of spring-loaded and 3-point tank mountings to ease stresses. These worked after a fashion but at the expense of more weight and complication.

In an era before canned motor oil, filling stations stocked their oil in barrels and dispensed by hand-operated drum pumps. Tank trucks carried oil in big containers stored on catwalks beside the gasoline tank. These had to be manhandled off the truck at service

A 1937 Ford straight truck with Brantford stake body.

Electrics were still getting attention in the thirties when the T. Eaton Company fitted out this 1-ton Walker with a custom window-van body. A big Toronto laundry used Walker electrics all through the war years, while other trucks were laid up because of gasoline rationing. There appears to be scant head room behind that steering wheel.

The 1930 Ford Model AA 1½-ton chassis showing the rear cantilever springs and torque-tube drive which characterized Ford trucks for years. However, some early Canadian-built AAs also used Hotchkiss drive with open driveline and torque arm.

The Republic was another popular American-made truck in the twenties and early thirties, when it became the LaFrance-Republic. This is a 1929 model with dump body and a cab with "dormer" windows. The Republic was assembled from stock components.

One of the last Packard trucks, used here as a tractor and coupled to a Lapeer semitrailer which had brakes, an advanced feature in 1923. The Lapeer fifth wheel was a large turntable which served as a raceway for the castor wheels that carried the weight.

The Christensen, an early-day air-brake arrangement, with the air cylinder located between the shoes for direct action, similar to hydraulic brakes. The system didn't catch on in 1925-26 and was soon displaced by the less complex Westinghouse air brake.

Fruehauf's first Canadian trademark, circa 1940.

GOOD THINGS IMPROVE WITH AGE.

Fifty years of Canadian trucking—and you're getting stronger all the time. At Fruehauf we're proud to have contributed to those great years. And we want to help make the next fifty even better—for all of us.

This wing-like escutcheon identified the popular Fruehauf Aerovan in the 40's and 50's.

The Fruehauf logo and the "Long Ranger" star, emblematic of the industry's first 5-year warranty.

SINCE THE YEAR ONE FORD HAS BEEN BUILDING BETTER TRUCKS.

Ford Motor Company of Canada

stations to replenish the drums. Attempts were made to keep the oil clean, but the constant pouring from one container to another didn't help at all.

An Ontario truck operator had a big choice in makes by 1925, in fact the heyday of the assembler. He could have an Acme or an Acason, a Clydesdale or a Commerce, also a Ward or a Walker both of which were electrics. But there was little demand left for battery-powered vehicles. However, a big Toronto laundry was much pleased with its fleet of Walker electrics and hung on to them until 1939 and the war. It was a wise move; the Walkers proved useful all through the conflict when gasoline rationing forced the firm to lay up many of its gasoline units.

Some makes were leaving the market. One was the Ruggles, though the company struggled on in the United States until 1928. There was nothing very distinguished about the Ruggles except that many Ontario operators had used them in earlier years and had a sentimental attachment for the make. Ruggles operated a London plant from 1921 but declining sales ended the operation.

In 1926 the Ruggles was assembled around stock components: Hercules engines, Brown-Lipe transmissions and Columbia, Sheldon and Wisconsin axles. The range that year consisted of five trucks in capacities from 1 to 3 tons.

The Federal was another American make which proved popular in Ontario all through the twenties and thirties. An assembled job, the Federal competed strongly against such rivals as Stewart, Diamond T and Republic. Federal produced a complete range of trucks, with the larger sizes commanding a big share of the market. Federal claimed Canadian status briefly in the 1930s with a Windsor plant.

Truck operators were cautious of a new development in 1925, four-wheel brakes. GMC offered two units with the new feature that year, Model K-17, a 1-tonner and the 1½-ton K-32, both with 4-cylinder engines. The external contracting brakes were rod-operated and seemingly quite effective. They also added $150 to the price, a steep $2500 for the K-17 and nearly $3000 for the 1½-tonner.

Four-wheel brakes were new in passenger cars, too, and the deflection of light front axles and frames designed for rear-wheel braking caused problems at times, such as front-end skidding. This was worse if the exposed linings were damp and brake-grabbing resulted.

Early four-wheel brakes perhaps didn't deserve the reputation they earned as being "tricky" and skid provoking; they weren't always used with good common sense. Drivers rejoicing in new-found stopping power often stunted with their brakes, applying them suddenly to throw unsuspecting passengers off their seats. These antics were also hard on following drivers who couldn't stop as quickly with two-wheel braking.

This behavior was so widespread that manufacturers cautioned in their handbooks that four-wheel brakes be used with caution and courtesy. Until the novelty wore thin, four-wheel brakes took an awful toll in heavy tire wear and spring failures through excessive windup. Ontario highway authorities were so concerned at the mounting incidence of rear-end collisions that a regulation was introduced requiring all vehicles equipped with four-wheel brakes to carry a warning. This was the familiar little red triangle bearing the legend "Four Wheel Brakes" which had to be prominently displayed on the rear of vehicles so equipped.

The development of four-wheel brakes for trucks took time. The time was needed to re-engineer and beef up frames and front axles to accommodate brake reaction, also to provide protection for linings against dampness through development of internal expanding brakes with enclosed shoes. Four-wheel brakes were becoming general by 1929, even among the heaviest trucks where progress with brakes had been slower. One exception was the Mack AK, a chain drive with braking on the rear wheels through the jackshaft; other Macks had four-wheel braking.

Another development gained momentum during the mid-twenties—automotive air brakes. Westinghouse introduced the idea in 1923 (with two-wheel braking on a Pierce-Arrow), while the Christensen system was another which attracted some attention at the time. Compressed air afforded far more pressure than a driver could exert by his foot through mechanical linkage.

With the air system, brakes were applied through an air circuit maintained by an engine-mounted (SAE standard) compressor. Brake actuation was by air pressure in a flexible line that could be routed anywhere, as opposed to straight runs of linkage and the complexity of rods, cams and equalizers.

Air braking opened the way to much wider use of the semitrailer, even two trailers in early-day train combinations.

Trailer brakes had been a problem; many didn't have any brakes before the air system appeared. Mechanically operated brakes were difficult to connect with the tractor; with air, connection with the brakes on the trailer was simply a matter of using quick connectors. Then both vehicles were linked by a common, fully equalized system. It was a big advance, though air brakes were expensive and there was maintenance to consider. There still is! Air braking led to variants of the concept, such as actuation by vacuum and air-over-hydraulic systems, up to the more complex sensor-directed systems we have today.

The semitrailer shared development with the heavy-duty truck. Solid tires were replaced by pneumatics and heavy structural steel frames gave way to lighter pressed-steel construction.

Trailer manufacturers pursued their own "systems" in the early twenties and there wasn't much interchangeability among makes. If an operator used Lapeer trailers, he had to use Lapeer fifth wheels which wouldn't interchange with, say, a Fruehauf, Warner or a Trailmobile trailer.

This changed in the late 1920s with the widening use of trailers in fleet operations and an obvious need for interchangeability. The "automatic" fifth wheel came first, during World War 1. This was automatic to the extent that the driver merely backed his tractor under the trailer for contact and locking with the upper fifth wheel pin on the trailer, the way it's done now.

Previously, the driver had to position his tractor ahead of the trailer, get out and elevate the trailer, then get back in the tractor and back it under the trailer. After all this, he had to get out again, this time to make sure the coupler between the two units was locked. Then, with any luck, he could drive off. It took a lot of time and the new automatic fifth wheels were a big improvement.

The tandem trailer saw some limited use from 1928 on, but had no real popularity until the late thirties and the pressure of new weight regulations. The tandem, or two-axled trailer, was inspired by greater acceptance of the three-axle truck and the guidelines established by Goodyear's experimental vehicles in 1918 and 1919. Mack had a factory-built 6-wheeler in 1927, but in most cases a 6-wheeler was merely a conventional vehicle with the addition of an extra or "bolt-on" third axle attachment. The Canadian-made Dominion third axle was popular for this purpose and there were many others on the market.

A characteristic of many medium and heavy-duty trucks during the twenties and thirties (even today vestiges of the idea survive) was radius-rod drive, as opposed to Hotchkiss drive. With Hotchkiss drive the springs not only carry the vehicle's weight but also absorb braking and driving forces. These tend to rotate the axle and cause "windup" of the spring, sometimes markedly so.

In an era of bad roads and solid tires, operators were plagued with broken springs. But, if the axle was located by radius rods, at least the springs would be spared from braking and driving thrust since these functions would be assumed by the radius rods.

Radius rod setups varied. Some were dead rigid, as when the radius rod also served as a torque arm; in other cases the radius rods allowed some slight rotation of the axle for cushioning. They also added weight, considerably so on heavy-duty trucks where the radius rods were usually massive forgings, and needed to be! Wear could be heavy too, since the rods had to pivot at both ends to allow for axle movement.

Radius rods were essential with chain drive, but for a different reason. Here the need was to maintain alignment between the axle and the jackshaft; adjustment of the rods back and forth also permitted tensioning the side chains.

Some truck manufacturers never did use radius rods on shaft-drive models. International considered them too rigid, as did Mack; the latter used rubber-insulated spring hangers for just enough movement to damp out vibration and impact shock that would otherwise be transmitted through to the truck frame. Leyland stayed away from radius rods too, as did other British manufacturers, perhaps because of much smoother British roads and lower speed limits.

The radius rod principle was revived in 1950 when Diamond T introduced a variable-rate suspension in which the axle was located by a spring leaf separate from the main spring. The axle was located yet it was also free for controlled rotation to absorb braking and driving stresses. With variable-rate springs the ride was improved and, overall, there were savings in weight and maintenance, essentially through the elimination of spring shackles as such.

All of these features had been used before, some for many years, but not in quite the same combination as

the Diamond T development. Its layout appealed to other truck manufacturers who picked up the same idea, collectively making it a popular suspension on many makes today.

International introduced a range of heavy-duty units of unusual technical interest in 1929, the HS series from 2½ to 5 ton. These were offered with shaft or chain drive, according to the model. All were powered by a novel engine, a big 4-cylinder Hall-Scott.

The Hall-Scott was more than an OHV, it was also an OHC—overhead valves plus overhead camshaft. The result was a very efficient high-output engine, one that was easy to service and maintain. A premium engine, the Hall-Scott's specs weren't far removed from those used in racing cars of the day.

International used several of these engines, the largest of which had a bore and stroke of 4-¾ x 5½ in. developing 57 hp at 1800 rpm, excellent output for the times. The firm was still using the H-S engine in its W series units as late as 1934.

International and other truck producers preferred big-bore, slow-speed 4-cylinder engines that rarely exceeded 2000 rpm. These produced high torque at low speeds for the much-desired "pull", as well as long life. Five-ton trucks weren't expected to be nimble in traffic and operators were satisfied with 30 to 35 mph on the highway.

Ontario truck operators were much impressed by the new Ford and Chevrolet trucks when these appeared at the end of the 1920s. Ford came first in 1928 with a new Modeal AA 1½ ton to replace the old TT 1-ton truck. It was an entirely different vehicle, as was the Model A passenger car compared with the long-lived Model T.

Gone was the TT's 2-speed planetary transmission in favor of a new 3-speed conventional-type transmission with a floor shift. There was a new 4-cylinder engine, too, developing 40 hp.

Another change was the rear suspension, now by cantilever springs to replace the TT's transverse spring. Early AAs used worm-gear axles until a switch to a spiral-bevel unit in 1930. Torque-tube drive was retained from the TT as well, though revised for the new model. Torque-tube drive was another approach in dealing with the requirements served by radius rods and torque arms, but quite a different layout.

The front suspension, while new, was still based on transverse suspension, now with a heavier spring than the TT's.

More obvious was the improvement in appearance. There was simply no comparison between the AA and the angular TT. The AA's new crowned fenders and shapely sheet metal attracted customers as much as the vehicle's mechanical specs.

Shortly after the AA was announced, Ford introduced a strange variant of the new model. This was unlike any Ford yet seen, having part or quasi-Hotchkiss drive instead of Ford's traditional torque-tube drive. Instead of the AA's worm-gear axle, a spiral-bevel Timken axle was used and there were other changes from the basic AA specs. It was produced only in Canada and why Ford offered it at all remains a mystery.

It was an oddball truck, presumably serving as some sort of a heavy-duty option to the Model AA. But, combining Hotchkiss drive with the AA's new cantilever springs, which had been conceived for torque-tube

The ride wasn't all that great with solid tires but the Gotfredson is fondly remembered by senior operators of the 20s and 30s. Model and year of this big one aren't known—it could be a 1928 4½-tonner. Buda engines were used and Timken worm-drive axles. Gotfredson was proud of its big cast aluminum radiator. The dump body has an underbody hoist.

Rear View of Model SD with Gravity Dump Body

Model SD

Early gravity-tip dump body on an International chassis, popular with contractors on into the thirties. Construction then was a fair-weather undertaking so there was no need for a cab or lights. Note the short ¼-elliptic springs to reduce frame overhang back of the axle.

drive, was by no means the best of both worlds. A torque arm, on one side only, did not successfully restrain the axle under driving and braking forces. Another oddity was the cable-operated braking system which, because of the springing and resultant axle movement, would constantly be out of adjustment.

Operators who liked Fords and who bought thousands of this truck mutation were pleased when it was replaced in 1930 by a new version of the Model AA truck. Gone was the AA's worm-gear find drive, being replaced by a spiral-bevel axle in conjunction with torque-tube drive. The new axle had a two-piece housing, the familiar split housing which would characterize Ford trucks for years.

The new Chevrolet 1½-tonner was introduced in 1929 and the big news was a 46 hp 6-cylinder engine, a novelty at so low a price. And, like the Nationals, Capitals, Superiors, and all the Chevs that had gone before, it was an overhead valve unit, the "Cast Iron Wonder" as this engine was affectionately known. It would stay under the hoods of Chevrolets for the next 25 years, though eventually updated with insert bearings, full pressure lubrication and aluminum pistons.

What the Chev engine lacked in pinnacle efficiency it more than made up for with its hard-wearing qualities and the ability to "slog" in tough going with only minimal care and maintenance. That's why Chevrolet stuck with it for so many years.

Other details of the new job included much better looks, a choice of single or dual wheels (the latter new for Chev) and a 3-speed transmission. As with the Model AA Ford, the new Chevrolet was a volume seller right off the bat.

The basic 1929 6-cylinder Chevrolet truck served Canadian operators well for many years and through successive changes and modifications. In 1930 a 2-ton version was introduced. This had the basic 1½-ton chassis, modified with a heavier axle and other changes for more payload. This led to a familiar vehicle many senior fleetmen fondly recall, the Maple Leaf.

Dodge Brothers trucks (then just plain Dodge by the mid-thirties) found plenty of customers among Ontario fleetmen in 1929 and with reason. It was an unusually wide range of units, from ½ ton to 3 ton, also bus chassis. Thus DB covered the market more comprehensively than Ford or Chevrolet with 1½-ton rating.

Heavier Dodge Brothers trucks were an outgrowth of the earlier Graham Brothers which Dodge dealers had sold during the twenties in capacities from ¾ to 2 ton. Dodge didn't have a truck line of its own at the time, apart from a light-duty delivery job, so the GBs rounded out the line with heavier units. With the Dodge Brothers takeover of Graham Brothers, the trucks bore the Dodge nameplate.

GBs had been assembled from many Dodge Brother car components, essentially 4- and 6-cylinder engines, and the vehicles were well regarded by truck operators. By the mid-thirties Dodge offered an unusually complete line of trucks, now up to 4 ton and powered by Chrysler 8-cylinder engines, though few of these were sold.

The same year, 1929, also saw a new truck name with close Dodge/Chrysler associations, the Fargo. Initially it was a light duty ½- to 1-ton unit with specs which varied somewhat from the lighter end of the Dodge

Brothers line. Eventually the name was applied to all Dodge Brothers units to enable wider marketing through different dealers.

In the context of what has just been said, if a few Ontario operators started toward success over a rocky and difficult course driving Model T Fords, almost as many in later years made their mark with a Graham Brothers truck. It was a popular make at the time and it sold well and widely.

The Rugby was another favored make in the late twenties and early thirties. The Rugby was an offshoot of the earlier Star Fleetruck, both American units and produced in Ontario by Durant Motors of Canada Ltd., Toronto. Rugbys were offered in capacities from ½ to 1 ton and, later on, 1½ ton, all powered by 4- and 6-cylinder Continental engines. The Rugby was considered a cut or two above a Ford or a Chev but less money than a Reo or an International. Later, they were available with 2-speed axles. If Ontario operators liked Rugbys, so did the farmers in Western Canada who bought them by the trainload.

There were a few odd units on the market in 1928 and 1929. One was the Willys-Knight truck, in capacities from 1 to 2½ ton, powered by a 6-cylinder sleeve-valve engine. The sleeve-valve design, as opposed to the poppet-valve type (all others) was considered to be quieter and to have a very long life. It was excellent on both points but it was a costly engine to produce and to service. Sliding valves called for close manufacturing tolerances. In any event, by 1929 the poppet-valve engine was much improved and differences between the two were slight. Still, a number of operators used Willys-Knights and liked them, at least until an overhaul was needed!

The Federal-Knight and the Yellow-Knight were somewhat earlier examples (1926) of Knight-engined vehicles that achieved limited popularity in Ontario. Both were 4-cylinder, rated at 1½ ton and, like the Willys-Knight, excelled in smoothness. A trait of the sleeve-valve engine was exceptionally heavy oil consumption when sleeves were worn, although to a degree carbon deposits helped to seal them. Cold weather starting with the drag imposed by sleeves was another drawback.

The British-built Leyland was an excellent seller. Leylands were heavy-duty vehicles, with cabs and bodies built in Canada. In particular, the Leyland Lioness with its low bus-type drop frame appealed to oil companies who used them as tank trucks. Leyland used 4- and 6-cylinder engines in a wide range of models. The Leyland Terrier found a good market. This was a 6-wheeler (War Office type) and many were sold in Northern Ontario from 1930 on, where off-road operators made good use of the dual-drive axles and superior traction.

Another British make, the Thornycroft, appeared on the Ontario market briefly at the end of the 1920s. Very few were sold and it vanished from the Ontario scene in 1930. As with Leyland, 6-wheelers were a specialty, although the company sold some smaller trucks as well. Ontario fleetmen weren't remotely interested in the Morris-Commercial, a popular British truck for light and medium service, when it put in a brief appearance on the market in the thirties. But there were always a few customers for light duty (very) Austin 7 and Singer vans in the late thirties. Apart from Leyland, no British manufacturer made any headway in the Ontario market, though a few tried.

The American-built Relay was another oddity that attracted customers in Ontario in 1929 and 1930. The Relay was an assembled unit (Buda engine for the most part, Brown-Lipe transmission and Columbia front axle) and its big feature was the Relay Drive Suspension. The Relay's drive axle wasn't fixed as in other trucks; it was free to float back and forth slightly under driving thrust. It was unsettling to see a Relay start up. As the driver let in the clutch, the rear axle moved ahead, apparently free of the rest of the vehicle. Then the truck caught up and the axle centred itself in the yoke that provided restraint. The idea was to boost tire life; Relay claimed tires were consistently good for 60 to 70,000 miles, high for the time.

While quite a few Relays were sold in 1929 and 1930, the novelty wore thin in time. Operators usually blocked the axle so it couldn't move, since maintenance was a problem when wear set in.

The 1930s saw few radical changes although refinement and an increasing sophistication was the order of the day. After all, what manufacturer could top the industry's collective gains of the past decade, an interval that ushered in the 6-cylinder engine, four-wheel brakes, electric lighting and starting, plus new levels of driver comfort and convenience.

Speeds were increasing, so was reliability, both going hand in hand with new standards of durability and performance. One might object to the trite expression of "evolution not revolution", but that's what it was. And it paid off.

By 1931 any heavy-duty truck engine was good for 40 to 50,000 miles without lifting the head to scrape out carbon, reseat burned valves, or replace the piston rings. This was a big improvement from, say, 1926, when 25,000 miles was about the limit before engines needed complete overhauling.

This was achieved in a number of ways. Fuels and lubricants had improved, as had engines. Nowhere was this more apparent than in the valves, now of high-duty chrome and nickel alloys resistant to heat and, more important, to corrosion from the combustion process. These were far superior to earlier materials. Much more attention was given to proper cooling of the valve seats to transfer heat out before it caused damage. Full-length water jackets helped enormously.

The new and superior precision insert bearing was fast coming into general use to cope with bearing loads in the higher compression engines, now used in trucks as well as passenger cars. Antiknock fuels permitted much higher outputs from compression ratios of 5:1 and 6:1 although, as ever, conservative manufacturers in the heavy-duty field played it safe with lower compression ratios.

Progressive truckers were no longer content with tradional truck speeds of 30 or 35 mph. Operators of medium-duty vehicles wanted better performance, as did the motoring public after much experience trapped behind slowpoke trucks on choked highways. Heavier vehicles often breathed hard to get over manhole covers; steeper hills and grades reduced their passage to an agonizing gear-grinding crawl.

A number of truck manufacturers responded with a short-lived novelty, the straight-eight engine which was all the rage in passenger cars at the time. But truckers

Rugby trucks were favored by Ontario fleetmen in the late 20s and early 30s, partly because they were built in Ontario (Toronto). There were larger units, as well as this sleek ½-ton panel, powered by 4- and 6-cylinder Continental engines. Quality was good and prices competitive.

*A 1937 fleet lineup. From left: a popular Maple Leaf, really a beefed-up Chev;
a Chevrolet and an earlier GMC. Cabs were wood-framed, the Maple Leaf and
Chev factory-built, the GMC custom-built. Tuckey Transport people shown
are, from left, Ben Tuckey, Ed Ward and Eric Campbell. Seated on the
bumper is Edgar Hunkin; atop the cab, Ben's son Ross.*

didn't take to it. Straight eights had the power, but they
were expensive. A few truck companies had some success with them; Reo had one in 1932, so did Pierce-
Arrow and Dodge. Studebaker was early with a straight
eight in 1929, but primarily for its bus chassis.

The Stewart Eight of 1932 was easily the most popular of the eights in Ontario, as it was in the U.S. This
featured a big AE series Lycoming with an output of
130 hp at 2800 rpm, well above the maximum 2500
rpm for a big 6-cylinder truck engine in the thirties.
Stewart used this engine in a 3½-ton model, also another and smaller Lycoming eight in lighter models. The
straight eight had merit, but manufacturers chose the
wrong time to introduce it—the Depression was on.

Other truck manufacturers saw the need for more
power and better performance but went about it in a
different way. One was the big White "12" in 1935
with its opposed-type 12-cylinder engine developing a
whopping 143 hp. This was a "pancake" or flat engine
and White used it in several big COEs in a setup White
called "Underslung Power". The engine was mounted
on a roll-out tray to facilitate servicing. White discontinued the COE in 1938 as it was an expensive vehicle
for depression times, although the big engine was continued in some of its buses.

In a novel move, Diamond T adapted passenger-car
styling and "streamlining" to its trucks, original thinking at a time when trucks were square and boxy, quite

practical but rarely easy on the eyes. This changed after
1933 and Diamond T's new streamlined models offered
passenger car "looks" and comfort. After that, veed and
raked radiator grilles, two-piece windshields and deeply
skirted fenders became the fashion, matching the new
pace Diamond T had set.

From 1933 on, the COE moved back into the mainstream of truck operations. It had been out of the picture as a popular type since 1914. Autocar never
dropped the type, the Autocar EUS was a specialized
unit throughout most of the twenties appealing to contractors who used them as dump trucks.

Although the EUS had been long gone as a highway
truck, this changed with a new Autocar in 1933. It was
still called the EUS but now it was aimed at carriers
who wanted a short, close-coupled straight truck or
tractor. Success was immediate, despite depression-
cramped budgets for new trucks.

While the Autocar was the first of the new breed in
production-type COEs, a small Chicago custom-truck
builder, Hendrickson, seems to have produced the first
of the "modern" COEs. This was in 1932 and it was a
custom-built truck that exploited the COE design in
terms of compactness and big payload. Ontario fleetmen
couldn't buy Hendricksons because they weren't sold in
the province, but they could buy Internationals
equipped with Hendrickson tandems, which they did in
considerable numbers. In fact, some big Internationals

in the thirties were more Hendrickson than International, since the former did a great deal of special and custom work for International.

Changing weight regulations and heavily congested city streets were factors in the COE's success although it was a more expensive vehicle to build. With the cab over the engine, more weight could be carried on the front axle for better weight distribution. The shorter length of the COE was an attractive feature when the unit was used as a tractor, since it could accommodate a longer trailer than a conventional-type tractor. The COE came back into style in a big way and it's been popular ever since.

Mack responded to the interest in COEs with two blunt-nosed "Traffic Types" in 1933, which sold quite well in spite of stiff prices. GMC brought out several too, as did White. Studebaker and Reo were early in the field among volume producers and by the late thirties all manufacturers could supply these units. But Ford, Chevrolet and Dodge were relatively late starters, announcing their COEs in 1938 and 1939 as additions to their conventional lines.

While the straight eight's reception had ranged from cold to no more than lukewarm, there was another eight-cylinder engine coming along. It would shake the industry and capture the imagination with its flashing performance. It was a vee-type eight this time and the name on the radiator was Ford!

The V-8 entered Ford's car and truck lines in 1932, the automotive sensation of the year. The new engine produced 75 hp at 3800 rpm, high revving for the day but Ford matched it with a 4-speed transmission for lively performance in a 1½-ton model. The Ford V-8 engine marked the onset of a trend that developed very rapidly.

It also brought an increasing interest of automobile manufacturers in the truck business. Ford, Chevrolet, Dodge, also Studebaker to a lesser extent, brought out a succession of "Depression era" models which posed increasingly difficult competition for old-time truck producers.

The 1934 Dodge K30 1½ ton was a good example. Customers got a 6-cylinder engine with an output of 70 hp, a 4-speed transmission, a 6 in. frame and hydraulic brakes. The chassis price was about $800 FOB Windsor, or some $1300 complete with cab, delivered and taxes paid.

All of the trucks that made up this segment of the market, i.e. the inexpensive vehicles produced by automobile manufacturers, cost about $150 less than a comparable unit from, say, International, GMC or Reo. These heavier units were worth the premium with their larger tires, greater power and huskier frames. But with a depression on, price counted for more than sales features, better performance, even improved durability.

Inexpensive 1½-ton trucks were easily and cheaply upgraded for heavier loads. Oversize tires, heavier springs and a reinforced frame could boost the capacity from 1½ to 2½ ton, often a good deal more. Obviously there wasn't enough power and torque for good performance; perhaps just as well as these upgraded vehicles were usually as underbraked as they were underpowered. But they "worked" well, which is what counted in hard times. Repairs and exchange engines were cheap; a factory exchange Ford V-8 ran around $100—installed.

This combination of the mid-thirties had a GMC T60 tractor, converted to diesel by Smith Transport using a British-built Gardner "oil" engine. Originally this, and other similar units, were powered by GMC (Buick) gasoline engines. They gave excellent service on the Toronto-Montreal run well into the postwar years.

White hit the Ontario market with a new range of low-priced units in 1936, the 700 series, in capacities from 1½ to 2½ ton and prices starting at a low (for White) $1555. They were powered by 6-cylinder 70 and 81 hp engines driving through 4-speed transmissions. Tires at 7.00-20 were far larger than the base units offered by the Big Three. A 7-in. frame also impressed customers.

White also had its Indiana, an assembled truck introduced to counter competition from the assemblers—Diamond T, Stewart, Federal and one or two others. But the emphasis in 1936 was on the new 700 series.

Styling was important and White retained a noted American automotive designer for the job, Count Alexis de Sakhnoffsky, who had styled a number of passenger cars and was chief stylist for Hayes Body at one point. His outstanding reputation was enhanced by work in Ontario where he designed a large number of striking truck and trailer bodies for Canadian brewers, from 1936 on.

Mack met its sales needs with a new line of trucks in 1936, the Mack Junior. These were powered by 6-cylinder engines in outputs from 72 to 85 hp. Prices started at $727 for the ½ ton, while the 2 to 3 ton listed at $1400. These trucks were built by Reo—they were Reos in every way—for distribution through the Mack organization. Sales were brisk, justifying the move.

Other truck manufacturers did the same. International had a particularly comprehensive range of models, introduced in 1934—the famed C-Line. Prices were low: the C-1½ ton listed at $581, while the C-20 a 1½ ton and one of the last 4-cylinder units on the market, carried a price tag of $794. International was also active in the promotion of 6-wheelers with a good lineup of Hendrickson-equipped units. This helped enormously to establish the Hendrickson bogie.

While the old-line truck producers were adding lighter and less costly units to their lineups, the Big

INBUILT QUALITY

Experience in MACK operation has taught men in all lines of business that strength lies not only in the most important parts of these hardy haulers but also in the lesser parts—down to the last bolt and nut—*all the strength that can be put there.*

A few of the many exceptional mechanical features of MACK Trucks are: case-hardened crankshaft, the biggest to be found in a motor truck; unusually long connecting rods and pistons to lessen side pressure and wear on wrist pins and pistons; exceptionally wide faced transmission gears, oversize axles, etc.

All MACK Trucks are of remarkably light weight for their rated power and capacity. Capacities 1 to 7½ tons. Trailers to 15 tons. Bodies for all needs and special loading and unloading appliances. Write for catalogue.

INTERNATIONAL MOTOR COMPANY, NEW YORK

"PERFORMANCE COUNTS"

Mack Trucks Canada Limited
300 The East Mall
Toronto, Ontario M9B 6B7.

reprint from an early 1920 Saturday Evening Post

We've been part of it

since the start of it.

Firestone

Three were increasing the capacities of theirs. It was an upward move into still heavier weight categories.

In 1935 Ford introduced a heavy-duty version of its V-8 truck, with a 2-ton rating. This was in response to the successful Chevrolet-based Maple Leaf. The new Ford HD was generally similar to the Maple Leaf concept—a standard Ford truck modified with a reinforced frame, larger tires and more power, 90 hp as opposed to 80 hp in lighter Fords.

Chevrolet countered this move in 1936 by upgrading its 1½-ton chassis to a 2-ton rating and the Maple Leaf rating to 2½ tons. The 2-ton Chevrolet, introduced earlier in the thirties, had been dropped in the interval.

In 1938 operators also had their choice of Ford and Maple Leaf cab-over-engine models, new that year and offered in similar ratings. The Maple Leaf COE was a Canadian-only variant of the GMC COE. Chevrolet got its own COE in 1939, as did Dodge the same year. Dodge had offered a COE earlier, the Montpelier COE conversion of a standard chassis. Ford had taken the route too, before its own factory-built COE got into production. It was known as the Dearborn COE conversion. Curiously, the Maple Leaf and the 2-ton Ford were only sold in Canada; there were no precise counterparts in the U.S. where Ford and Chevrolet restricted their trucks—different vehicles admittedly—to only 1½ ton.

The Ford HD and the Maple Leaf were created to serve the Canadian market with its differences to the U.S. in manufacturing and distribution. Both lines were typical of the steady upward climb in ratings among the lighter vehicles offered to Canadian customers. These trucks didn't go to the impending war in all cases, but their engines did!

Diesel power in the mid-1930s promised new and radical savings for truck operators. This was an achievement, with gasoline selling for only 25 cents a gallon. Still, a saving was a saving and it was worth going after.

There was a drawback; diesel-powered trucks were expensive. For instance, in 1936 an Indiana 3½ ton powered by a Hercules diesel engine cost $3750. The same truck with a gasoline engine was $3400, still expensive when 3½ tonners were available for as low as $2300 from other manufacturers. But it took a heavier vehicle for diesel power; it had to be a premium unit in terms of its components. Then the engine itself represented another $300, so who could afford a diesel? Few operators could.

Moreover, the diesel engine was a radical innovation as far as Ontario fleetmen were concerned, although operators in Europe liked them. Their roughness and high noise level didn't reinforce the claimed long life and freedom from repair. Then there was "diesel knock" from the combustion process, which didn't win the new engine many supporters.

In its way, the diesel aroused as much comment and speculation as the gas turbine does now for automotive applications.

Exponents of diesel power, principally Leyland in 1932-39, came into the Ontario truck market through a back door, selling their engines, not to truck fleets, but to busmen. Then, as now, the profit margins in public transportation weren't high and the diesel could help. Too, a premium engine with a life expectancy of 500,000 miles, and 200,000 miles between overhauls, looked good.

A few truck operators tried diesels on long hauls. Smith Transport had a large fleet of them by 1939, after good results with a trial engine in 1935. This was the British-built Gardner "oil engine" offered with 4, 5 and 6 cylinders. Smith Transport used this engine to repower its 1929 and 1930 GMC T-60s.

They were memorable conversions. The new Gardner was longer than the original Buick engine in the GMCs and the flywheel bellhousing, while standard SAE, was higher. Smith Transport overcame the problem with a novel solution; move the radiator ahead and extend the hood, raising the cab in the process to clear the bellhousing. There were no problems and these trucks were sufficiently rejuvenated to run all through the war years, although they were old units by then.

The *Toronto Star* put a Cummins-powered Stewart into service in 1936, then followed up the conversion with three Walters powered by the same engine. Metropolitan Transport made a similar move with a repowered Mack. The diesel was off to a good, if not overly spectacular start. The postwar years would see real strides with diesel power.

Commercial vehicle development didn't stop with the outbreak of war in 1939, it was simply redirected. The emphasis wasn't so much on design details and engineering innovations as it was on keeping vehicles in service. This called for good maintenance practices. It also meant the salvage and restoration of some unlikely vehicles as well.

Canadian truck operators scoured and ransacked junkyards for vehicles which had been scrapped just before the war started. Maybe they could be rebuilt to help out in an emergency. Many could.

A strange assortment of Reos, Macks, GMCs and Internationals from the late twenties and early thirties took to the roads, fresh from overhaul shops. Many would stay in service well into the postwar years, until new replacements were available. Another manifestation of wartime equipment shortages was the large-scale conversion of car transport trailers into "crowd busters" — big semitrailer buses. They worked well after a fashion, although the conversions resulted in a desperate shortage of car-haul trailers after the war. No other type of vehicle took quite so much steel as a big car transporter and steel was in short supply for several years.

Truck technical development was apparently stalled during the war years—there were advances but these would take years to show up in new vehicles, in many cases well into the 1950s. But there was much ingenuity at the maintenance level, in the upkeep of fleet vehicles. War-weary trucks had to be kept on the road and it was a tough fight all the way for hard-pressed operators and maintenance men.

Worn crankshafts were ground and reground, then ground again to clean up main journals and crankpins. In general, prewar limits for this amounted to a maximum of .030 in. undersize, but operators took as much as .060 in. off worn shafts to clean them up. But there were limits to the grinding a shaft would take. This led

International's DS-30 model was an all-purpose vehicle in the late 1930s. It was produced until 1940.

to a radical technique, metallizing, or the welding back on of new metal. It was expensive and it didn't always work, but when it did a worn shaft could be restored to as-new condition, with original factory dimensions.

Another innovation that proved to have more lasting benefits was hard chrome plating, the application of a hard-wearing chrome "film" to cylinder bores to improve durability and build up worn surfaces. It was a wartime development that had immediate application on the civilian front, although it was a costly and complex process. Hard chrome plating was later applied to compression piston rings and is now a universal feature of all heavy-duty engines for its excellent wearing qualities.

Detergent engine oil was a military development to meet some specific problems in the operation of diesel engines. Although described at the time as "self cleaning", it was really an oil that resisted sludging and the buildup of engine deposits.

Up to this time, fleetmen had used the only lubricant available, straight mineral oil, for which no claims were made other than to lubricate. If oil changing was neg-

lected there was a tendency for the oil to form sludge, a problem compounded by inadequate crankcase ventilation.

The new detergent grades largely overcame this problem by holding the sludge-forming compounds in suspension for eventual removal with the oil when it was changed. The effect on engine cleanliness and service life was remarkable.

Along with the benefits came some early problems. Occasionally the detergent oil worked too well in engines that had been in service for some time. Loosened engine deposits were picked up by the new oil and, in extreme cases, caused heavy damage by plugging up oil passages. But truckers soon learned how to avoid trouble and avail themselves of the benefits of advancing oil technology. Heavy-duty detergent lubricants came along, followed by the all-season multi-viscosity grades of engine oil.

Engine manufacturers, in conjunction with the petroleum industry, now have taken much of the choice away from the user, laying down strict specifications for lubricants required for satisfactory engine performance.

The early postwar years were not outstanding technically. Operators were hearing about such innovations as plastic cabs and automatic transmissions but, as it turned out, they were years away. Postwar strikes delayed deliveries of new vehicles that were much the same as 1939 production.

But the selection was greater—not necessarily new models but more diversity in the types of vehicles they produced. For instance, the Chevrolet Maple Leaf in 1948 now carried a 3-ton rating and it had more power, 100 hp.

Ford had a 3-ton vehicle too, now with less horsepower (88) but more torque with a high-torque camshaft—"pull" still meant a lot to truck operators. This engine was a variation of the standard Ford V-8 truck engine that developed 97 hp with 175 ft lb of torque at 3600 rpm. With the high-torque camshaft, torque was upped to 183 ft lb at the same rpm. Ford offered the 97 hp V-8 in lighter models.

Besides Ford trucks, operators also had their choice of Mercury units. Ford introduced the Mercury line in 1946 to widen the company's truck distribution, countering competition posed by the Chevrolet, the Maple Leaf and the lighter end of GMC's range. Give or take a few grille details and minor chassis changes, the Mercury was a Ford truck and it was offered through Ford's Monarch and Mercury dealers.

The COE was much in demand by 1949. White introduced a novel one that year, the company's new 3000 series with a cab that tipped hydraulically in 30 seconds. It had to—the White L-head engine was mounted so far back in the frame that a radical approach was needed to aid servicing and maintenance.

It wasn't a new idea, White had a tipping cab unit in 1938; Sterling had produced similar models for years, while the concept can be traced as far back as 1912. But the White 3000 was a production unit that sold in considerable volume, exerting much influence in the marketplace and stimulating a new interest in tipping cabs. The White cab was a stylish all-steel structure designed for driver convenience and excellent vision.

White offered the 3000 series with straight frames initially, later adding drop-frame variants for bottlers and other customers who needed a low frame to ease loading and unloading. The White 3000 sold well, though its features made it an expensive unit.

International brought out six new COEs a year later to meet the rising demand for this type. All were powered by 6-cylinder engines, but the cabs didn't tip. Access to the engine was through a tilting panel at the front. This was known as the forward-control type, a variant of the COE. As with most other truck manufacturers, International had offered COE units of various types since the late thirties.

Diamond T introduced a very good COE in 1951 with a cab that tipped through counterbalancing. This proved to be a good seller too and in time the same cab was adopted by International in a sharing of compo-

White introduced its advanced 3000 series tipping cab COE in 1949, kept it in production until the 1960s. Although not the first of its kind, the 3000 was the first tipping cab COE to sell in volume. Originally offered with a White-built gasoline engine, diesel power later became available. The trailer is a Fruehauf.

ers. Glass-lined tanks in stainless steel and aluminum, either trailer-sized or mounted on trucks, provided a new and economical way to transport milk. But it didn't happen all at once and the traditional farmer's milk can was good for a few years yet.

Diesel power progressed rapidly after the war, although the Gardner had disappeared and the Leyland diesel was less prominent. Now there were new engines. Mack had produced its own diesel engines since 1939, while other American truck producers who didn't build their own used the General Motors Diesel or the Cummins, among others.

As a group, these were 6-cylinder engines, though GM had and still has a 3-cylinder engine for light-duty vehicles. Engine horsepower demands were on the upturn in 1952. But a 150 hp diesel was a big engine and all that Diamond T needed that year for its largest truck, a tractor with a gross vehicle weight rating of 50,000 lb. There was no particular demand for more power in gasoline engines. The International KR-11, with a gvw of 27,000 lb. did all it had to do with a 6-cylinder, 149-hp engine. The KR-11 was a giant, the largest 4-wheeled or single-axle vehicle International produced. With 150 hp tops for the heaviest units, all that customers got was 90 to 120 hp among the general run of lighter vehicles.

Trailers underwent much refinement. A new type was coming into general use by 1957, the monocoque or frameless trailer which was light and well suited to bulky dry freight. In general, it had no framing; the stressed-skin construction was based on standard aircraft practice. Fruehauf, Trailmobile, Can-Car, Highway, in fact all trailer manufacturers were producing them. Aluminum was the standard choice because it was 25 percent lighter than steel, although a few steel ones were built. All were tandems.

New and more liberal weight regulations favored the tandem-axle trailer, as they did tandem trucks. A variation of the tandem trailer, the slider, incorporated a sliding tandem to permit conformity with conflicting provincial weight regulations on long hauls. Movement of the slider tandem bogie under the vehicle altered weight distribution on the axles, though sometimes they didn't slide all that easily.

The same weight regulations that influenced the tandem trailer also resulted in a new type of tractor for long hauls, the ultra lightweight. A premium job throughout, this used aluminum for just about everything, short of the engine block and axle housings. Weight reduction of a ton or so was achieved. Sometimes weight was pared too much and durability suffered. But, in the main, ultra-lightweight equipment (including trailer) allowed profitable payloads in circumstances where heavier conventional equipment couldn't earn a profit. Weight-saving equipment is still a big factor in the industry.

Regulations also permitted longer vehicles, then wider ones with an increase in overall width in the 1960s. It was needed; operators were increasingly involved with bulky but lightweight freight that ate up van space but scarcely depressed the vehicle's springs. New and shorter COE tractors permitted use of the longest possible trailers, built right out to maximum legal widths. The trend for equipment of this type and

size has continued to this day for loads with a bulkiness out of proportion to their weight.

Speeds were also on the increase and the need for better performance triggered a new generation of gasoline engines in the late 1950s. It was the high-efficiency, high-compression V-8, a legacy from the passenger car field, where similar engines had been introduced in 1950. The big car makers, Ford, General Motors and Chrysler introduced similar engines to their truck lines, as did International and Reo. By 1960 the V-8 truck engine was widely used in medium-duty vehicles. Most manufacturers offered them as standard power or as an option to 6-cylinder engines. The six had a strong following and still has, but the overhead-valve V-8 established a new era in engine design.

Characteristics were generally the same—overhead valves and compression ratios of 7.5:1 and 8:1. This was a substantial boost from the approximately 7:1 in the 6-cylinder engines, which they either replaced or supplemented as a new option. An old idea in engine design, replaceable cylinder sleeves, was revived for some of the new V-8 and 6-cylinder gasoline engines. Diesel engines had used them for years.

Another feature was the short stroke giving a "square" engine with bore and stroke the same, or approximately so. This meant high revving but lower piston speeds. Outputs were impressive, about 150 hp at a brisk 3000 rpm. They revved higher but the short stroke improved durability. Crankshafts had five main bearings for a rugged "bottom end" and there was a good potential for even more power as development progressed.

The same upgrading was also applied to the 6-cylinder engine. Four bearing crankshafts were replaced by massive seven-bearing shafts to handle the higher compression ratios. They matched the efficiency of the V-8 although outputs were generally lower with the popularity of the six for city work. But one cannot generalize as many operators preferred the big six for highway operations. Truck manufacturers offered both to cover their markets.

In 1960 GMC introduced its big Twin-Six gasoline engine, a V-12 developing an impressive 275 hp at 2400 rpm. The idea was to blend the good torque characteristics of diesel power with the smoothness of a gasoline engine. Torque was outstanding; a high 630 ft lb at 1600 to 1900 rpm, coupled with 275 hp for good highway performance. GMC used it in its own trucks as an option to its diesel engines. While the big Twin-Six was a good performer and durable, it was costly to produce and it was soon discontinued.

Another truck manufacturer who had much success with big V-8 gasoline engines was Reo with its Gold Comet. This followed the same formula as the smaller high-efficiency V-8s, but on a larger scale. Outputs were high at 207 and 235 hp and it was a popular choice in 1961. Before leaving the "new" gasoline engines mention should be made of GMC's line of V-6s introduced in 1960. They were in the 150 hp range and were more compact and lighter than the V-8. The same concept was applied to its Toro-Flow diesels and for the same reasons.

The tipping cab, which raised for engine access, was a general feature on COEs by the 1960s and there was variety in the method used. White's cab tipped hydraulically while Ford, Diamond T and International used a variety of coil spring and torsion bar counterbalancing

International MOTOR TRUCKS for Heavy-Duty Work

Heavy "Duty" is right. The duties of a motor truck in every-day service for the average busy concern are "heavy" to say the least. Heavy loads, hard pulls, fast work—demand real, true "bone-and-muscle" construction.

This is one reason why a nationally known concern has upwards of 300 International Motor Trucks in city and country service where road conditions are exceptionally severe.

International Motor Trucks are built as strong as expert mechanics can accomplish, using the highest grade of material obtainable. Further—each truck is watched and inspected by International road engineers at regular intervals—*as long as you own it.*

This is a combination that means cheaper hauling for you, in your business. Let us demonstrate at your own work.

SIX CAPACITIES		**INTERNATIONAL HARVESTER COMPANY**	INTERNATIONAL

SIX CAPACITIES
Model S Speed Truck
" 21   2,000 lbs.
" 31   3,000 "
" 41   4,000 "
" 61   6,000 "
" 101   10,000 "

INTERNATIONAL HARVESTER COMPANY
OF CANADA Ltd

INTERNATIONAL
SPEED TRUCK
BUILT IN
CANADA
AT CHATHAM

Ad Circa 1922

A fleet of motorized and horse-drawn road tankers and delivery vehicles outside a British American Oil Company depot in the mid-1920's.

Serving the Ontario Trucking Industry over the years and miles

GULF OIL CANADA LIMITED

Up, up, with never a knock, never a falter, never a strain or conscious effort, but with a smooth, accelerating speed that flows through the engine as though some Giant of Power gently swept your gliding car to the top of every hill.

When your car has hard work ahead, drive up to a British American gasolene station, where the Giant of Power awaits you.

The BRITISH AMERICAN OIL COMPANY LIMITED

AUTOLENE ENGINE OIL

Whatever science and invention have devised for the improvement of lubricating oils is incorporated in British American Oil Company's product — Autolene . . .

No price penalty—no extra charge for extra quality.

Giants of Power
that sweep your car up every hill

PEERLESS—This British American Product is the Company's proudest achievement. Peerless Gasolene is unequalled for Purity, Uniformity and the full limit of POWER. Our 22 years of scientific production have achieved PEERLESS—the most superb Gasolene sold in Canada.

SUPER-POWER—An above-the-average Gasoline selling at an average price. For ordinary motoring Super-Power is ideal. At the price it is unsurpassed by any Gasolene.

The POWER *that* DRIVES
the Cars of Canada
The British American Oil Co., Limited
Refiners and Distributors of the Celebrated Peerless *and* Super-Power *Gasolenes and* Autolene *Engine Oils*

This advertisement was in the "Mail and Empire", Toronto, April 24th, 1928, promoting B-A fuels and lubricants to owners of bus and truck fleets, cars, tractors and motor-cycles.

A 1962 International DCO single-axle tractor hauling two Fruehauf 20 ft semitrailers in Muskoka. The tractor featured a short bumper-to-back-of-cab dimension for minimum overall length.

nents and manufacturing between the two firms.

A new make (to Ontario fleetmen) was starting to appear in the province, the Kenworth. Kenworths, then and now, were big custom-built long-haul units. Model K-522, a COE and typical of Kenworth's trucks in 1952, featured a big Buda diesel driving through a 10-speed Fuller transmission. An interesting feature was the provision of temperature gauges to monitor oil temperatures in the engine, transmission and both rear axles, since the vehicle was a tandem. An all-aluminum chassis was another departure from standard practice at the time.

Several British trucks were available to Ontario fleetmen in the early 1950s. The Commer was one, reintroduced after an absence of 36 years in conventional and COE types. The COE was a much more advanced unit, powered by a 109 hp 6-cylinder engine, with chrome-plated cylinder bores for long life.

The Austin 3 ton was another, a conventional type with a slightly dropped frame (not a full drop, but lower than a straight frame) and a 6-cylinder engine. An all-steel cab and a spiral bevel axle were other Austin specifications. Ontario fleetmen could also buy big Czech-built Tatra tandems with air-cooled engines—but didn't. Similarly, British Fodens and Scammells found few, if any, buyers.

The fifties saw an important development—mechanical refrigeration for long-haul vehicles. Refrigerated trucks and trailers had been around for a long time, using ice and holdover plates as the refrigerant. Now compact gasoline-powered refrigerating plants were available and they were small enough to build into a trailer. Thermo King and Universal did much pioneering but their units were anything but cheap at prices ranging around $5000. What they offered was cooling capacity down to zero for the most perishable of commodities such as fish, ice cream, and other products of a new and booming frozen-food industry.

Reliability was somewhat uncertain at first but the new means of refrigerating didn't "burn" loads as dry ice could, nor was corrosion a problem as it had been with natural and dry ice. But maintenance was heavy and operators who got into the new field had much to learn, as did the manufacturers. The arrival of mechanical refrigeration put a new meaning into long-haul trucking. Now it really was long haul, with Ontario operators working regular schedules between cities in the province and distant points in Florida and Texas.

A related development was a growing interest in bulk-milk hauling in insulated tanks. Much had been learned about insulation from experience with mechanical refrigeration and this was now applied to milk tank-

A 1962 Mack B-61 tandem with diesel power owned by Active Cartage. The Mack B series was built for about ten years and was widely sold for construction and other heavy-duty applications.

This 1962 White 4000 series conventional tractor has White's Super Mustang gasoline engine and extra long-range fuel tanks. Box at upper right of the lead Can-Car refrigerated trailer records inside temperature during trip.

The Dodge 1000 series tractor was introduced in 1960 and continued until Chrysler left the heavy-duty truck field in 1975. With Cummins diesel power, this 1960 model is hooked up to a vintage ouutside-post Trailmobile tandem semitrailer.

The broadening application of specialized tanker equipment is apparent in this combination of 1961 White Freightliner tractor and Highway tri-axle tank semitrailer. The trailer was built by Trinity Steel of Texas.

Another unit typical of the early sixties is this Mack C series diesel-powered tractor with single drive axle hooked up to a Can Car trailer.

arrangements. Truck manufacturers still use different systems, according to the model and capacity. GMC raises the cab on its smaller COEs through a spring arrangement, reserving hydraulic operation for its big long-haul COEs.

Aluminum COEs became popular, typically the White-Freightliner, Kenworth, Hayes and the GMC Astro. Riveted construction was used, not welding as in all-steel cabs; in this respect it had some resemblance to aircraft practice. More recently, welded aluminum cabs have been introduced, though riveted cabs are holding their own. Aluminum trailers were built the same way. Aluminum construction had been available since the 1930s when aluminum panels were often applied to wood-framed bodies to cut weight. And a good many trucks in the twenties, including the Mack AC Bulldog, had aluminum components such as crankcases to reduce weight. In fact aluminum has almost as long a tradition as steel in commercial vehicles.

If cabs on COEs could be tipped for easy access to the engine, why couldn't the hoods on conventional-type vehicles also be tipped? This reasoning in the 60s resulted in the tipping hood, a complete hood unitized with the fenders that tipped forward exposing all of the front end of the chassis.

GMC, in 1965, was early in the field with this feature, as were Mack and International with their heavier units. Not only did hoods and fenders tip but they were also of plastic material to reduce weight and minimize minor impact damage.

The automatic transmission made good progress in the late 60s after a slow start in trucks in the mid-fifties. It was not a success then but later units, principally the Allison, were quite different. By 1964 they were generally available as rather expensive options in many light and medium-duty vehicles, usually for city operations and difficult off-road requirements. The advantages were the same in both cases, no manual gear-changing and a "cushioned" drive to eliminate impact shock in drive-train components. Now they're available for large diesels, mostly for specialized operations, although the automatic is making significant gains in long-haul highway operations.

Methods for improving the riding qualities of heavy-duty vehicles have attracted designers for years, but progress has been slow. Air suspension, a very old idea, was adopted by a leading truck manufacturer in 1957 for heavy units. It wasn't a success and was soon dropped, although the system was satisfactory on buses.

However, air suspension for third or "tag" axles for trucks, also as the suspension medium for tandem trailers, has become widespread practice today.

Similarly, independent front suspension for heavy-duty vehicles failed to make progress. The semielliptic spring is still dominant in front suspensions of heavy-duty trucks.

The diesel engine offered "big power" for trucks by the late 1960s. Mack, Cummins, Detroit Diesel and Caterpiller each had a wide range of engines with outputs of 350-plus hp. They came in many forms; the basic in-line six, also V-6s, V-8s and V-12s, depending on the manufacturer.

Diesel development also brought forth the mid-range engine of 150 to 200 hp. This was aimed at smaller vehicles used on short hauls and in city service where peak horsepower wasn't important but economy was. This was a new market for the manufacturers of diesel engines, although progress has been slow against the entrenched gasoline engine.

The gas turbine appeared on the truck engine scene in the 60s. It worked well in aircraft and truck applications were expected to show similar advantages. But there were problems that still persist. High fuel consumption and noise acted as a brake on the gas turbine's progress in the automotive field. Virtually every manufacturer had prototypes for working demonstrations, but that's about all that has happened so far.

Still, the gas turbine holds considerable promise with its high output, low weight (1000 lb as opposed to 2000-plus lb for a diesel) and compactness, although air intake and exhaust systems are bulky. Enthusiasts for the gas turbine claim that its appetite has been curbed somewhat and fuel consumption now approaches that of a diesel.

Ontario truck operators entered the 1970s with a total of 426,307 commercial vehicles in service. Technical development took a new turn to meet changing conditions, less influenced by the truck marketplace than pressures stemming from an avalanche of government regulations and an uncertain fuel situation.

As it had in the passenger car field, safety and environmental measures loomed large in the engineering of commercial vehicles. The trend had started in the 60s, gaining full momentum by the early 70s. Most of the new regulations were of American origin, but they were an influence in Canada because the vehicles which operators used were American-designed. The Canadian

The Peninsula, a short-lived all-Canadian tractor appeared in 1960. About ten were built. Engine options were Rolls-Royce, Cummins and Detroit Diesel, driving through Fuller transmissions and Timken axles. The semitrailer is a Strick.

government's legislation, when it arrived, was quite similar to that in effect in the U.S. It was a new ball game for everyone, operators and truck manufacturers alike.

The upshot was a blinding complexity of directives and requirements which truck designers had to engineer into new vehicles. There were a lot of these "standards"; it took a 500-page binder to accommodate them in 1976 and they're still coming through, with manufacturers well on the way to a second volume.

The outcome was a new generation of vehicles designed around government directives calling up standards for in-cab and external noise, exhaust emissions, vehicle braking and other safety requirements. For most of the new safety-related government standards there's also a tough timetable setting forth increasingly stringent standards on into the 80s.

Before operators and truck manufacturers had become accustomed to new circumstances and the pressure of legislation, another crisis developed to disrupt what calm there was left in the truck business. This was a new and an all-absorbing concern for fuel conservation. It seemed for a time that trucks might be denied fuel with events as they were in the Middle East. This

didn't happen, but fuel became a soaring expense and now, in the spring of 1977, there's a good deal of uncertainty about fuel supply and price.

The technical response was immediate from 1973 on, with new engines achieving higher levels of efficiency. Engineers turned to their notebooks for design ideas to boost fuel economy. There were quite a few of them. Lower compression big-bore engines would do nicely on unleaded gasoline, while even more turbocharging improved the diesel's economy.

Derated and high torque-rise engines provided better operating economy and there were benefits as well in reduced gear-changing. There were other areas besides the engine in the quest for new economies. Steel-belted radial tires had less rolling resistance, while streamlined air deflectors on top of the cab smoothed out the flow of air at highway speeds for further economy.

Efficiency is the operative word in the economics of trucking and the industry will continue to pursue it—at ever-higher levels. Obviously it's what Simpson's and Parker's had in mind when they got into "trucks". The idea is still the same, only the vehicles have changed.

WHITES EARN MOST MONEY!

Reduced budgets have effected timely economies in many businesses. Intelligently applied, these economies prove of great benefit—but too often the quest for economy leads to unwise buying.

Operators of transportation equipment who pigeonholed their experiences to buy "so many trucks for so much money" have found their operating cost sheets blooming with red ink.

Transportation equipment is not bargain merchandise regardless of what the price tag says. Trucks and busses make money only when they operate dependably and economically over a long period of time.

White sells cheap transportation, not cheap trucks. Owners' records prove Whites deliver the lowest-cost transportation money can buy—operating over money-earning miles five to ten years after cheaper trucks have been retired.

© The White Company

THE WHITE COMPANY, *Cleveland*

Officers & Directors
Ontario Trucking Association
1977

EXECUTIVE COMMITTEE

CHAIRMAN OF THE BOARD: M. W. DONNELLY
PRESIDENT: G. M. HENDRIE
1ST VICE-PRESIDENT: W. MacKINNON
2ND VICE-PRESIDENT: C. V. HOAR
SECRETARY: K. ZAVITZ
TREASURER: L. K. ASH
EXECUTIVE VICE-PRESIDENT: J. O. GOODMAN

DIRECTORS

EASTERN REGION (i)
PERKINS, J. A., JR.
    Taggart Service Ltd. — Ottawa
RODGER, T.
    Hurdman Bros. Ltd. — Ottawa

EASTERN REGION (ii)
RANSOM, R. C.
    Kingsway Transports Ltd. — Montreal

LAKE ONTARIO REGION
CATHCART, J. M.
    Cathcart Freight Lines (Peterborough) Ltd. — Peterborough
HAGGARTY, R. M.
    Lafferty-Smith Express Lines Ltd. — Belleville

NIAGARA REGION
BAIRD, P. G.
    Canadian Freightways Eastern Ltd. — Hamilton
FURNESS, G. L.
    Walmer Transport Co. Ltd. — Hamilton
ZAVITZ, K.
    Zavitz Brothers Ltd. — Wainfleet

GEORGIAN BAY REGION
CAIN, W. R.
    Cooke Cartage & Storage Ltd. — Barrie
TUDHOPE, G. C.
    Tuchope Cartage Ltd. — Parry Sound

CENTRAL ONTARIO REGION
ASH, L. K.
    The Toronto-Peterborough Transport Co. Ltd. — Scarborough
AUSTIN, D. H.
    Direct Transportation System Ltd. — Toronto
ERDMAN, H. H.
    Inter-City Truck Lines Ltd. — Toronto
HENDRIE, G. M.
    Hendrie & Co. Ltd. — Toronto
HUME, A. T.
    Hume's Transport Ltd. — Toronto
KEMBEL, L. O.
    Motorways (Ontario) Ltd. — Rexdale
THOMPSON, V. J.
    Smith Transport Co. Ltd. — Toronto

LAKE ST. CLAIR REGION
NUSSEY, A. M.
    Nussey Cartage Ltd. — Tilbury
THIBODEAU, L. J.
    Thibodeau-Finch Express Ltd. — Windsor

LAKE ERIE REGION
WARING, R. A.
    Dixon Van Lines Ltd. — London

HEAD OFFICE

MID-WESTERN ONTARIO
MacKINNON, W.
    MacKinnon Transport Ltd. — Guelph
ST. DENIS, G.
    Peplow Transport Ltd. — Guelph

NORTHEASTERN ONTARIO REGION
GOODINE, F.
    Soo Van & Storage — Sault Ste. Marie
MONETTE, J. R.
    Star Transfer Ltd. — Timmins

LAKEHEAD-NORTHWESTERN ONTARIO REGION (i)
SMITH, H. W.
    Lakehead Freightways Ltd. — Thunder Bay

LAKEHEAD-NORTHWESTERN ONTARIO REGION (ii)
REIMER, D. S.
    Reimer Express Lines Ltd. — Winnipeg, Manitoba

ASSOCIATE
HARPER, M. R.
    Harper Detroit Diesel Ltd. — Toronto
McNAB, R. D.
    General Motors Truck Centre — Toronto

CLASS 'C' CARRIERS' DIVISION
SINCLAIR, J. W.
    All-Ontario Transport Ltd. — Malton

DUMP TRUCK OWNERS' DIVISION
McKAY, C.
    D & M Transport Ltd. — Weston

ONTARIO MOVERS ASSOCIATION
NAYLOR, B.
    Tippet-Richardson Ltd. — Toronto

HEAVY-SPECIALIZED CARRIERS' DIVISION
BARLOW, W.
    Barlow's Cartage Ltd. — Cambridge

LIVESTOCK TRANSPORTERS' DIVISION
THUR, W.
    W. Thur & Sons Ltd. — Elmira

ONTARIO MILK TRANSPORT ASSOCIATION
BARTLETT, H. V. — Dunnville

PRIVATE CARRIERS' DIVISION
KRON, J. W.
    Canadian Tire Corporation Ltd. — Toronto

REFRIGERATED TRUCKING ASSOCIATION OF ONT.
ROBINSON, D.
    Zip Express Ltd. — Hamilton

REGULAR ROUTE COMMON CARRIERS' DIVISION
STALVEY, W. B.
    Dominion-Consolidated Truck Lines Ltd.   Toronto

TANK TRUCK CARRIERS' DIVISION
DAVEY, M. H.
    Provost Industrial Tankers Ltd.   Toronto

ONTARIO UNIT MASONRY TRANSPORTERS' ASSOCIATION
THOMSON, R.
    Tombro Trucking Ltd.   Streetsville

ECONOMICS & FINANCE COUNCIL
WYLLIE, W. R.
    J. D. Smith & Sons Ltd.   Downsview

THE OPERATIONS COUNCIL-ONTARIO
POLL, B. J.
    Red Star Express Lines of Ontario Ltd.   Toronto

SALES & MARKETING COUNCIL
HOFLAND, E.
    Laidlaw Transport Ltd.   Hamilton

INDUSTRY & PUBLIC RELATIONS COUNCIL
FLEMING, W. R.
    International Harvester Co. of Canada Ltd.   Hamilton

DIRECTORS-AT-LARGE
(Past Presidents)

M. D. DAVIS, Toronto
W. J. HINES, Toronto
C. V. HOAR, Agincourt
G. M. PARKE, Toronto
B. W. TUCKEY, Exeter

OTA STAFF

Executive Vice-President	J. O. Goodman
Executive Assistant	Albert W. James
Director, Industry and Public Relations	John N. Nickell
Co-Ordinator, Agricultural Activities	John D. Wishart
Co-Ordinator, Educational Activities	Alex Smith
Director, OTA Security Council	Colin Venning
Director, Economics and Finance	Robert A. Bentley
Director, Membership Services	J. G. M. Beerens
Director, Legal Services	Gordon V. Meakings
Solicitor	Jack R. Armstrong
O.M.T.A. Field Representative	Charles H. Baillie

Mark Ahmeo
Mrs. Audrey Burnett
Miss Anne Coggon
Mrs. Carol Hayward
Miss Debbie King
Mrs. Judy McClelland
Miss Debbie McCormick
Mrs. Dorothy Myles
Mrs. Lucy Nakao
Miss Trudi Norris
Miss Elizabeth Parker
Miss Sherry Reilly
Mrs. Marilyn Sandford
Mrs. Marlene Warwick

PICTURE CREDITS

In the main photographs are from the Canadian Road Transport Archives, a project of the Ontario Trucking Association. With thanks, sources, where known are listed: 4. Inter-City Truck Lines; 5. Harpham Bros.; 6. C. S. Koven; 8. Emco-Wheaton; 9. (a) Ontario Hydro; (b) Wright Motor Transport; 10. Slichter's Ltd.; 16. Manning Bros.; 17. Meyers Transport; 18. (a) Lewington's Flowers; (b) W. J. Pickard Ltd.; 19. J. M. Schneider Ltd.; 24. White Trucks; 25. Brantford Coach & Body; 27. Batten Ltd.; 36. C. A. Fraser Ltd.; 39. Howard Sober, Inc.; 42. (a) Dominion Truck Equipment; (b) International Harvester; 54. & 55. Fruehauf Trailers; 57. Warner Bros.; 79. Micklethwaite; 80. (a) White Trucks; (b) International Harvester; 91. (a) Fred Muscat; (b) Canadian Pacific; 92. Reimer Express Lines; 94. (b) Ford of Canada; 108. Creative Photographic; 114. Richard Mathews; 122. Feature Four Ltd.; 128 (a) Parker's Dye Works; (b) Canadian Electrical News; 131. G. Bureau; 132 & 133. The Commercial Motor; 135. The Overland Express; 136. Bennett & Wright; 137. T. Eaton Co.; 140. (a) & (b) R. L. Jerry; 141. J. Sercombe; 142. Canadian Cartage System; 144. National Sewer Pipe Ltd.; 146. J. Walter Thompson Co.; 148. (a) (b) (c) R. L. Jerry; (d) Wilke Movers & Cartage; 150. Manning Bros.; 152. R. C. W. Percy; 153. (a) L. R. Gray; (b) Hendrie & Co.; 154. C & D Sugar Co.; Dixon Van Lines; 157. (a) Manning Bros.; (b) C. E. Shelton; 158. (a) Canada Decalcomania Co.; (b) Finch & Sons Transport; 160. (a) Ford of Canada; (b) T. Eaton Co.; 161. (a) Ford of Canada; (b) T. Payne; 162. (a) Smith Bros. Body Works; (b) R. L. Jerry; 167. (a) C. E. Shelton; (b) International Harvester; 169. Canadian Railway & Marine World; 176. International Harvester; 177. White Trucks; 181. Canadian Pacific; 182. (a) Mack Trucks; (b) Micklethwaite; 183. (a) Fred Muscat; (b) Herb Nott & Co.; 184. White Trucks; 185. Welland Studios